Gender, Media and Interface

About the Author

Shital Jimmy Tamakuwala is currently a faculty in Social Work Programme, Department of Sociology, Veer Narmad South Gujarat University, Surat. She took her early education in Mumbai, received master degree in Sociology from SNDT University, Mumbai and was awarded PhD Degree from Veer Narmad South Gujarat University, Surat. She has deliberately worked in different projects and did field work in rural and urban areas of South Gujarat.

While association with NABET as a Functional Area Expert in Socio-Economic Aspect she has widely contributed on researches on the impact and assessment of industries on villages in several states. She has successfully prepared projects on CSR (Corporate Social Responsibility) to sensitize the industrialist to accomplish their duties towards the society.

She has attended several National, International Conferences, seminars besides presenting papers on Gender Studies, women empowerment, social problems and environment.

She is a life member of Indian Sociological Society and Indian Association for Women's Studies.

Gender, Media and Interface

Shital Jimmy Tamakuwala

CONCEPT PUBLISHING COMPANY PVT. LTD.,
NEW DELHI-110059

ISBN-13: 978-81-8069-975-7

First Published 2013

Published and Printed by

Concept Publishing Company Pvt. Ltd.
A/15-16, Commercial Block, Mohan Garden
New Delhi-110059 (India)
T: 25351460, 25351794, *F*: 091-11-25357109
E: publishing@conceptpub.com, W: www.conceptpub.com
Editorial Office: H-13, Bali Nagar, New Delhi-110 015, India.

Cataloging in Publication Data--Courtesy: D.K. Agencies (P) Ltd. <docinfo@dkagencies.com>

Tamakuwala, Shital Jimmy.
Gender, media and interface / Shital Jimmy Tamakuwala.
p. cm.
Originally presented as the author's thesis (Ph. D.)—Veer Narmad South Gujarat University.
Includes bibliographical references (p.) and index.
ISBN 9788180699757

1. Sex role. 2. Sex role—India—Gujarat. 3. Mass media and women. 4. Mass media and women—India—Gujarat. 5. Stereotypes (Social psychology) 6. Stereotypes (Social psychology)—India—Gujarat. I. Title.

DDC 305.3 23

Foreword

Gender stereotypes continue to persist worldwide with varying degrees blocking attitudinal changes. These archaic notions are socially embedded in patriarchy controlling women i.e. their thoughts, body and their labour. It is a simple common sense that these unilateral gendered assumptions generate gender violence time and again. The nation, in fact, the entire world is still afresh with the brutal Delhi gang rape in December 2012. Same story everywhere. In Liberia, West Africa, an aid group known as More Than Me rescued a ten year old orphan who had been sexually abused. In Steubenville, Ohio, high school football players rape an unconscious girl of sixteen; and the list is endless. There are umpteen rape cases across India - some are reported while many go unreported due to social stigma. Yet in some cases rape is endemic. More often than not the victim is on trial! That in Delhi, out of 635 rape cases reported in 11 months last year, only one ended in conviction speaks volumes.

Be that as it may, gender violence is one of the world's most common human rights abuses. Several studies point out that women worldwide between 15 to 44 years of age are more likely to die or be maimed because of male violence than due to cancer, malaria, war and traffic accidents combined (New York Times, Sunday, January 2013). The World Health Organization has stated that domestic and sexual violence affects 30 to 60 percent of women in most countries. Having said so, social awakening by concerned civil society groups from various strata across rural and urban belts like students, youth, activists, academia, workers, judiciary, state etc. can rectify and reform the prevailing unequal misogynic social order.

In this context the study by Shital Tamakuwala on Gender Stereotypes in Media is not only significant but also relevant today. This is a revised version of Ms. Tamakuwala's doctoral thesis submitted to V.N.S.G. University, Surat–India under my supervision in 2010, for which she has been awarded Ph.D degree in Sociology. She analyses meticulously sociology of gender and the impact of mass media through television serials and advertisements on women and men by contextualizing with empirical data from college students both in rural and urban settings. Accordingly, she projects some significant revelations on gender stereotyping and thus observes that television advertisements invariably reinforce consumerism on the audience, while the market economy has successfully harnessed the role of electronic medium between the producers and consumers. Meanwhile mass media takes special care to package patriarchal value system in subtle ways.

On the whole the present research by Dr. Shital Tamakuwala is a welcome departure from the mainstream in Sociology of Women and Communication Studies notwithstanding some drawbacks.

I wish her success in her future endeavors.

February 28, 2013

Dr. Suguna Pathy
Chattanooga, TN
USA

Preface

This book has been inspired from my PhD thesis. This book is intended to help the youth readers on degree courses and modules which are concerned with media studies, and, to some extent, with the study of culture.

I take a holistic and dynamic view of the relationships between media and society. This book tries to focus on my views and debates about the media impact on the society, but at the same time I do not intend to subscribe to pessimistic opinions about the influence of media on society. Nor do I go along with what I regard as over-optimistic views about audience autonomy and power. It seems to me that the media exists in evolving and difficult relationships with their audiences, and also with institutions of the state.

You will find that the book keeps returning to the concepts and nurture ideas about ideology, discourse and hegemony. The media industries are meaning producers. All acts of communication produce meanings. It is the power of these meanings, which results in relationships, exercises influence, models reality, generates behavior of domination and simultaneously feelings of subordination. To me, Culture and communication are deeply intertwined and interdependent. Culture without active support from communication is incomplete and communication without adequate backing from culture will be ineffective and ecliptic. Hence, Marshall McLuhan was strong in his belief in media technology, particularly television, as driving mechanism behind cultural change.

This book examines the development of television in India since 1990s and its implications for Indian society more widely. This book explores the transformation, explaining how television, a medium that developed in industrial west, was adapted to suit Indian conditions. Considering the full gamut of Indian television- from national networks in English and Hindi to the state of regional language networks- this book elucidates the transformative impact of television on a range of identity formation, cinema, popular culture and the youth.

The very phrase women and TV serials incorporate about the coherence of a group of people labeled women who can be represented collectively. This representation of women may be in part be inspired by cultural assumptions and attitudes- stereotypes are never simply invented by media. But it is also in part a creature of market forces.

In this book I want to engage with some textual features of soaps in terms of their female gendered nature and also how this features have 'bled' into much other drama programming on Indian television. This book will also open up questions about the female reader and empowerment. The persistence, indeed the expansion of the soap opera form is some kind of tribute to its attractions and culture validity. If soaps seduce us with myths, then it will also be useful to examine some of those myths, not least in relation to discourse and ideology. In critical terms, and with relation to their production, content, structure and consumption, television serials and advertisements have raised a number of issues. For example, there is the matter of their relationships to the lived experience of a largely female audience. There is the squaring of their traditionally low culture status with their high culture profile, and with evident pleasures that women from all backgrounds gain from viewing Television serials. TV serials are the absolute bottom of the television hierarchy, lumped with stereotypical representation of women, dramas, melodramas etc.

In terms of structure of this book you should know that the first two chapters are intended as an overview of institutions, gender, stereotypes, media and their relationship. The remaining chapters are the findings and conclusions of the research work. The research work exemplifies and develops issues, concepts and debates. In particular, you will find the chapters return to ideas about mass media, gender, representation and globalization. Each chapter raises questions for two reasons; one is that they raise problems and issues for discussions around the chapter topics. The other is that they then inform what follows. But the overall idea is to get you thinking, to encourage you to ask your own questions. I stand responsible for the nature of my explanations, and especially for interpretations, comments and views of my own. I hope that you find this entire book useful for your studies. I hope that you will find at least some of it interesting and better still provoking.

Acknowledgements

Acknowledgements may be traditional in book publishing but they are nonetheless a heartfelt on my part. This book has been part of my life for sometimes and, that life includes people who have helped me make it happen. The present book is piece of research work which hopefully I feel will be benefited to many young and talented scholars.

I am deeply indebted to my supervisor Dr. Suguna Pathy, Professor and Former Head, Department of Sociology, Veer Narmad South Gujarat University, Surat for her incredible guidance which enabled me to complete this work and therefore express my deep sense of gratitude and heartfelt thanks for her constant stimulation and constructive criticism throughout the research. I sincerely believe that without her this research would not have seen the light of the day. She has not only encouraged and motivated academically but also morally to broaden my perspective as a researcher. I have no words to thank her. I would also like to agree to that without her motivation this book would not be possible.

I have greatly benefited from the insightful discussions and suggestions of Prof. Parvez Abbasi, Head Department of Sociology, who has always kept faith in me and helped me keep up the pace of production. My thanks are due to him for suggesting title of the book and much other editing work. He has always provided me constant support in enhancing and perceiving my academic endeavour.

I like to thank my colleagues in the Department of Sociology and Master of Social work Programme of Veer Narmad South

Gujarat University for providing me with an eclectic intellectual atmosphere and with friendship. I would feel happy to thank Dr. Samiullah Ghanchi, Centre for the Study of Exclusive and Inclusive Policy, for helping me at different levels in the study, particularly in its initial stages.

I also wish to thank Mr. Bahadursinh Vasava, Mrs. Rekha Mistry, the staff of MSW programme for donating their valuable time to discuss various aspects of the study.

My special gratitude to Dr. Kiran Desai, Centre for Social Studies and Dr.Kalpana Rao, Department of Mass Communication who helped me in my academic venture. My thanks are also due to Ashish Nikam, Dr. Seema Shukla, Heena Shah, Ashokbhai Pawar, Centre for Social Studies and Neha Gutkar, Research Scholar, Department of Sociology.

I would be failing in my duties if I do not express my sense of gratitude to all the respondents of VNSG University, S.P.B. College and Olpad College for their cooperation in data collection for this study. I wish to acknowledge the Central library of Veer Narmad South Gujarat University, Centre for Social Studies library staff for the necessary help during my research.

My friends have always shared my pains and pleasures during the course of the study. The friendly cooperation of Kunal, Bhavin, Viral, Nimmi, Nimisha, Rujal, Pratiksha are acknowledged.

Finally, I must appreciate the patience and cooperation of my husband Jimmy who always stood by me throughout the tenure of this study and always made free from the family obligations. My parents as well as parents-in-law are also acknowledged because they are responsible for what I am today. Above all my son Dhyey is appreciated for bearing my absence during the long journey of research.

Lastly, I thank God for his Enlightenment and Unconditional Blessings; I dedicate this book to my entire family's sacrifice who has sustained me in the times of darkness.

PLACE: SURAT
January, 2013 **Shital J. Tamakuwala**

Contents

List of Tables

1

Understanding Gender: A Sociological Perspective

The concept of gender, as we all know came into existence during the early 1970s. It was used as an analytical category to draw a line of demarcation between biological sex differences and the way these are used to inform behaviours and complexes which are then assigned as masculine or feminine. The purpose of affirming a sex/gender distinction was to argue about the actual physical or mental effects of biological difference which was exaggerated to maintain a patriarchal system of power as well as to create a consciousness among the woman that they were naturally better suited to domestic roles. The conception of gender varies according to different contexts and time period. A common core sediment of meaning that the gender concept carrier while engaging with how different cultures work in, through and off gendered realities. Though gender has always been a part of societal realities everywhere, its emergence as a concept and a discursive tool is a recent and modern phenomenon.

Meanwhile analyzing gender as a keyword today involves the formation of certain vocabularies surrounding culture and society and the interpretive accretions they gained over time, but also about contexts that enable or disable meanings. It is often assumed that gender is a self-evident category and that its field of reference is transparent and uncomplicated. A static meaning of gender concept has aligned itself with a range of idea clusters from time to time, making it impossible to explain it by tracking its etymological roots alone. While such alignments on the one hand extend originally or grammatically and on the other hand, they make for re-routing of meanings that stretch the very matrix on which the gender concept is based.

The concept of gender is addressed in various specialized disciplines for instance in literary studies, history, anthropology, etc. each of which retrieves and refigures the concept differently. Centrally speaking the gender has been the issue of sexual difference and its manifestations and their consequences. The debate usually is found amongst man and woman and even women themselves, which implies the combination of biological and socio-historical factors in the definitions.

In the present exercise, we try to understand the major conceptual concerns on which the gender concept has been laid out working through the related terms such as sex/gender, inequality and biology/culture, in the first part. While in the second we would analyze the notions of gender, equality, sex and how these intersect with caste, community and religion in Indian context. Though gender is a complex of individual rights, identity, and equality, this complex often intersects with positions delineated by caste, creed, community, religion, etc. Despite the flexibility of meaning of the term gender, it also appears to retain a certain core reference to the social organizations of power relations between the sexes (Scott, 1988). Accordingly, every culture as well as every contextual configuration of elements within a culture, draws on this core, yet reconfigures the meaning of gender, gender relations, or gender inequalities differently under specific political and cultural contexts.

Gender and Inequality

The concept of gender emerged as a reaction to the marginality of women in existing critical frameworks, and sought to initiate changes in the substantive context and philosophical theory of knowledge of these disciplines. In social sciences, it became natural to analyze the society in terms of caste, class and race alone was not sufficient because it neglected to take into account relations of asymmetry between men and women. This term emerged to challenge the new categories and ways of understanding that could account for the nature and organization of male-female relations and the ways in which they are overlapped in a larger context of power relations. Thus, gender is inspired by a number of studies on different aspects of women's lives, but the interface of this with existing explanatory paradigms has remained a complex issue. Today, though gender has emerged as a major analytical category, it is marked by an interpretive angle wherein only certain questions can be raised in certain ways. The universal association of gender with inequality is one such rendering, where gender is read as coterminous conflict between the sexes and is issued to go beyond patriarchy.

Patriarchy term refers to male domination and female's acceptance and internalization of that dominance. 'Sylvia Walby' in her book theorizing patriarchy describes patriarchy "a system of social structures and practices in which men dominate, oppress and exploit women". Women have been socialized in such a manner that they love being dominated Feminists claim that the home and family are responsible for women's oppression. Our culture demands separately from male and female. Feminists like Carol Gilligan and Ned Noddings answers differ by arguing that women tend to stress on relationship and responsibility while men emphasize on rules and rights, which make both of them different. Here, it can be referred to Dipankar Gupta's concept of 'hierarchy and difference' where he mentions that stratification can be always straddled in two forms of axes, one vertical and another horizontal. Thus, inequality comes into Question when difference is arranged hierarchically while elements like language, race and culture should be straddled on the horizontal scale (Gupta, 1991: 9).

Our male dominated society have frequently claimed that the development of the child requires the mother to denote herself completely to the welfare of the child and it is the primary duty of the mother to shower all kinds of affection and care to the child. The father does not perform any of those duties. Our patriarchal system most peculiar feature of most societies is that the child bears the surname of her this father. Moreover, she is first considered the property of her father and after marriage of her husband. The feminist argue that her surname should not be changed but that is considered futile. Moreover, the child should also bear her surname, in order to challenge patriarchy. But looking deeply the surname of the mother is also the surname of the mother's father which would be like reinforcing patriarchy once again.

The world of man and a woman has been divided into two halves, forming many pairs of binary opposites. It is a world of body *Vs* mind, nature verses culture, emotion verses reason, private verses public. These dichotomies stand in chain to each other that shape the culturally constituted roles for men and women. (Gender, Culture and History, 291: 2).

Body Vs Mind

A woman's existence is centrally because of her body she bears and rears children. Besides her laudation functions has made the functional abilities of her body more prominent. The society has burdened her with childcare, assigning no role to men. Other than breastfeeding, there is no work involved in childcare and household chores that a man's anatomy prevents him from doing it. Our culture with its patriarchal ideology, has been exploiting women in the name of motherhood, which our culture has prescribed as the primary duty of a woman. The woman suffers a lot due to her body. Simon de Beauvoir said that menstruation interrupts a woman's routine, putting her in stigmatized state, involving various restrictions on her activities and her social contacts. Simon concludes that the female "is more enslaved to the species than the male, her animalist is more manifest".

Nature Vs Culture

The male dominated society clearly depicts the dominance of male and subordination of the women. Women were allocated domestic service and attending upon children while men did the rest. When a child is born, the mother is usually in most cultures in charge of breast-feeding the baby taking care and socializing it (Ortner, 1997: 16). As we all know infant and children are considered a part of nature and are unsocialized like animals. Moreover, women with their association with infants and children are tagged together with 'nature'. Since, men lack a natural basis meant for family orientation i.e., series they do not reproduce, the cultural reasoning seems to go that men are the natural proprietors of religion, ritual, politics and other realms of cultural thought. Thus, men are associated with culture i.e., the higher form of human thoughts involving art, religion and law (Human Rights, Gender and Environment, 242).

Private Vs Public

These physical and social roles of women and men have extended their association with private/public dichotomy. The private sphere popularly known as the domestic sphere has no economic-political or historical significance. The private realm stands in opposition to the public sphere. 'The private sphere needs to be nourished with understanding, co-operation, care, selflessness and of course bundles of emotions. However, the public sphere is a competitive would, which requires being aggressive, reasonable and ambitious with no trace of emotions. This we can say, as emotions are the greatest hindrance to the profit-making motive of the public sphere. Socialist feminist have pointed out that the private and public have different modes of production. Even though toil hard all through the day; they have been branded as useless, worthless, entities, whereas the man in the public sphere is given more importance. Things even worsen with working women as they shuttle between the two worlds, which has different kinds of expectations systems altogether. At one point they need to be competitive and at other point they need to shower their blessings, love and affections.

The exaggeration showing in early feminist writings is to cast the analysis in terms of gender exploitation is nothing but only a reflection of its overlapping in a series of groups such as equality/ inequality, which set up male dominance or superiority and female subordination (inferiority) as opposite poles of relation under one system of power. There have been two lines, however, along which the analysis has sought to be extended in the later writings i.e. the first is to work with a more variation understanding of patriarchal relations as neither homogenous nor unitary in nature, which varies across time, space, and economic position within the same society. The second is to focus on the potentialities of women engaged with patriarchal patterns. Both are recognized as various agents and the agendas of power exercise, but it cannot be determined without the operated knowledge fields. This clearly stressed that patriarchy relations took historical specific forms, as the diversity of forms and cultures led to differences in the way of gender are issued.

Be that as it may the conjoining of gender with inequality has been the most significant moves which predefine the field of gender studies. This difference of social inequality could be broadly presented as stratificational. Such a framework has tended to present a range of social differences such as class/gender in terms of common underlying principles of equality, which means that many layers of difference are all understood as manifestations of inequality. Socio-anthropological debates on the nature of Indian society, suggest that the hierarchal logic with social differences which is quite varied with the egalitarian principles defining the western social ethos. A non-western cultural context forces one to look into a range of similar questions of gender, particularly as to whether the joining of gender identity and gender inequality is the understanding of an individual, which itself is inseparable from an ideology of rights, liberty and equality. Since, identity is seen, much more in terms of a person's location within a group for e.g. it has been pointed out that concepts of person in India do not derive from an epicenter of an individual with a sovereign unitary identity, but are revealed as an identity that is other-directed (Marriott, 1990).

The perception of the self as a fluid entity, where there are no individuals, but dividual selves places the burden of self-definition on interpersonal relations with the other. Such twofold dimension is symbiotically linked to sociality and than referring to the ways in which social relation between persons and very nature of social action is constituted. It is very necessary to understand the concept of gender where persons are seen as composite beings, which are composed of many layers of social relations. We find hierarchical principle clearly within the caste society and social junctures also. Social relations are considered hierarchal whole and while disadvantage is expressed within these space are always to be key questions of gender. More often than not in India, the concept of gender is adopted, as a framework of equality *vs.* inequality and in this context, the structure of hierarchy needs to be investigated. Then only analyse gender relations rather than as a purely oppositional category where one is defined against another.

Inequality and Gender

Sex role theory proved inadequate to explore the variations in gender definitions, which requires deeper examination of the variations within the category of men or women. Such theorizing enables to see the relationships between and among men-women as structured relationships not as abstract set of relations. A movement, which relates to social change, for e.g. feminism or gay liberation, ultimately becomes movements that expand role definitions and even change role expectations. These movements lead to options of opportunities for individual men and women whose lives are constrained by stereotypes. However, whenever we see we find that social and political movements are not only about expanding the options of availability for individuals of inhibiting sex roles but also permit themselves to emerge or evoke. This would result in reallocations of resources, and reducing forms of inequality that are studded in social institutions and sex role stereotypes. The social constructionist approach emphasizes conflicting relations between and among groups of people within social institutions.

In this connection (Hacker, 1993) argued that largely the position of women and blacks have much in common as systematic structural inequality produces a "culture of self-hatred among the target group. And yet we do not speak of race-roles". This is illogical because the difference within each race are for greater than the differences between races and needs to be analyzed in the context of the socially based power relations between white and non-white people movements for social equality are much more than expanding role options. Role theory cannot explain race of gender relations in isolation of the wider socio-cultural and political framework.

We may argue that gender is about difference as well as inequality and power. At gender relations level, gender is about the power that men as a group have over women as a group, and it is related to certain men over other men or some women over other women. Gender and power collide and exist together—not because power is the consequence of gender difference—but because power is what produces those gender differences in the first place. However, we hold that gender is an unequal power relation between men and women. Thus, theories of gender need to explain both difference and domination. While other theories explain male dominance as the result of sex differences.

That symmetry breaks down if we try to imply to men. Men always feel themselves to be equally constrained by a system of stereotypic convections that do not allow them to live a life which they are entitled to Men as a group are powerful than women, but visualizing single man compared to woman in it not so. The feeling of powerlessness is one reason why so many men believe that they are the victims of reverse discrimination.

Gender, Biology and Culture

The understanding of gender based on commonsensical perceptions of the differences between male and female vary everyday. Gender is not found as self-evident and unproblematic but also found as naturally given. Moreover, the evolution of gender as a concept has also been a consequence of the realization of the pitfalls in relying on "woman" as an analytical category. Though the large numbers of empirical and descriptive women centered studies were indeed, largely constituting women as a field for analysis counter several problems.

For instance, early studies of the status of women in India invariably obscured the cultural and contextual heterogeneity of the category of women, whose attributes and activities have varied in relation to the diverse intersections of caste, class, age, kinship, religion, region and so on (Chakravarty, 1989; Menon, 1999). The category of women was reduced to woman as a biological category. The concept thus emerged in an early distinction posited between sex and gender. Recently the cultural conditioning and experience found that going beyond the category of sex, which referred merely to the sexual or biological differences between male and female.

The cluster of meanings of gender has very close connection with the feminist movements the world over. Feminist theory during the 1970's subscribed to the equality position, denying differences between women and men and arguing that women must be equal to men in all respects, but not calling an end to inequality based on biological difference. By the 1980's however, certain trends within this body of theory veered around to an essentialist position, affirming and celebrating women's bodies and creative capacities, arguing that these be given equal social recognition (Rhode, 1990). Though the positions differed in terms of their angle towards sexual difference, the equality principle was kept out of analysis. In the recent years the concept of difference rather in terms of equality and inequality has itself been largely critical as some indicating the need to distinguish between difference as a biological fact and equality as a socio-political one. This attempt is centralized on the notion that biological sexual difference generates power relations.

A large number of heterogeneous voices from within the women's movement have tried to draw attention of difference in women's experiences and lives—likewise through caste, class, colour, sex, nation and so on. These voices prove that not only biology is the marker of gender but the various aspects of cultural context also shape gender experiences in innumerable ways. The recognition that notion of femaleness and maleness are largely social and psychological products also paved the way for a perception of gender as concept as Scott observes that gender becomes a way of denoting "cultural constructions"—the entirely social creation of ideas about appropriate roles for women and men. It is a way of referring to the exclusively social origins of the subjective identities of men and women. Gender is in this definition, a social category imposed on a sexed body (Scott, 1980: 19). Typically studies not just in literary criticism, but also anthropology and history came to focus on the different ways in which femininity and masculinity are culturally constituted, the tension between biological constitute and cultural construction has come to configure most modern debates on gender.

Reconfiguring Gender: Some Issues

In spite of the advance, gender analysis represents today over the earlier sexual difference argument, the distinction made between sex and gender has given rise to number of questions related to the relation between women and their bodies such as—What are bodies? Do they exist prior to gender? Does one belong to a gender or does one become a gender? Female body is a natural fact, and there is nothing-cultural expression or external something. The reluctance, which speaks about the female body other else than symbolic or cultural terms, has often led to over emphasis on femininity. The problems which often arouse related to sex/gender distinction have become more apparent and omnipresent.

Gatan (1992) argues that the federative dimension of gender in earlier researcher now seems to be constraining analysis, largely due to the perception of gender as attributes inscribed upon a neutral body. To delink sexual difference from gender, suggests that femininity is something that has been removed from it. In reality the body is not a receptacle but the medium through which meanings are produced.

To put this misleading issue in place it is very much essential to reestablish the co-relations among the two principal axes, that define female subjects in specific socio-historical context, namely femininity (as an acquired attribute) and its grounding in the female body respectively. The point is that we need to go beyond both biological essentialism (gender as an essential trait) as well as cultural constructivism (gender as culturally constructed). It does not just understand how gender is defined, structured and experienced within a culture but also sensitivity to the variations, in the content of gender across and within cultures. Different from the other approaches, the sexed body is neither a mere symbol nor an inert biological foundation onto which gender ideas are written. Gradually, the body becomes the very medium through which femininity is constituted. In Indian context, a great deal of significant work has been done regarding the construction of female bodies and sexuality, consisting the interrelations of gender subjected with caste, class, colour, socio-cultural ethic, political events (John and Nair, 1998; Sangari and Vaid, 1989; Rajan, 1993). Meanwhile, the superficial separations between sex and gender (or even body and mind) are impossible. By asking how women inherit and live through a female body, one can open up several issues, for scrutiny, such as how women inhabit the body, what are the socio-cultural meanings 'invested in the female body, how does' the women body occupy space and exist and so on. Such a formulation highlights the interface between the material body and representational body, and the ways in women activate these constitutive conditions.

Though the early theories of patriarchy and female subordination give little room for an active female subject, later theories of gender has raised the issue of agency. The issue of agency is central to contemporary debates found in India, and the agencies extensively are used as a means of transformation, largely in political action. These perceptions raise questions that are based and related to identify certain kinds of actions of women as agential and others as not. This helps us to understand the domains of power. The delineation of spaces as both public and private, the positing of public as a political domain (power), women's lack of entrance of this field and their consequent characterization of powerlessness aspects of this rendering. This seems to be problematic, as this does not explain the varied actions of the women. As Sangari (1993) has noted, such a view would be not only historical but also distortive in predefining women's agency in specific ways. Another way of achieving and recording women's agency has been the documentation and examines instances of women's resistance within a larger frame of domination (O'Hanlon, 1991; Raheja and Goldi, 1996). Among these would figure women's implicit acts of resistance, unplanned, often non-confrontational in that to avoid a direct conflict with authority structures. In spite of their differences, what seems problematic in both tendencies is that we may be speaking of women as group or woman as individual, without proper and sufficient clarification of the identity. A consideration of how women's bodies are lived and imaged, how they are spoken about the perceived, and the narratives such as community, honour, morality, nation, etc. as well as how women respond to these mediations, which would enable us to better address the question of women's agency i.e., to understand women's agency and gender as to how women live (in) their bodies and how they contend with what cultures makes of these bodies. The answer to the queries related body's sexuality and its cultural mediations, or female embodiment occurrence can be identified. Precisely, the influences such as cultural beliefs and practices regarding the body, ritual prescriptions and norms of female conduct that orient speech, etc. all can be included in 'matrix of sexualization'. Such matrix specifies certain domains of moral conduct within a community and is often responsible for the emergence of conceptions of feminine and masculine. Beside it also includes ideas and concepts of shame and honour, the authority of fertility through marriage, an outline of appropriate spaces for women, codes of manliness, etc. Often women's perceptions and their bodily experiences are routed through such a matrix. Therefore, indeed we can say gender can be implicated within socio-cultural practice regulation of sexed bodies.

The most significant neglected parameters that define this grounding matrix of sexualization are space and spatiality. It may be argued that the femininity/masculinity and the activities of women and men are negotiated within socio-spatial parameters that define physical space for e.g. the meaning of inside and outside of these spaces are elaborated in symbolic terms. In rural South India, for instance, the terms inside and outside are not just indicators of physical space, but has various dimensions of meanings depending on how they are used. For an instance sitting outside, for women denotes that she is menstruating, avoiding from inner spaces reflects ritual dimension. While similarly, delineations of inside and outside also define work opportunities for women. When used socially related in a village, "outside" could be the area inhabited by the so-called low castes reflects economic and social dimension. These socio-spatial usages define relations between persons, different castes, or even religious groups. These meanings are context circumscribed and could be differently exhibited in other localities, such as urban and semi-urban spaces. The point is to analyze the power of this matrix for understanding how gender is figured locally as socio-spatial matrix of sexualization helps to perceive women's lives and their social structures. On one side, it demonstrates how norms of space and movement are written into definitions of the female body giving detail study of their lives acts of speech. On the other hand it indicates the manner in which the woman or female body becomes central to the drawing of boundaries within the communities. In broad terms gender refers to the social organization of differences between the sexes (Cornell, 1987; Scott, 1988). What is being emphasized here is the space and spatiality is a vital idiom through which gender (and other) differences are articulated and channelled in multicultural contexts.

It is a fact that issues related equality, female agency and body have been the main debate in the feminist movement highlighting explicitly gender concept in many ways. Since last decade or even more, we find that the discourse on gender has been the central space in women's studies. Having said so we also need to accept that some the term monolithic feminism has existed and the world are being feminist studies exclude the histories and struggles of women who do not belong to dominant group sections of society in India. In other words there is an urgent realization that the way in which we are positioned as women, and how this positioning occur with the range of other identities matters a great deal to our experience of oppression and subjugation.

In Indian context issues related to gender equality are being addressed at different levels and by various agencies both academic as well as action. Thus attempts were made to highlight asymmetries in gender relation, such as vulnerability of women workers, sexual harassment, health care and development regarding women. These concepts of women's rights were made on legal rights of system to be more concern about the gender inequality. These actions and movements of women directed in actions towards the government transforming them as state policies, in the areas of law, health and employment. Subsequently the mobilizations around issues of rape, dowry, and attributes compelled the state to take effective measures of women's issues, and also to consent women's groups while formulating policies on a wide range of issues. Viewed thus at one level are expression of women's agency within the space of civil society; at another level are the struggles for equality within the framework of the democratic state itself, a struggle alongside other groups for better access to resources has been on engagement (Gandhi and Shah, 1992; Kumar, 1993). In addition to the women's concerns, women's movement/struggles are also addressing gender issues in the context of globalization particularly liberalization policies, rising communalism, fundamentalism, subtle casteism, etc.

Therefore, it has become necessary for Indian feminism, to redefine itself in the face of these developments, a task rendered all the more difficult due to the different kinds of identity policies in which religious, caste, and economic groups have been engaging (Tharu and Miranjana, 1999).

Gender is not simply a system of classification, by which biological males and females are sorted, separated and socialized into equivalent sex roles. Gender goes beyond these seemingly existentialist platitudes to the universal inequality between women and men. For, when we speak about gender we apparently speak about hierarchy, power and inequality, not simply difference. In order to underscore this issue, most social and behavioural scientists now use the term gender in a different way than we used the word sex. Sex refers to the biological apparatus, the male and female, our chromosomal, chemical, anatomical organization. While gender refers to the meaning that are attached to those differences within a culture. Sex is male and female whereas gender refers to the meanings that one attached to those differences within a specific culture. Sex is male and female; gender is masculinity and femininity—what it means to be a man or a woman. To cite Justice Antonin Scalia, 'The word "gender" has acquired the new and useful connotation of cultural and attitudinal characters distinctive to the sexes. That is to say, gender is to sex as feminine is to female and masculine is to male' (Kimmel, 2006).

By and large if not all but some men are ubiquitous in universities and professional schools and in the public sphere in general. When we study specific books yet we do not find the word women but very often we notice the word, men. Every course, which is not "women's studies", is obviously a course of "men's studies", be it history, political science, chemistry, literature, geography and so on. But when we study men, we study and have really meant them as political leaders, military heroes, scientists, writers, poets, etc. Everywhere one turns there are courses related to men, but no information on masculinity. Until a person thinks himself generic universally generalizable, he doesn't understand that race, class and gender didn't refer only to the people who are marginalized by race, caste and gender privileges. For example, only white or upper caste people in the society have the luxury not to think about race or caste every minute of their lives. Likewise only men have the luxury to pretend that gender does not matter. Needless to mention that how power is so often invisible to those who have it—the privilege and gender.

The interplanetary theory of gender assumes, whether through biology or socialization, that women act like women wherever they are and men act like men wherever they are.

One of the most celebrated anthropologists to explore these differences was Margaret Mead, whose research in the South Seas (Samoo, Polynesia, Indonesia) remains, despite some significant criticism, an example of engaged scholarship. Mead was clear that sex differences were "not something deeply biological", but rather was learned and once learned, became part of the ideology that continued to perpetuate them.

Every society reveals some differentiation between women and men and, therefore, the society intends and exhibits the patterns of gendered inequality and male domination in specific ways. We all are familiar that gender differences and gender inequality exists more or less in the society. Economic, political and social variables tend to produce different cultural configurations. Researcher points out those different cultures in society who need more physical strength and highly developed motor skills, the more will be the differences in socialization between males and females. The studies also reveal that larger the family group the larger the differences between women and men.

It needs no special mention that one of the main key determinants of women's status has been the division of labour around childcare. Women's role and responsibility of reproduction has limited their social and economic participation. No society in the world assigns childcare to men. If the men take care and responsibility of childcare more compared to women then the status of women will be surely higher than men. Relationships between children and their parents have also been seen as key to women's status. Sociologist Scoot Coltrane found that the close the relationship between father and son, the higher the status of women is likely to be. The more mothers and father share child rearing the less men belittle women. Margaret Mead also emphasized the centrality of fatherhood by arguing that most cultures take women's role in child rearing as a given, whereas men must learn to become nurturers.

There is much at stake, but nothing inevitable "every known human society rests firmly on the learned nurturing behaviour of men. Such issues are not simply incidental for women's lives either; it turns out that the more time men spend with their children, the less gender inequality is present in that culture. *Controversially, the more free women are from childcare the more that childcare is parceled out elsewhere and the more that women control their fertility the higher will be the status.*

Daphne Spain (1992) argues that "societies with men's hut are those in which women have the least power, if you spend your time away from your hut, off at the men's hut with the other men, you'll have precious little time, and even less inclination to spend with your family and sharing in child rearing". Therefore, it may be mentioned that males and females can be trained for a vast arrangement of characteristics and individual variations with overlapping order. Since, we find very less difference between girls and boys, yet we take into consideration for their ineffectiveness of socialization activities such as televisions, toys, play, schools, etc., in shaping the behaviour of children in psychological experiments. It seems that boys and girls perform similar tasks without labelling the tasks as gender appropriate. The social environment is filled with gendered messages and gendered activities. Even if the child possesses no fixed and permanent gender roles, social arrangements will automatically reinforce gender differences. If so in a gender - neutral experiment, social requirements are removed, the child does not behave in accordance with a gender stereotype. Often, the first time we hear that gender is socially constructed, that means that we are not responsible for what we do. Small wonder as we hold often "society made me like this," so it's not my fault." When we say that gender identity is socially constructed, we mean that meanings and behaviors rs that we construct from the values, images, and prescription we find in the world around us. Our gendered identities are both voluntary, we choose to become who we are and perused, we are pressured, forced, sanctioned and often physically beaten into submission to some rules. We neither make up the rules but gradually peruse them nor adopt them in our social life. Social constructions thus build on the other social and behavioural sciences adding specific dimensions to the exploration of gender, inequality and difference (*ibid*). To explain the institutional dimension, social constructionism, moves beyond socialization of gendered individuals who occupy gender—neutral sites, to the study of the interplay between gendered individuals and gendered institutions.

The famous phrase by Simon de Beauvior, One is not born woman but becomes one, a basic statement which shows distinction between sex and gender. Society takes up the task of converting a biological male into a man and a biological female into a woman by prescribing masculine and feminine qualities to them. According to Ann Dakley, "gender is a matter of culture" (Dakley, 1985: 16). She asserts that gender distinction constructed by society, based on sex differences, which are biological in nature as not only, is the division of labour by sex is not universal but also there is no reason why it should be. They own their creation to human, inventiveness rather than invisible biological forces.

Culture is a learned way of behaviour that is transmitted from generation to generation. Moreover, it is shared by a group and historically accumulates over a period. Therefore, it is said to have a historical growth, which is linked with the past and the future. There are certain norms, values and beliefs in any society that are culturally determined and socially transmitted. Culture pertains to the learned aspects of society rather than the inherited ones the way in which children and other new members of society learn the ways of life in that society is called socialization. It is a process of transmitting culture consisting of "complex processes of interaction through which the individual learns the habits, beliefs, skills and standards of judgment that are necessary for effective, participation in social groups and communities" (cited in Shankarwa, 1993: 241). Socialization is a process that not only allows the baby to know about the basic norms of society, but also helps in the gradual development of one's self. Development of the self on the ego comes with the help of role-playing where a child put himself/herself in somebody else's shoes and tries to get his/herself image through other's perception (Mead cited in Shankarwa's 1993: 252). Thus the child comes to learn about the norms, expectations and different roles to be played in the group through the process of socialization. A child learns about his/her gender identity by learning what is she/he expected to do by others for instance a male child learns to confirm to his own gender group by negating all the activities that a girl child does. Thus, a male child becomes violent and plays hazardous games and keeps way from dolls and kitchen set else he would be branded a girl. Socialization is continuous process that helps learn the normative behaviour, which mostly happens to be the stereotypic behaviour. The very first thing the child is socialized about is the idea regarding his/her gender identity, socially constituted gender role from stereotype.

Gender Construction

At a very early age, the title boy develops an object-cathexis of his mother, which is originally related to the mother's breast... his father the boy deals with by identifying himself with him. For a time these two relationships exist side-by-side, until the sexual wishes in regards to the mother become intense and the father is perceived as an obstacle to them. This gives rise to the Oedipus complex (Freud, 1957: 219). So in repressing the erotic feelings towards the mother and accepting the father as a superior being, the boy identifies with the father and become aware of his male identity. (Freud cited in Giddens, 2000: 110). The child suffers from worthlessness and shame and through the process of identification; he tends to internalize the voice of the torturer. It is similar to what the Indian felt about their oppressors during the British rule. This is the form where identification is established with the oppressor (Nandy, 1983: 7). In this case, the farther acts as the 'other for the boy child'. (Mellody cited in Baker and Galanski, 2001: 90) But this 'others' adds to the masculine identity (the self) construction of the boy child. The girl slowly realizes that she is not like her father because of certain anatomical differences. Therefore, she should be like her mother—then she starts identifying with the mother and when she grows up, she seeks her father in her lover. She loves being dominated by men, which represents the dominance of the father (Storey, 1993: 132-133).

But Nancy Chodrow has something else to say. She reverses Trend's statement by saying that masculinity rather than femininity is defined by a loss the forfeiting of close attachment to mother. She emphasizes more on the role of mother in the development of a child's identity rather than the role of father as Trend did (cited in Giddens, 2002: 111). Accordingly Chodrow argues that attachment with the mother is broken at some point of time in order to achieve a separate sense of self. And this process takes place in different ways for boys and girls. Girls remain closer to their mother and imitate her. In Chodrow's view this tends to produce characteristics of sensitivity and emotional compassion in women. Boys on the other hand reject the closeness to the mother in order to forge their understandings of masculinity from what is not feminine. They learn not to be sissies or mummy boy. So, they remain unskilled in relating closely to others they develop more analytical ways of looking at the world emphasizing on achievement and repressing their ability to understand their own and other feelings (Giddens, 2002: 111). Thus, male identity is constructed through separation. So men fear close associations while women feel endangered in the absence of one as their self-esteem and identity gets damaged.

The recent news item reported women in European countries suffering from domestic violence. Domestic violence is a common feature, but it had a strange link with love. 18 per cent of the mistreated women in trance told that they were still in love with their violent partners. Many among them were guilty that they failed to become good wives and lovers, as they were unable to sympathize with their violent partners. So, these women felt they deserved thrashing. (Gyanarajan Swain, *The Hindu*, 2004).

Economic development is thus no longer considered synonymous with economic growth, it is a wider concept, which includes growth plus many other objectives necessary for the upliftment of an economy. To quote Michael Jodaro, "Economic Development must therefore be conceived as a multi-dimensional process involving major changes in social structure, popular attitudes, and national institutions as well as acceleration of economic growth, the reduction of inequality and eradication of absolute poverty. Development in its essence must represent the whole gamut of changes by which an entire social system, tuned to the diverse basic needs and desires of individuals and social groups within that system, moves away from conditions of life widely perceived as unsatisfactory, towards a situation or condition of life regarded as materially and spiritually better.

Sex Discrimination

With the release of the Census 2001, UNFPA began a journey to address the growing sex-ratio imbalance. Calculated based on the number of girls per 1000 boys in the 0-6 year age group, the child sex ratio showed a sharp decline from 976 girls to 1000 boys in 1961 to 927 as per the 2001 census. What becomes newly apparent is how far the urban, educated middle class has gone to ensure birth of sons and not daughters. In addition, with this it became clear that the problem is not one deficiency as is seen in the case of malnutrition or poverty but a new expression of choice by largely urban families. The use of ultrasound to determine the sex of the focus was to contribute to the rapid decline in the child sex ratio. Adversely, a greater dip is seen in the ratios of urban cities and districts, educated and those access to resources and technology. In India, small families are becoming the preferred option, and deselecting daughters are achieving this. Couples want small families but not without son(s). Possibly, the employment of women outside the home and inherent recognition of the value of the girls within the culture can contribute to the survival of daughters.

In conjunction with the patriarchal influences on women's status, an analysis of patterns seen in the countries across Asia reveals three key factors that influence the sex selection. Sociologists and demographers conclude that sex selection will take place wherever there is a rapid fertility decline, with continued son preference, and access to technology and illegal abortion services. A distinct feature of sex ratio imbalance is that it is conditional in nature. Emerging data shows that it is often families without sons who are most likely to indulge in sex selection for their next child. Even in India, the Census office's Special Fertility and Mortality Survey (1998) shows that the sex ratio at birth is adverse for girls at higher birth orders. The ratio is as high as 139 boys to 100 girls for the third child when the two previous children are girls. If cultural conditions favour boys, then technology is already catching up to meet a latent demand. This is making the practice of sex selection almost irreversible and widespread.

Psychologist Warren Farrell called mate power a "myth" since men and women have complementary roles, and equally defamatory stereotypes of "Sex objects" and "success objects" (Farrell, 1993: 100). Farrell often uses the analogy of the driver to illustrate his case. The driver is in the driver's seat. He knows where he is going wearing a uniform. We think that he is in power but from his perspective someone else is giving the orders, so he is not powerful at all. From this analogy we can say that individual men are not powerful, the group of men is powerful and dominates. The relations between and among men emerge also as relations of power—power based on class, castes, race, ethnicity, sexuality, age and the like. It is groups of men, not men in general, who are oppressed within patriarchal sexual relations give rise to situations in different ways to overall subordination of women to men.

The social construction of gender relations has three main related issues present in its formation are identity, institution and interaction with regard to gender difference and inequality. Gender is less a property of the individual than is a product of our interactions with other we play in front of them. According to West and Zimmerman gender is a "managed property" which is contrived with respect to the fact that particular ways women and men are distinctively of social groups, constituted in concrete, historically changing and generally unequal social relationships" ("Doing Gender", 1987).

Thompson observes that class applies equally to gender as gender "is a relationship, not a thing"—and like all relationships, we are active in its construction. We do not simply inherit a male or female sex role, but we actively—interactively constantly define and redefine what it means to be men or women in our daily encounters with one another." (Cited in "The Making of English Working Class": 1966). James W. Messerschmitt argues, "Gender is a situated accomplishment in which we produce forms of behaviour seen by others in the same immediate situation as masculine or feminine." (Zemmerman, 2005: 29). Gender is what we bring to these interactions and what is produced in them as well. Social world is a built on systematic, structural inequality based on gender. Social life reproduces both gender difference and gender inequality. The study of sociology reveals and understands both what is different between women and men and what is not different but only seems to be whereas gender difference is the product and not the cause of gender inequality. Therefore, we can say that we are gendered people living gendered lives in a gendered society.

Taking world apart, gender starts from the family's environment where the child learns, and adapts his thoughts and actions. If one of the chief purposes of the family is to maintain both gender inequality and gender difference between the parents, then its other chief purpose is to ensure that those gendered identities are imparted to the next generation. It is in the family that the seeds of gender difference are first planted, that we first understand that being a man or woman, a boy or a girl, has different and unequal meanings. Gender socialization begins at birth and continues throughout our lives. Throughout childhood gender difference and gender inequality are created and reinforced through play, media, and the school. At later ages the girls are encouraged to move away but never as much as boys are parents interest building independence seems to explain this difference. As a result of gender stereotypes, mothers believe that boys rather than girls should be independent and encourage them to explore their world. And parents in general are more restrictive with their daughters and create more limits on their acceptable behaviour from a very early age.

Parent's early treatment of their infant is not usually to teach the child regarding a "proper" gender role, but rather reflects the fact that the parents themselves accept the gendered roles for men and women. Even though universally sturdy and active girls are still thought to be more delicate and gentle.

Researchers have found that people interact with infants based on assumptions rather than characteristics of the child itself. For example subjects in one experiment consistently gave gender specific toys (dolls for girls—hammers for boys) to infants they were told were either boys or girls (*ibid.*). As they were not knowing the sexes they described boys as strong, big, and soft and pretty for girls. One experiment showed a videotape of nine months old reactions to a jack in the box, a doll, a teddy bear and a buzzer. Half the observers were told the child was boy and half were told it was a girl. The expressions of anger, fear and pleasure they found were at emotional levels different when the child cried. Those who thought that the child was a boy found it angry and those who thought it was a girl found it afraid. When the child moves from infant to the toddler stage, boys are told, not to cling to their mothers are told that boys do not cry. Boys are expected to be independent aggressive and suppress his emotions. And whereas girls are encouraged to express emotions and control aggression. It is an established truth that the shops have different design toys especially for boys and girls. Girls are given dolls and doll houses while boys get trucks and buildings blocks. These labels originally come from the adults. Often we have noted that at the age of 2 or 2/6 years boys prefer to play with dolls but parents consider them to be girl's toys. Besides we find colour segregation among gender i.e. blue for boys and pink for girls which clearly shows our views and ideas regarding gender for example we think about the kinds of images boys and girls see in comic books and television shows. Boys are showed playing mythic heroes (cowboys, Indians, soldiers, superheroes, Ninja turtles) while girls often play mothers, nurses and teachers. Though this has changed significantly in recent years, it has changed for more for girls than for boys. Girls now play soccer but the direction of change has tended to go in only one way. For boys, the opportunities to play at girls games are rare, the label "sissy" is more negative than the label 'tomboy' while girls have more 'boy's toys' than boys have girl's toys.

Girls think they would be better off as boys and many of them declare that they would rather be boys than girls. By contrast, boys tend to see being girls as a fate work than death. "If I were a girl", one grader said, "Everybody would be better than me because boys are better than girls".

Coming to gendered politics of housework we have noticed through a historic fundamental transformation of a family. And it reveals that the greatest single shock the family has had to absorb has been the entry of women into the workplace. That women work outside the home as a matter of economic necessity and of ambition that will dramatically alter the life of modern family. Several studies observed that working mothers report higher levels of self-esteem and are less depressed than full time housewives. However, they report lower levels of marital satisfaction than do their husbands of traditional housewives. The reason is women's work multiplies increases at home and work twice more than men while the men work only outside home. Perhaps this must be the reason why women are so tired and unhappy. Arlie Hochsehild has called, "The second shift" the housework and child care that every family must do to function properly. More often than not women do housework and child care because they have to, not because they want to. To quote Mary Hallock Foote, "I am daily dropped in little pieces and passed around and devoured and expected to be whole again next day and all days and I am never alone for a single minute" (Gender and Space, 156; West and Zemmerman, 156).

The family as a gendered institution also depends on interpersonal relationship among family members, on the gendered division of household labour that produces male dominance in society. Gender inequality is expressed in the housework and childcare performed by men and by the different trajectories of men's and women's lives following divorce. It is maintained too often by the real or implicit threat of violence (Niranjana, 2001: 156).

A child who experiences love and nurturing from his or her father or mother will come to see that nurturing is something that adults do, not something that men and women do, so all the children, both boys and girls, will expect when they become adults. Similarly, it is related with work, the child will see adults working and not men or women working. The two experiences that trend himself identified as the most crucial elements of healthy adult life are love and work.

Coming to gender difference in school the classroom setting reproduces gender inequality. There are some signs of change; this nursery school experience is reproduced in every classroom in every town and city, everyday. Boys and girls learn and teach each other—what are appropriate behaviours and experiences for boys and girls, and make sure that everyone acts according to plan. "From elementary school through higher education, female students receive less active instruction, both in the quantity and in the quality of teacher time and attention," note Myra and David

Sadker, summarizing the research, failing at fairness. Many teachers perceive boys as active, capable of expressing anger, quarrelsome, while they perceive girls as affectionate, obedient responsive and tenacious. Many teachers assume that girls are likely to "love" reading and "hate" mathematics and science, and they expect the opposite of boys.

Status of Women in India

The Constitution of India guarantee women, as it does to all citizens, equality in all spheres besides making special provisions for them. The situation of women as it exists is one of low status, powerless, endangered by development suppressed by poverty and oppressed by patriarchy. Traditional structures have not failed to make room for them as equal partners in the decision neither making process, nor has the system ensured that their interests and concerns are reflected in development plans and local programmes. They are ignorant, unaware and ill informed about how they could live better lives with less drudgery, morbidity and fear of violence. Even though nature has endowed them with superior biological strength, the environment stifles their development.

Policy implements consider women as demographic tool to be used in the battle against population growth. Their health-care as women are of little concern but majority of women centre round pregnant or lactating mother. They are the beasts of burden, attending to all domestic chores, fetching fuel, fodder and water, from dawn to dusk on family farms, or enterprises with no reward, no asset and no recognition in the system of National Accounts. Women constitute 48 per cent of the total population in India. Among these 72 per cent live in rural areas. Even after 50 years of Independence these women continue to live in a state of neglection and exploitation. They generally have lower incomes and seldom have equal opportunities to develop their capacities. Given empowerment in terms of knowledge information, the right environment and proper skills, women can lead the nation to greater heights socially, economically and culturally (Hasan and Menon, 2004).

Education is one of the most important factors promoting economic development. The empowering role of woman's education is multidimensional, affecting not only every aspect of women's lives, but also the lives of their children and others who depend on them. Many developing countries exhibit considerable gender inequality in education, employment, welfare, health, etc. For e.g., girls and women in South Asia and China largely suffer with discrepancies in education (Klasen and Wink, 2000).

Assuming that boys and girls have a similar distribution of innate abilities and that children with more abilities are lesser abilities than girls have greater chances to be educated. The average innate ability of educated children is lower than what it would be if boys and girls had equal education opportunities. Assuming that the amount of human capital of a person is the outcome of a combination of innate abilities and education, gender inequality in education would therefore lower the average level of human capital in the economy and therefore slow the economic growth. For the same reason, such gender inequality in education would lower the impact of male education on economic growth and raise the impact of female education (Doller and Gatti, 1999; Knowle, Lorqelly and Owen, 1999).

Single-sex education for women often perpetuates detrimental attitudes and stereotypes about women that "by nature or situation girls and young women cannot become successful or learn well in co-educational institutions" (Dobbs, James, 1929).

Gender Discrimination in the Workplace

For many years, the chief obstacle facing women in the labour force is sex discrimination. Discrimination occurs when we treat people unequally because of personal characteristics that are not related to the job. To exclude one race, caste or gender from housing, educational opportunities, or employment would be a form of discrimination. With regard to gender discrimination in the workplace, employers have historically referred to a variety of characteristics about women to exclude them.

The basis for the discrimination may not rely on any stereotypic ideas about male and female differences, but it must be based on some occupational requirement that either only men or women could perform.

Employment is the most natural and best way to achieve the objectives of economic growth, poverty eradication, social justice, social stability and peace. The participation of women in economic activities is an important factor in the economic and social empowerment of women, as employment is not only a source of economic independence, but also gives women a sense of self worth. Over the last decade, the participation of women in the labour market i.e., paid work has increased in most part of the world. Women's global economic activity rate in the age-group between 20-54 climbed from 54 per cent in 1950 to 67 per cent in 1996 and is expected to reach almost 70 per cent by the year 2010 (ILA, 1996). Besides, the economic development, industrialization and demographic factors cultural and ideological factors play a role in determining the degree of feminization of the labour force.

Female heads of the households and women from poor families in particular have increasingly allocated their time to productive activities and taken up any kind of work available in their home countries to help contribute to family incomes, often at the expense of the household work, family care and their own leisure time. Their role in the labour market continues to remain invisible in many cases, and in numerous countries, the notion that the supply of female labour is easily available when needed, and dispensable when not needed, still persists. The increase in the quantity of women's employment, however, has not been matched by improvement in the quality of their employment. Majority of women go for typical forms of the wage work or self-employment, rather than stable fulltime wage employment in the formal sectors of the economy. These forms of work are mainly associated with low earnings, lack of training opportunities or promotion, and they tend to be highly unstable.

Women in Organized and Unorganized Sectors

Among rural women workers, majority is employed in agriculture as labourers and cultivators. 55.6 per cent of women workers followed manufacturing, 21.4 per cent agriculture and allied occupations 9.8 per cent and finance, insurance, real estates and business 4.9 per cent. In 1997, women workers employed in factories, mines and plantations constituted 14 per cent, 6 per cent and 51 per cent respectively of the total work force. More than 80 per cent of female workers are engaged in the agriculture sectors in rural India. In the urban areas, female workers participation in the tertiary sector has increased appreciably from 37.6 per cent in 1983 to 52.9 per cent in 1999. The distribution of female work participation and status employment indicates that there is a pronounced declining trend in the importance of self-employed category in both rural and urban areas and an overall increase in the casualization of the women work force from 31.4 per cent in 1972-73, to 40.9 per cent in 1997, in rural India with a marginal decline to 39.6 per cent in 1999-2000 (Government of India, 2002: 53).

Women in Agriculture

Women farmers provide enormous services at almost every stage of agriculture practice. The tradition of producing, selecting, storing and replanting seeds dates back to at least 5000 years. A major characteristic of the India's labour force is the structural stagnation in its intersectoral distribution. About 70 per cent of the labour force is concentrated in agriculture. The small women force has been at about 28 per cent. With increased population pressure on land, the choice of determining work status lies with the men folk who cultivate their land and the women land up as labourers. Hence, the occupational division of labour, women have slipped down from better skilled jobs to lesser skilled ones. Apart from poor participation of women in the workforce, there has been an increased uncertainty of women's employment. Acharya and Patkar (1983) have shown that employment uncertainty of poor women is four times more than that of men in the same category. The causes of overall uncertainty in employment have their origin in demographic, technological and social factors like caste, class or genders.

Thus difficult skill access and employers inhibitions contribute to female non-acceptance in the organized sector. On the other hand, the unorganized sector, in the industrial and services sector, employs women in large numbers.

Though gender discrimination is extremely difficult to justify, but far more mysterious mechanisms maintain gender inequality. Amongst them ubiquitous of these is sex segregation. Sociologist Barbara Reskin writer refers to women's and men's concentration in different occupations, industries, jobs and levels in workplace hexarchies and argues that sex segregation becomes, itself, a sexual division of paid labour in which men and women do different tasks, on the same tasks under different names or at different times and places. Different occupations are seen as more appropriate for one gender or the other, and thus women and men are guided, pushed or occasionally showed into specific positions (Barbara Reskin, "Sex Segregation in the Workplace" in women and work, 1999).

Sex segregation starts early and continues throughout our work lives, which has its significant consequences on incomes and experiences. If sex segregations were simply the product of socialized differences between women and men, we should expect that professions would have roughly comparable gender distributions. But they do not for e.g. In New York city, there are only 25 women out of 11,500 fire fighters, In Europe most dentists are female. In Russia half of the doctors are women.

To discriminate against individuals on the basis of average between group differences ignores the differences within each group. Such behaviours rely on stereotypes and should be prohibited under law. Logically, stereotypes fall into a compositional fallacy—assuming what is true of some is true for all. For example, "all human are animals but not all animals are human".

Another main reason for increasing wage gap in that men and women experiences different in the labour force for e.g. when men enter labour force, they enter for good, while women occasionally take time out for child bearing and parental leave. This has vast effect on women's wages, and fuels the growing gap across the life span. In fact, women who dropout of the labour force have lower real wages when they come back to work than they left.

Sexual harassment is one of the chief ways that men resist gender equality in the workplace. The increased reporting by women of their experiences at work, the re-labeling of behaviours that men used for granted.

The result of several historical and social developments is that the gendering of intimate life—of friendship, love and sex. In this century, we have witnessed a dramatic transformation in the gendered division of emotional labour. Since the 1970s, studies of friendship have taken a different turn, divided in two different events. One hand, feminism began to celebrate women's experiences as a source of solidarity among women. Women's greater experiences of intimacy and emotional expressiveness were seen not as a liability but as an asset in a culture that increasingly elevated the expression of feelings as a positive goal.

Most women, according to surveys, believe that women's friendship are decidedly better than men's because they involve personal care, concern, intimate sharing and more emotional exchange, while men's friendship were seen as more likely to involve work,. sports, business and other impersonal activities.

Sociologists Lynne Davidson and Lucille Duberman, "Even though they report little investment in the personal and relational levels of the friendship". Despite the findings that both women and men say, they disclose equal amounts of personal information and say that they are completely open and trustworthy to their friends, the authors conclude that women actually disclose more to their friends.

Without such relationship maintenance, men's friendships experience greater attrition than women's over time for example, Pilcher (1999) draws together a range of British research evidence that shows the gendered character of education and training, paid work, household work and caring, love and sexuality, body related technologies, popular media culture, crime and criminal justice, and politics. Adkins describes her research as concerned with the 'gendering' of the contemporary labour market. It focuses on the processes through which power relations between men and women in employment are constituted and how "advantage and disadvantage, exploitation and control, action and emotion, and meaning and identity are patterned through and in terms of a distinction between male and female" (Acker, 1990: 146; Adkins, 1995: 1). Adkins calls 'sex-workers', working both for the public and for their male colleagues and bosses. In other words they were required to fulfil conditions related to the production of an "attractive" female workforce (*ibid*, 145). This gendering of production practices meant that women and men employed in the leisure parks were qualitatively different kinds of workers. To be workers, women had to be "attractive" workers and carry out forms of sexualized work, whereas men did not have to do this (*ibid*, 147). Adkins argues that the labour market is gendered prior to job differentiation. In other words, women workers in the leisure parks had to fulfil the conditions of being sexualized workers regardless of their specific occupation. The thought about gender as a noun, which focuses on the distinctions between men and women can be noticed actively produced by "gendering" process, while the terms of "gendering" and engender give a clear emphasis to the ongoing, processed quality of gendered relations. The gender is said to be a patterned system of ideological and material practices, performed by individual in a society, through which power relations between women and men are made and remade as meaningful and worth. Only a gender order of a society forms codes, norms and standards of masculinities and femininities which are created and recreated and then organizing the relations amongst them.

The concept of the gender order was first developed by Jill Jullius Mathews (1984) in her study of historical construction of femininity. According to Mathews, the idea of the gender order gives recognition to the fact that every known society distinguishes between women and men, as systematic ways of creating social women and men and of ordering and patterning relations between them, it is not logically necessary that gender orders should be hierarchal, inequitable or oppressive (1984: 13). In her study she draws an analogy with the concept of the economic order or mode, which shows that systematic ordering of people's relationship to the means of production and consumption, may vary likewise it may be capitalist, feudal or communist in its specific content.

It seems that a gender order could be equalitarian or matriarchal, rather than patriarchal. To cite Mathew "The specific nature of content of any gender order is constantly in process, being formed and changed. It is fashioned by actions of individuals who are themselves formed in that interaction. It is created in the struggles and power strategies and contradictions and unintended consequences of a multitude of social groups and individuals and interest. The femininity and masculinity that are forged of these countervailing forces are never constant but always changing and more often than not internally in consistent if not contradictory" (Mathew, 1984: 14-15).

R.W. Connell (1997) in his study observed that the relationship between the body and gender is a central issue for gender theory and he opines that gender is the outcome of recurrent interpretations of the reproductive and sexual capacities of human body, and its multiple effects are femininities and masculinities. In his analysis, gender is a recurring creation of human agency, which also acts to constrain individual agency. For Connell's empirical research covers three major structures of gender relations which are labour, power and cathexis (concerned with emotional relationships, including sexuality). For Connell, as for Mathews gender relations are regarded as the outcome of human practice or agency subject to resistance as well as conformity and as acceptance. All this implies that gender relations are open to change in the contemporary gender order of industrialized world. For example, in family relationships the state policies interprets in the legitimacy of men's domination over women such as for ex. -- *via* laws on divorce, domestic violence and rape within marriage, pensions, taxation, etc. for married women who work outside home. Connell argues that gender inequality can be eradicated through individuals and groups, collectively and on a mass scale. Marshall (1994) finds the concept of the gender order valuable for the analysis of gender, particularly for understanding the relationship between individual gathered subjectivities and gender as a social structure. Marshall believes the gender order provides the mode of interpretation though individuals constructing an embodied subjective and social identity. For Marshall, though, a fuller account is needed of the formation of gendered subjectivities in the configuration of power relations especially in relation to understanding why it is that knowledgeable acting subjects may nonetheless tend to participate in the legitimation of conditions that reproduce their position (Marshall, 1994: 117).

In evaluating the concept of the gender order, critics point to its advantages over the concept of patriarchy. Pollert (1996) for example describes Connell's theory of the gender order as open to more diversity than patriarchy, emphasizing more on gender as an ongoing process than human agency. Similarly, Marshall also points out that the approach allows a description of a society as patriarchal, without lapsing into the trans-historical, agentless conception of patriarchy (1994: 116). For some critics however, the concept of the gender order has not overcome the problem of how to theory gender in relation to class and race. For example, West argues that Connell's (1987) approach fails to include either race or ethnicity or caste as key concepts (1989: 1489). Pollert criticizes Connell's theory of the gender order for its 'dualist' conception of gender and class arguing that it is based on diffuse (1996: 650). Despite the lack of clarity around the interrelations between gender, class, caste and race others (Maharaj, 1995; Pikher, 1999; Fiaser and Nicolson, 1989) feel that Connell's theory of the gender order goes some way toward satisfying the criteria of a postmodern gender theory as in that it is explicitly historical and attuned to cultural specificity in terms of time, place and diversity.

Gender segregation, which also is one of the most current issues faced in our society, occurs when women and men are located separately from one another. For example, in some countries, where there is educational provision for both boys and girls, rather than being educated together in the same institutions they are segregated on the grounds of gender and are educated separately, in single-sex schools or universities. Gender segregation in education can also be said to occur in the way that boys and girls often study different subjects.

Many researchers have focused on gender segregation in paid work in their analyses of power inequalities between women and men. In Hartman's (1982) account, there is a mutual accommodation between patriarchy and capitalism, which results in a vicious circle of disadvantage for women. Job segregation means that it is men who hold the job with greater material rewards, not relatively high wages compared to women. The lower wages earned by women in their jobs keep women dependent on men because they encourage women to marry. Married women must perform domestic chores for their husbands. This domestic division of labour in turn, acts to weaken women's position in the labour market. Thus, the hierarchal domestic divisions of labour are perpetuated by the labour market and *vice versa* (*ibid*, 448).

Segregation is at the most extreme level of jobs. Since occupations are clusters or aggregates of jobs, this grouping together of jobs may obscure the full extent of segregation. For example, if we find in teaching profession 'teacher' obscures the pattern that women predominate as teachers in primary schools and men in secondary schools. Similarly, the occupational classification 'cleaner' obscures the predominance of men as 'street cleaners' and women as 'office cleaners' (MacEmen, 1994: 5). We are not born with perceptions of gender differences, these emerge during the process of socio-economic change. The conflicts concerning are gender identity interaction particular ways that boys experience the processes of differentiation of the formation of sex. Both sexes establish separateness in relation to their mother, but because the mother is a woman, these experiences differ by gender. Though children of both sexes are originally part of her, a mother unconsciously and often consciously experiences her son as more of than her daughter. Reciprocally, a son's male core gender identity develops away from his mother.

While core gender identity for a girl is not problematic in the sense that it is for boys. Girls and women do not define themselves as 'not-men' or 'not-male' but as female. However, girls and women may have problems with their sense of continuity and similarity.

Men's and women's understanding of difference and gender difference must thus be understood in the relational context from which they are created. As we all know that the main stem of relation of boys and girls to their mother is the primary caretaker, love object and object of identification and is a woman in sexual and gender organized world. These developments create a gender difference which is central for males and not central for females. It gives men a psychological investment in difference that women do not have.

According to psychoanalytic accounts since Freud, it is very clear that males are "not females" in earliest development. But, because men have power and cultural hegemony in our society, a notable thing happens. Men use this hegemony to appropriate and transform these experiences. Both in everyday life and in theoretical, men have come to define maleness as that which is basically human, and to define women as not men.

Needless to mention that the subject of women is an ancient as the prehistoric period an evolution of man and society. From ancient time woman is always been seen as a part of male. She does not have her own recognition. Even that Eve was created out of a 'supernumery bone' of Adam Michelet describes woman as the relative being. According to Brenda"... Man can think of himself without woman. She cannot think of herself without man. And she is simply what man demands, thus she is called "the sex", which means that she appears essentially to the male as a sexual being. For man, woman is sex—absolute sex, no less. He is the subject, he is the absolute—she is the other (de Beauvoir, 1952: 19). The position of women in Primitive society is difficult to ascertain women's situation in pre-agricultural period. But women worked hard as she was the burden carrier. The terrible obstacle was the bondage of reproduction as menstruation, pregnancy and childbirth reduced their capacity to work. The domestic labour that feel to her lot because they were reconcilable with the cares of maternity imprisoned her in repetition and immanence; they were repeated from day-to-day in an identical form, which was perpetuated almost without change from century to century; they produced nothing new" (de Beauvoir, 1952: 71). While the position of men is totally in contrast to women. Initially man has been the inventor through numerous inventions, he proved himself self-realistic. Men's success has always been celebrated with festivals and triumphs. As hunter, as a warrior man proved by endangering his life for a purpose, that life was not of the supreme value for men. "For it is not giving life but in rising life that man is raised above the animal; that is why superiority has been accorded in humanity not to the sex that brings forth but to that which kills" (de Beauvoir, 1952: 72). Thus, women's subordination began with the society's development. Men's activities were always appreciated while women's undermined.

Historical Materialism and Women

According to historical materialism, human being is not only an animal species, but also a historical reality. In their opinion women could not be treated simply as a sexual organism, their position has also been determined by techniques, attainment and economic organization. Engles retraces the history of women according to the materialist perspective (Engles, 1952: 19). He further explains that in the Stone Age, when land was common to everyone in the clan, the rudimentary character of the spade and hoe limited the possibilities of agriculture, so that women's strength was adequate for gardening. In this primitive division of labour, the two sexes constituted in two classes and equality was found between them. While man hunted and fished, woman ran the home. Thus, women played a large part in economic life. With more inventions and refined agricultural devices, man's work expanded, as he takes on more men to help in production, hence slavery and private property appear. The man as master of slaves and of the earth becomes the proprietor also of women. According to Engels this was "the greatest historical defeat of the feminine sex" (*ibid*, 20).

With this change in the value of work of man and woman, the maternal authority gave into paternal authority. The property was inherited from father to son and no longer from woman to her clan. Thus, the private property gave rise to patriarchal family, and from here began the subjugation of woman. She was seen as Earth, Mother or Goddess, but not as fellow creature in man's eyes; It was 'beyond' the human realm that her power was affirmed. Hence, she was 'outside' of that realm. "Society has always been male; political power has always been in the hands of men; public or simply social authority always belongs to men" (de Beauvoir, 1952: 79).

From the beginning of humanity, men's biological advantage has enabled them to confirm their status as sole and sovereign subjects. They have always affirmed their power. Frazer puts more aptly: "Men make the Gods; women worship them. Women's place in the society is always which men assign to her; at no time has she ever imposed her own law" (*ibid*, 87). With the ownership of land, man claimed also ownership of women. Since woman owns nothing, she does not enjoy the dignity of being a person; she forms a part of the patrimony of a man, first of her father, then of her husband. The crux of the problem is that the two sexes have never shared the world equally. Even today the woman is heavily handicapped as her rights are legally recognized in the abstract, while tradition and custom prevent their full expression. Thus woman's position is lower than man in all spheres of her social, political and economic life.

Many historians have defined the working class 'defector' as working men. Occupational, skills, wages, relations of production, the labour process itself, have been and still discussed as if social production were an exclusive male prerogative. More often than not consciously or unconsciously, the world has been conceived in the image of family, the husband is the breadwinner and the wife remains at home attending to housework and childcare. Both the household itself and women's domestic labour within it are presented as the state to the world of real historical activity. The labour historian has ignored women as workers in the labour market and within the household, consequently women's contribution to production and to the reproduction and maintenance of labour force as well, has been dismissed. This is partly because the labour and economic historians, who first wrote about the working class, wrote about the organized and articulate labour movement, accessible through its trade union records, its newspapers and the occasional autobiography. Only recently have the inaccessible areas of working class life has been approached, but even here the focus has remained on the working man. In every respect women's participation in history has been marginalized (Alexander, 1976).

It was but for the feminist history that released women from their obscurity as the wives, mothers and daughters of working men. The feminist perspective meant that the production is not simply the class struggle between the producer and the owner of means of production. But it is also the development of a particular form of sexual division of labour in relation to the struggle. The relation who is changed drastically can be because of the dislocations created by industrialization and modernization of the industries. The stress of the working class may be due to the rapid increase in the population, the movement of population into towns dramatized the class antagonisms, which always created anxiety among the class. This industrial and political activity was strict which resulted and gave birth to the Victorian middle class ideology in western context, which is a blend of political economy and Evangelicalism. The natural laws included political economy and the laws of capitalist production. While the woman's roles as wife and mother was centralized and therefore, it was expected from them to guard and function the religious and socio-cultural values. Henceforth, we can say that women's wage-work was supposed to be in harmony with the home, the family and domesticity.

The biological features and characteristics resulted role determinants of the division of labour and resulted in domestic roles of women received enormous emphasis. Thus for woman 'home' became the primary occupation and if they opted job it was the secondary salaried job. Over the recent decades, women in general have been liberated considerably from the domestic drudgery by the introduction of modern domestic appliances. But despite this and due to changing family structure, the burden of women's work has increased. Their working hours have been doubled. Once Lenin described women's domestic work, as monotonousness and lack of job satisfaction which stands so appropriately in the present period. Housework is most unproductive, the most barbarous and the most arduous work a women can do. It is exceptionally petty and does not include anything that would in any way promote the development of the women (Lenin, 1983 quoted in Alexander). The drudgery of women's work is also accompanied by psychological tensions and depression, fear and anxiety. Rice emphasized the enormous burden placed on women by their 'housewife role...' in the large majority of homes. The woman is ...the slave without whose labour the whole structure of the family tends to collapse (Rice, 1939: 14).

Hinduism provides a conception of the world in which women are necessary, but powerful and dangerous. Traditionally this power and danger has been controlled through religious laws prescribing women's proper behaviour as being under the control of men. As such, women provide an alternative role that of the dutiful wife. Women's religious and ritual practices emphasize kinship and family relationship, reinforcing the view of woman's as wife. Thus despite the ideology of the powerful aggressive woman, most Hindu women probably will continue to be motivated by the Hindu conception of the women as dutiful wife, and will perform their yearly rituals for their husband's long life, the presence of many sons, etc. Housework does not matter and is not considered productive, but now everyone throws the importance of women and its work. The same housework if she performs outside the home than it will be considered productive, as because she earns for that. Even men have understood the essentiality of women's productive work and in clearly seen in the society with new more hopes and horizons each day, encouraging women.

Practically seeing the family is the basic unit of production where housework is essential to sustain our social and economic structure. But at the same time it is petty, isolated, monotonous and required virtually unending hours of work, much of it being hard and unrewarding. It requires high labour, yet it is unpaid. In spite of women's labour intensive domestic work, in the modern industrial society it is believed that "woman does not work". Even the housewives themselves express resentment over their not being the part of paid work. This is the result of the process in which women lost their economic autonomy as producers in their own right as farmers, craft workers or traders and became increasingly dependent on the wages of men. As an outcome, they were more confined to "private sphere" and middleclass ideology pushed women towards unpaid labour.

In the pre-industrial period, the father, who was head of household was engaged in land or urban craft or trade, which determined the family's principal source of income. The law of God and the law of nature, both sanctioned authority to male patriarchy. The entire family, men women and children participated in production and contributed to the family income. A woman's work was vital in the family allocating between domestic labour and work in production as per the family's economic demands. Most of the women in the pre industrial production, which was largely agrarian, worked as weavers, spinners, gardeners, mashers and agricultural farmers. But their work in the fields was ancillary to their work at home and restricted to supplementing for husband's earning.

Industrialization and Capitalist Production

The Industrial Revolution in Western Europe upset the existing demand and supply so drastically that structure of job composition rapidly changed with the mushrooming of textile industries. As a result the demand for women and children increased. This driving force pulled the women from home to the labour market. Women have always been responsible for the clothing of family, but with the commercialization of the cotton industries they became wage earners rather than small independent producers. By the 18th century the production of textiles came under the control of the merchant capitalists, as a result, women worker's flight was more severe and miserable. Thus, the change from the home to the factory involved a crucial change in the sexual division of labour. The introduction of technological change brought crucial social consequences. "...when the number of spindles was considerably increased the jinni's were gathered into small workshops and worked by men and after the appearance of the male in 1779, women spinners were soon superseded. Heavier machine required the strength of men, and spinning of the male quickly became highly skilled work monopolized by a new class of men spinners. Thus within the space of one generation, what had been women's hereditary occupation was radically changed" (Pinchbeck, 1981: 111). According to Pinchbecks description since women were physically unable to handle machinery, so male spinning became defined as a skilled male occupation therefore women were excluded. The bodily difference between women and men were socially defined thus inducing discriminatory practices because "A small physical difference in size, strength and reproductive function is developed into an increasingly relative physical advantage to men and vastly multiplied by differential access to technology. The appropriation of muscle, capability, tools and machinery by men is an important source of women's subordination indeed it is a part of the process by which females are constituted as women" (Cockburn, 1981: 144). The physical distinction between the two sexes became the prime cause of their displacements from textile cotton industries. Women's work is always invariably characterized by low paid, lack of craft traditions, weak union and unskilled status. Such radical changes confirmed that the capitalist mode of production was predetermined by the division of labour that had existed within the family in the West when household had been the unit of production.

The capitalist economy, changed the labour process in such a way that women's entry into the trade was restricted and technical know-how denied to them because knowledge of the skills involved in the work process was confined to formal apprenticeship. Thus, women who were denied access to socially reorganized skills, formed a source of cheap labour power for the unskilled unorganized units of production developing outside the cooperate sections. This formed the basis of the industrial reserve army, which according to Karl Marx, became "the precondition and necessary product of the accumulation of capital" (Marx, 1971: 495-6). The capitalist intervention into the sexual division of labour confirmed the economic subordinators of the married women. By doing so, capitalism ensured and made distinction between the production for use and the production for exchange. In Alexander's words, "manufacturer provided the economic conditions for the hierarchy of labour from the family into social production which ensured that it was women who moved into the subordinate and auxiliary positions" (1982: 226).

By and large in all societies both developed as well as developing women's employment shows certain distinct features such as occupational segregation wage differential, unskilled labour, low-paid jobs, low value attached to their work and part time jobs. Occupational segregation is the function of gender norms and biological role of a woman. Gendering in occupations generate 'female' and 'male' jobs. Men are also segregated in some specific jobs, but there is a difference between the segregation of the two sexes. Men's jobs are prize catchy, characterized by higher level of technical knowledge, higher wages, prestige, autonomy and supposed to be 'skilled'. Thus men dominate the labour market, decide, and frame the policies regarding labour operations. Women's concentration in unskilled and semiskilled occupations arises from two sources i.e. from social construction of men's job as skilled and from the exclusion of women from skilled ones. Male strategies of exclusion are crucial in the assignation of jobs. Fire (1992) discussed about two factors that prominently account for deskilling of jobs. Accordingly, the division of labour is subjected to restructuring as capital accumulation takes place and new methods of production, management and control are introduced. Secondly, certain amount of emphasis is given to the ideological role of gendering jobs, with the restructuring of the sexual division of labour depending upon and interacting with the pre-existing notions of femininity and masculinity in the allocation of jobs between two sexes (Tine, 1992: 249 and 77).

Where segregation is high, the associations between different jobs and gendering is strong. Williams (1989) explained this as, "highly segregated occupations take on the 'gendered' attributes associated with the sex of their work force secretaries 99 per cent, kindergarten and preschool teachers 98 per cent and domestic workers 95 per cent are all expected to be emotionally sensitive and nurturing reflecting the feminine quality of workers. Exhibiting stereotypically masculine quality engineers 96 per cent, airline pilots 99 per cent, auto-mechanics 99 per cent are assumed emotionally reserved and detached, concerned more with the caring and support of people.

Apart from the handful of women who are doing skilled jobs in organized labour market, the many of population are performing unskilled or low skilled jobs. History reveals that women have been participating in all kinds of work, but despite this they have been unable to learn and master specific skills. This happens because of two reasons—firstly their participation in paid labour market was not visualized.

Secondly, the strategies for capitalist profit accumulation with automation and mechanization, which resulted in men's skills upgraded and women's skills degraded. Any job a woman performs is bound to be less skilled than that of men's.

Today, the statistics show improvement in women's economic participation. Although female labourers are increasing but they are getting jobs as part timer. Women's primary role of motherhood and homemaker compels them to take up jobs that they could manage part time. But gender ideology is the bigger force in making the women looks for part time. Domestic occupation always comes before any kind of employment. Employers have a tendency to strengthen such role biases. This helps them in profit accumulation. Women as cheap labour are readily accepted. Part time suits both the employer and family. These way women supplement the earnings of family and fulfil their roles both as wife and as mother.

It is a fact that gender biases are more acute in Indian society as the socio-cultural prescriptions create hurdles in women's educational achievement and which the difficulty they face in competing with the men in the labour market. In rural India, where agriculture is the central source of livelihood the subsistence production of women become an essential requirement. Technology has struck the traditional work of the women labour more drastically. The social, economic, political and environmental forces combine and force the women workers to take a backward step. The sexual division of labour is both the cause and effect of the virtual monopoly by men of the important positions in the socio-economic hierarchy and their control of main institutions of modern society like law, police, defence, politics, etc. Like these important institutions, history is also male dominated since it recorded only what men did or achieved. Thus gender biases are reflected in historical experiences too. The classical Marxist theory argues that the oppression of women reflects the inherent inequality and injustice of capitalism and class society, arising from the institution of private property. Hence, women's liberation requires the abolition of class society, through the abolition of private property and capitalism. Domestic activities are considerably out of the domain of commodity production. Since women perform household activities, thus automatically they are out of the sphere of commodity production. Hence, "domestic labour is viewed as private and defined as non-social and unproductive" (Acker, 1988: 18-19).

It seems that two mechanisms are important for understanding the structuring of the labour process and gendering of work i.e., the exploitation by men in the occupational structure and the active gendering of both people and jobs. It is observed that if men leave the jobs in case of promotion that women fill gap leftover positions. Women experience gender discrimination in labour market due to many reasons such as: Women have lower accessibility than men to productivity augmentation opportunity like schooling, required training and experience, continuity in career and regional mobility. This is referred to as pre-market discrimination because low level of education work experience, etc. is not consequences of labour market discrimination but the consequences of the discrimination itself. Sex role stereotypes limiting tastes for jobs belong to the category of pre-market gender differentials. Women receive less favourable jobs than do the men or they may not get any job because of their low less education and experience compared to men.

In addition women get lower wages than men for the same job. It occurs against women by creating sex-specific wage groups with lower pay for women. Another is by paying women less hourly wages than men for the same or similar work are. A third wage discrimination relates to the unequal treatment of women in terms of fringe benefits.

It is a well-known fact that men have more power, income and high status than women. These three measures of inequality power, income and status, are closely linked factors and mutually reinforcing dimension of inequality. In the labour market men occupy most of the higher position, in co-operated sector, educational, military, religious and political world. Even in the same occupation men's earnings are more than that of women. The power, income and status reinforce male dominance and female subservience.

Cultural Construction of Masculinity and Femininity

This socialization process is so strong in men and women that one can notices a deep chasm between them in terms of their perspective, priorities in life, their dreams and lifestyle and their vision of looking at things. Ned Noddings believes life is not just rules and principles but also individuals and responsibilities. And this is where the difference between man and the woman lies. The feminine that is associated with women is characterized as passive. Tenderness, consideration and physical weakness are synonymous to the feminine glare. The masculine is defined as dominant and encouraging male violence against women. Men are supposed to be high on physical strength and process. Both Noddings and Carol Gilligan believed that men and women have different moral orientations, men speak the language of rights and women the language of responsibility. It is interesting to note that education teach girls the language of justice and rights, because it is the language they need to learn in order to function in the world. However, educators' do not teach boys the language of care and responsibility because as so it would harm their success in the market.

Psychoanalysts believe boys from age 3 to 6 remain under a great turmoil, as they have to give up their identification with the mother and start to hate the women's way of doing things they even go to the extent of suppressing their affection towards. Their mothers but at the same time, it causes great pain to them. Perhaps, this is the origin of some grown up men's fear of intimacy (Hudeon and Jacob, 1979). Contrast girls never lose their identification with the mother. Thus, according to Judith Viorst (1986) in 'Necessary Losses' we all suffer loss, with boys giving up their identification with mothers and girls giving up mothers as a sexual object. Gradually, girls become nurturing and caring, always showering emotions by intimating her mother, whereas the boy is discouraged from showering any form of emotions.

The society does not have one single model of masculinity or femininity as Connell observes that there are many different expressions of masculinity and femininity, which are ordered in a hierarchy; one at the top is the category of hegemonic masculinity, which is dominant over all masculinities and femininities is associated with heterosexual marriage, which includes, authority, paid work, strength and physical toughness. Homosexual masculinity is the most subordinated form yet not accepted by many societies. At the level of society, these contrasting versions are ordered, which has one common premise—the domination of men over women.

In Connell's opinion, femininity can be of various forms. The most popular one is called, emphasized femininity complimenting hegemonic masculinity accommodating the desires and interest of men, featuring the embodiment of motherhood and sexual reciprocity. This type is the most prevalent image of women. Thus we have the subordinate femininity which includes feminists, lesbians, spinsters, witches, prostitutes and manual workers. It is high time that in terms of popularity 'hegemonic and emphasized femininity top the scale. All action heroes like Sylvester Stallone, Amitabh Bachhan, even the comic characters like Superman and Shaktiman represent 'hegemonic masculinity'.

Since women are economically disadvantaged than men and suffer from the effects of poverty in different ways and the multiple roles that they carry out keeps them under stress. Few feminists are of the opinion that women's condition can only improve if they give up their reproductive ability. Some studies observe that the men are biologically weak, but our culture has made women weak. Other than being biologically weak men suffer from stress and pressure because culturally, they are expected to be fulfilling the material needs of their family, and failing to do it builds a kind of pressure on them. However, women are the maximum sufferers of this gender-specific expectations as they suffer not only physically and socially but also mentally. This process of socialization is carried out by various institutions such as family, religion, school, media etc. that promotes the ideology of patriarchy, claiming that women are inferior to men.

The concept of gender has been central to debate on how to empower women to improve the quality of their life. Since women have multiple identities based on gender, caste, class ethnicity and age, at any given point of time, any one or combination of factors could oppress them.

There are three leading approaches to women studies which are as follows:

(1) The Neo-Classical School

The Neo-Classical School of thought considered to be the most dominant school in West which is based on the concept of utility. According to this school, the allocation of time by any individual is linked with the utility attached to it. Women's participation in labour force is a function of the utility derived from work. This participation or withdrawal of women from the labour force does not only depend on wage rate existing, but also on the household i.e. (husband's income). Gender-specific wage differential arises due to discontinuity in employment on account of bearing and rearing of children, or voluntary selection regarding lesser skills. Neo-classicists view pressures on wage gaps as not unjust but a natural outcome of choice.

This classicist explains marriage as a relationship for both individuals to maximize utility. Marriage is a two-person firm where women hire men since men earn more and men hire women because they are superior nursemaids.

(2) The Institutional Approach

This approach to women studies draws its theoretical rationale from the rigid quasi-rigid structural institutions among the society. Here the status of men, women and children are determined on the basis on race, caste, education, etc. The origin of gender specific social division of labour is traced to the hunting and fishing theories—where only men would venture and women would look after young ones. Some say or believe that women have to perform due to biological roles. This school of thought hypothesizes that there is possibility of change through social reforms, legislations and milder forms of rational social interventions.

(3) The Marxist School

This school adopts a historical perspective of any social situation. As per this view, production and capital accumulation is fundamental to the understanding of women's position. There are two different views, According to one view, articulation of the relationship between man, labour and capital and their integration with the larger market system is the key to the understanding of women's status. It refers to some methods such as splitting trade unions by gender, creating wedges between genders to break labour homogeneity exclusion of women from market production which are being adopted by the capitalists in accentuating capital accumulation (Himmdmeit and Mohum, 1977).

The second view within this broad Marxist stream is known as the Marxist-Feminist school. It views history as a system of relations between men who dominate and women who are dominated. In addition to the fundamental contradictions between capital and labour the Marxist feminists add yet another dimension to the system of contradictions and suggest a simultaneous struggle against caste and gender exploitation (Hartman, 1979).

Empowerment of women is necessary not just for their own welfare but the well-being of the entire country because it enhances both the quality and quantity of human resources available for development (Economic Development and Women, 259). The success of development efforts depends on the fruits of development reaching the whole population. Empowerment is the process by which the powerless gain greater control over the circumstances of their lives. It includes both control over resources and our ideology, greater self-confidence and an inner transformation of one's consciousness that enables one to overcome external barriers (Sen and Batliwala, 2000). Women's position and degree of empowerment is defined by gender and gender relation in society. Gender not only represents the biological sex of an individual but also the various rights and roles that society attaches to males and females. Whether, it is domestic life or labour market, sex differentiated roles, rights and obligations exist and they vary by class. All this goes to make gender a fundamental dimension of societal stratification (Women in Indian Society, Rehana Ghadially, 206).

The developing countries like India manifest and perpetuate the subordinate status of women. In India custom determines who has the greater access to education and to employment opportunities. Poverty is an overaching factor and a liability of life for vast majority of women in India. A correct solution or remedy to such a situation is women's right to gainful education and employment. Apart from being a question of survival this would increase their self-respect image and provide for greater autonomy within the household. Indirectly, this would also increase their direct participation in the community activities, leading them to under horizons. This will make women economically self-reliant, thus paving the way for their concurrent empowerment in the other factors of their lives.

Conclusion

Indeed, history talks of the interaction between gender and culture. Moreover, our culture is such that only men and their activities have been highlighted. One would only find women in the feminist context i.e. they have been in focus as somebody's daughter, mother, or sister. E.P. Thomson points and concludes that history needs to register the lived experiences, day-to-day life, aspirations and dreams of common man. Our culture has given enough space for ignoring women as secondary. It could be a deliberate attempt by historian to subordinate women or it could also be a result of our culture for which historians felt that it was not important to register the lives of women. But now the time is changing. Feminist come together and write on the issues of women and their life details.

The ideas and views of Amartya Sen who won The Nobel Prize for economics in 1998 for his work on the interface between Welfare and Development Economics have been enormously influential and can be quite visible in the World Bank's World Development Report, 2000-2001. Its topic was how to expand the entitlements, capabilities and freedom of poor people. The great challenge is to tackle the institutional structures of countries that continue to marginalize, discriminate against vulnerable selections of society. The state has a role to play in helping to empower women. Depriving women of their development rights amounts to violation of human rights. We should not forget that a nations destiny depends on the Mother's (female population)-"The hand the rocks the cradle, rules the world".

2

Gujarat State: A Brief Note

Gujarat state was carved from the present Marathi speaking region i.e. Maharashtra in the year 1960. Gujarat state is situated on the West coast of India between 20.1 and 24.7 degrees North latitude and 68.4 and 74.4 degrees East longitude. The boundaries of Gujarat are surrounded by the Arabian Sea in the West, Rajasthan in the North-East, Madhya Pradesh in the East and Maharashtra in the South-East. It shares a common border with Pakistan on the Northern side. Gujarat state gets a rainfall of South-West monsoon from the month of June to September. The land of coastal and central Gujarat is fertile, whereas the Northern part is dry and drought prone. The state covers 196024 km (75665 sq. miles) on the border with Pakistan. The rivers of Gujarat are Narmada, Tapti, Sabarmati and Mahi. The black soil is best suited for cash crops such as sugarcane, cotton and groundnuts besides that it cultivates crops such as rice and millets.

Archaeologists have found Stone Age settlements around the Sabarmati and Mahi rivers in the south and East of the state. The settlements probably date from the time of Indus valley civilization. There were also Harappan centres at Lothal, Rampur, Ameri, Lakhabanal and Rozdi, Rocky inscriptions in the Girnar Hills show that the Mauryan Emperor Ashoka extended his domain into Gujarat in 250 B.C. After the fall of the Maurya Empire, the Sakas and Scythains controlled the region from A.D. 130 to 390. Under Rudradaman the area formed part of the Gupta Empire, which was succeeded by the Maitrika dynasty. During the period 900 A.D., the Solanki dynasty came to power, when the state flourished in all fields. There then followed a long period of Muslim rule;

Ahmed-I, the first independent Musilm ruler of Gujarat, founded Ahmedabad in 1411 A.D. The Mughal Emperor Akbar conquered Malwa and Gujarat in the region remained under Mughal rule for nearly 200 years. The excavation of Harappa at Lothal in 1954 has revealed the existence of a flourishing part of city of the Indus civilization. The Indus Empire witnessed many changes. The city of Lothal was devastated by natural calamities at many times but reconstructed again each time. According to documented history, Chandragupta Maurya assimilated Gujarat an integral part of his empire as is evident from the engravings. In 415 A.D. Kumar Gupta I son and successor of Chandragupta II, ruled over Gujarat. After Gupta period Gujarat passed through the Maitraka period (470-780 AD) and Chalukya period (840-1304 AD) followed by a period of independent sultanates (1411-1573 A.D.). Under Chalukya tenures, Bhill Chiefs were conquered. In 1304 A.D. Muhammad Tughlak Ahmed Shah I founded the city of Ahmedabad which afterwards became famous for trade and commerce. Gujarat was divided into several small princely states. The Moghul King Akbar captured the region in 1573. Under Mughal governors this region developed foreign trade and commerce and initiated domestic manufacturing units (Choksi, 1984). After 1700 A.D. the Dutch, English, French and Portuguese established bases along the coastal region. The East India Company set-up its first head quarters in India at Surat in 1612. As British maritime supremacy developed, all but the British and Portuguese at Daman and Diu went back. The state came under the control of the British East India Company in 1818. After the First war of Indian Independence in 1857, the British government ruled directly, dividing the area into number of princely states. Following Indian Independence in 1947, all of Gujarat except Saurashtra and Kutch became part of Bombay State. However, the Bombay State was bifurcated into States of Maharashtra and Gujarat on May 1960.

The state has been divided into two distinct economic and geographic regions, namely, the main land Gujarat comprising Mehsana, Sabarkantha, and Banaskantha on the northern border, Ahmedabad, Gandhinagar, Kheda and Vadodara in Central Gujarat, Panchmahal in Eastern highland, Bharuch, Surat, Valsad, Dang District and Navsari, Tapi (Vyara) newly declared district and divided from Surat in south Gujarat which includes coastal as well as hill regions. The peninsular Gujarat comprise Kathiawad

(Saurashtra) and Kutch. However, the development in the state is uneven. Reflecting on the statistical data the population of Gujarat as per 2001 census is 50,671,017 including rural and urban population. The scheduled caste population is stated to be 7.09 per cent and scheduled tribe comprise 14.76 per cent. The sex ratio in Gujarat has declined from 942 females per 1000 in 1981 to 920 females per 1000 males as per 2001 census.

The architecture of Gujarat is famous for its fine detail. Besides, the region has a long tradition of handicrafts, such as bandhini (tie-dyed cloth), Jari (gold and silver embroidery), Patola (a beautifully patterned silk for which the thread is tied-dyed before being woven), perfumes and wood carving. Gujarat was the chief centre of wood carving in India from at least the 15th century. Even when stone as a building material handled with great ease and confidence. Wood carving in Gujarat in the Mughal Period (1556-1707) shows a beautiful synthesis of the indigenous and Mughal styles. Jain wooden pavilions of the late 16th and 17th centuries are richly sculptured with scenes from Jain mythology and contemporary life. and with imaginative floral animal and geometrical motifs; figural sculpture has a great vivacity and rhythm. Many wooden facades of the 19th century have been preserved but the ornamentation lacks the grace and movement of earlier work (Chaudhary, 1983).the architectural style of Gujarat is well known for its luxuriousness and refinement, as exemplified by the movements and temples at Somanth, Modhera and Thane. It is also famous for its art and craft products. Among the most durable and effective of the state's cultural institutions is trade and craft guilds known as Mahajans.

Demographic Features

Religion is an important and perhaps one of the basic cultural characteristic of the Indian society. Therefore, distribution of population by religion is of considerable sociological significance in its own right. There are cultural, linguistic and other socio-economic differences among the people belonging to different religions that are relatively persistent over time. The Hindus, Muslims, Christians, Sikhs, Jains and Buddhists are the major religious communities residing in the various states of India. It is therefore important to observe the percentage composition of the population of these religious communities.

The total population of Hindu communities is 4,51,43,074, among them males are 2,35,38,770 and 2,16,04,304 are women, male constitute 60.1 per cent and female represent 39.9 per cent of total Hindu population. Christians form 2,84,092 of the Gujarat State population, male are 1,42,881 and 1,41,211 are women. In Gujarat the population of Sikhs is 45,587 while 20,600 are women and men are 24,987. Buddhists population is 17,829 among them 8,390 are women and men are 9,439. The proportion of Jains in the State is 2,52,305 (Census of India, 2001). Muslims and Christians in Gujarat are more urban than other religious groups. In 1991, 58 per cent of Muslims, 54 per cent of Christians are based in cities or towns. There are 15 towns with a population of more than 100 thousand, where Muslims have a presence of around or more than 10 per cent. Their proportion in 7 of these towns is around 15 per cent.

Information on work status of the population reveals that 41.95 per cent have been reported as workers; the disparity being markedly prominent between the two sexes. Whereas work participation rate 54.87 (male) and 27.91 (female) respectively. Rest of the other religious communities has very little proportion to the State's population. According to Census 2001, Gujarat, with literacy rate 69.14 per cent ranks 17th among all the States/UTs. Male literacy rate is 79.66 per cent and the female literacy rate is 57.80 per cent. Rural population literacy rate 61.29 per cent and urban literacy rate 81.84 per cent while scheduled caste literacy is 70.50 per cent and scheduled tribe 47.74 per cent (HDR, 43-47, 2003).

Political Economy during Colonialism

Under the British the land tenure system was different in mainland region and peninsular region, i.e. Gujarat, Saurashtra and Kutch. In mainland Gujarat *Ryotwari* system was dominant wherein revenue was collected in cash. Intermediaries collected the revenue on behalf of sate from the tillers. These were mostly Patidar and Anavil Brahmins. In Saurashtra and Kutch region *Zamindari* system prevailed. These were mainly Rajput Girasdars, Bhayats and Mulgirasias and had property rights over their land. At least two-fifths of the entire Saurashtra are was under Ryotwari system (Mishra, 1961). Most of the villages in Gujarat exhibit the usual Ryotwari features common to western India (Baden-Powell, 1974). Further the most striking characteristics of the tenurial system in

1850 was the massive extent of land alleviated even greater in proportion then that in the southern Maratha country (Charles Worth, 1986). Nearly Rs. 30 lakhs of revenue were alleviated in Gujarat's four districts of Ahemdabad, Kaira, Bharuch and Surat through individual names resulting in a substantial size of land under the ownership of Brahmins, Rajput, Kunbis and Kolis. The system of tenancy and subtenancy was advantageous to the British as they could use the surplus for other purpose thereby halting agricultural production (Desai, 1986). In 1821 the land revenue situation was such that India was 'transformed into the revènue producing agricultural form of England' (Mukherjee, 1970). The relationship of talukdars and tenants were retrenching the peasants. Therefore, the Bombay Tenancy and Agricultural Act were passed in 1939 in order to control the tenancy system. In the course some tenants were evicted while other becomes permanent. In Gujarat the Kunbis and Kolis were cultivating the land for the rulers by paying tribute which was fixed by landlord. Throughout Gujarat there were 347 such villages in the mid nineteenth century of which the Bhagidari villages of Bharuch district numbered 244 and the Marwa villages in the Kaira District ninety respectively. The British changed the co-sharing system into *Ryotwari* system. It was the vested interest of Marwadars and Bhagidars that boosted these systems. Most of the Marwadars were Kunbis. The same broad caste group as the Maratha peasantry but of the assertive Leva sub-caste, gradually the name Patidar acquired a mark of improved status besides being a name and an ideal. In 1931 Census the name Patidar was given the official recognition as well. Thus under colonialism the Bhagidari and Marwa systems were means to organize, preserve and enhance the social authority of the cultivators in the prosperous western villages of Gujarat. By 1860, the talukdars were selling off the villages to settle creditor's claim at low price, resulting in Ahmedabad Talukdars Relief Act in 1862. The indebted estates could be taken over by a Talukadari settlement officer. Thus more than a third of talukdari villages came under the Act's provisions. The colonial government used the same mechanism as the talukdars for the Thakurs in Bharuch and Karia districts, through an encumbered Estates Act in 1877. This legislation did not affect the social structure of the area. It was the Marwadars and Bhagidars who emerged as cultivating castes in Bombay presidency. Inamdar and leading cultivator shared the power in some talukdari and Ryotwari villages. The colonial government was mainly interested in "collecting revenue maintenance of peace and the defence of Indian frontiers for their own sake" (Roy, 1994: 6).

Colonialism was favourable to the middle and Patidar landlords in Gujarat while the peasantry consist the ordinary farmers which were reduced to agricultural labourers. The peasants could not resist the oppression due to impoverishment besides natural and human made calamities that occurred frequently (Maheshweri, 1974). Till the first half of the eighteenth century irrigation was neglected. Hardly any money was spent on roads, canals, bridges and other works of public necessity as the over-pressed agrarian economy, failing to maintain even the previous rates of production and being further overburdened by ever increasing land tax demanded by the company and extracted from the starving peasantry with unexampled vigour, led to chronic famine conditions. The year of famine coincided with a major stretch of serious epidemic illness. All those calamities resulted in drastic reduction in population levels. The result was decreased in cultivating capacity which in turn resulted in a fall in agricultural income. Famine compelled the migration of population particularly backward castes and the landless labourers and the Indian urban population increased by only four per cent by the thirty years ending in 1914.

Table 2.1: Growth of Population in Gujarat since 1901

Census Year	Population	Decadal Growth Absolute	Decadal Growth Percentage	Percentages Progressive growth over 1901 (per cent)
1	2	3	4	5
1901	9094748	—	—	—
1911	9803587	+ 708839	+ 07.79	+ 7.79
1921	10174989	+ 371402	+ 03.79	+ 11.88
1931	11489828	+ 1314839	+ 12.92	+ 26.33
1941	13701551	+ 2211723	+ 19.25	+ 50.65
1951	16262657	+ 2561106	+ 18.69	+ 78.81
1961	20633350	+ 4370693	+ 26.88	+ 126.87
1971	26697475	+ 6064125	+ 29.39	193.55
1981	34085799	+ 7388324	+ 27.67	+ 274.79
1991	41309582	+ 7223783	+ 21.19	+ 354.21
2001	48387270	+ 7077688	+ 22.66	+ 432.03
2011	50596992	+ 9287410	+ 22.48	+ 456.00

Source: B.K. Bhatt, 2003: 142.

The above data shows that population has increased by 7.08 million in 10 years excluding the areas where census was postponed due to earthquake. The decadal growth rate of the decade 1991-2001 has increased in comparison to 1981-1991 from 21.19 to 22.66 while in terms of percentage population has increased by 432 per cent since 1901.

Table 2.1 points out that Ahmedabad retained its position as 1st in 1991. Surat and Vadodara also follow census according to size of population in 2001 respectively. The literacy of the males and females has increased over the decades in Gujarat. After the Independence total literacy in the State has increased from 21.82 to 69.97 per cent. Male literacy has increased from 30.32 to 80.50 per cent during 1951-2001. Female literacy accounts to 58.60 against the male literacy of 80.50 per cent. In terms of absolute number of literates, Gujarat was having 21.1 million persons as literates in 1991 Census; this number has gone up as 29.1 millions. About 8 million literates have been added against 8 million increase of population during the decade.
Source: Socio-economic Review, Gujarat State, 2006-07). The district-wise absolute number of literates can be seen in Table 2.3.

Table 2.3 reveals the literacy rate of various districts in the State. Highest male literacy can be seen in Gandhinagar (87.74%) and female literacy can be seen in Ahmedabad district (70.8%). The lowest literacy in males can be found in Banaskantha (66.47%) and females can be seen in Dahod district (31.28%). The highest total literacy can be found in the districts such as Ahmedabad (79.5%), Gandhinagar (76.59%) and in Navsari (75.83%). Whereas, the lowest literacy rates were found in the districts such as Dahod, Banaskantha, Dang and Narmada; there literacy rates were very low 45.15 per cent, 50.97 per cent, 59.65 per cent and 59.86 per cent respectively.

Architectural Heritage

Architecture, culture and arts have always been prime objectives for travel, and Gujarat with its high concentration of historical sites is certainly one of the most richly rewarding destinations for the heritage tourist. The architectural diversity Gujarat reflects its commercial and political importance over the last 4500 years. The State has some of India's most substantial remains of Harappan

Table 2.2: District-wise Population in Size 1991 and 2001

Rank in 2001	District	Population 2001	Per cent to total population of the State 2001	Population 1991	Per cent to total population of the State 1991	Rank in 1991
1	2	3	4	5	6	7
1	Ahmedabad	5808378	11.48	4587491	11.1	1
2	Surat	4996391	9.87	3397900	8.23	2
3	Vadodara	3639775	7.19	3038127	7.35	3
4	Rajkot*	3157676	6.24	2514122	6.09	4
	(Excluding earthquake affected areas)					4
5	Banaskantha	2502843	4.95	1981513	4.8	7
6	Bhavnagar	2469264	4.88	2069953	5.01	6
7	Junagadh	2448427	4.84	2091182	5.06	5
8	Sabarkantha	2083416	4.12	1761086	4.26	9
9	Panchmahal	2024883	4.00	1682333	4.07	10
10	Kheda	2023354	4.00	1786794	4.33	8
11	Jamnagar**	1913685	3.78	1563558	3.78	13
	(Excluding earthquake affected areas)					13
12	Anand	1856712	3.67	1642615	3.98	11
13	Mahesana	1837696	3.63	1640251	3.97	12
14	Dohad	1635374	3.23	1274123	3.08	15
15	Kutch	1526321	3.02	1262507	3.06	16
16	Surendranagar	1515147	2.99	1208872	2.93	17
17	Valsad	1410680	2.79	1087980	2.63	19
18	Amreli	1393295	2.75	1308867	3.17	14
19	Bharuch	1370104	2.71	1148252	2.78	18
20	Gandhinagar	1334731	2.64	1077406	2.61	21
21	Navsari	1229250	2.43	1085692	2.62	20
22	Patan	1181941	2.34	1036019	2.51	22
23	Porbandar	536854	1.06	469472	1.14	23
24	Narmada	514083	1.02	449376	1.09	24
25	The Dangs	186712	0.37	144091	0.35	25

* 2001 Census figures are presented including the estimated figures of Maliamiana, Morvi and Wankaner talukas where Census 2001 was postponed due to Earthquake

** 2001 Census figures are presented including the estimated figures of Jodia taluka where Census 2001 was postponed due to Earthquake.

*** Census 2001 was not conducted due to earthquake; the estimated figures have been taken into account.

Source: Socio-economic Review Gujarat State, 2006-7.

Table 2.3: District-wise Literacy Rate of Gujarat State, 2001

Sl. No.	State	Total	Literacy Rate	
			Male	Female
	Gujarat	69.14	79.66	57.80
1.	Kutch	59.79	70.39	48.59
2.	Banaskantha	50.97	66.47	34.40
3.	Patan	60.36	73.63	46.33
4.	Mehsana	75.22	86.20	63.65
5.	Sabarkantha	66.65	80.42	52.30
6.	Gandhinagar	76.59	87.74	64.58
7.	Ahmedabad	79.50	87.31	70.83
8.	Surendranagar	61.61	74.19	48.10
9.	Rajkot	74.16	82.61	65.20
10.	Jamnagar	66.48	76.25	56.18
11.	Porbandar	68.62	78.36	58.42
12.	Junagadh	67.78	78.74	56.43
13.	Amreli	66.09	76.44	55.78
14.	Bhavnagar	66.20	78.02	53.73
15.	Anand	74.51	86.09	61.94
16.	Kheda	71.96	85.99	56.90
17.	Panchmahal	60.92	75.91	44.94
18.	Dahod	45.15	58.88	31.28
19.	Vadodara	70.76	80.04	60.73
20.	Narmada	59.86	72.44	46.61
21.	Bharuch	74.41	82.98	65.11
22.	Surat	74.65	81.51	66.36
23.	Dang	59.65	70.68	48.51
24.	Navsari	75.83	82.77	68.61
25.	Valsad	69.15	77.90	59.62

Source: Census of India, 2001.

Civilization, one of the world's oldest, at sites like Lothal and Dholavira that offer an insight into the town planning and industry of the 2600-1600 BC period. The recorded history of Gujarat begins with the Mauryan dynasty which ruled one of the most powerful empires of ancient India spanning from Assam in the East to Baluchistan in the West. Though originating from Bihar, the Mauryan Empire had a stronghold in Junagadh ratified by the third century BC rock edicts of emperor Ashoka and rock cut caves from the Mauryan and Gupta periods in and around the city. Gujarat's Maitraka dynasty that grew after the decline of Gupta power in the 5th century was also responsible for many Buddhist monuments in Saurashtra. The most important period in the history of temple architecture in Gujarat was the reign of the Solanki rulers in the

11th and 12th centuries when the Sun temple at Modhera, the Toranas of Vadhnagar, the Rudhramalaya at Sidhapur, temples at Somanth and the some of the earliest Jain Temples of the Kumbhariyali, Taranga, Girnar and Palitana complexes were commissioned, all of them justly famous for their exquisite carvings. A unique feature of this period was the creation of huge temple complexes on sacred summits like Shatrunjaya over Palitana and Girnar outside Junagadh, which are today among Gujarat's greatest tourist attractions and India's most spectacular sites. The prosperity that followed trade with the affluent western countries is also reflected in the havelis, the courtyard the houses of the merchants. Wood was imported for the façade of these houses and carving techniques where perfected to embellish the *jarokhas* (balconies) and their brackets, window frames, doors, columns. These wooden houses can be seen in polls of Ahmedabad, old quarters of the cities of Gujarat, and at village like Vaso. The princely states too thrived and their rulers built great palaces, some of which are open for viewing as museums or have been converted into heritage hotels where tourists can stay.

The UNESCO listed world heritage site of Champaner as one of the most remarkable archaeological zones in Gujarat with Hindu temples and stepwells at neighbouring Pavagadh, the regional capital city built by Sultan Muhammad Bhegada in the 16th century with mosques that are considered perfect examples of the Gujarat Sultanate's Indo-Saracenic architecture. The Jami Masjid and Nagina Masjid have exquisite sculptures on the pillars and along the *mihrab*. Ahmedabad became capital of Gujarat in 1414, replacing Patan, and since then became the centre of architecture. The first mosque built is referred as Ahmed Shah Masjid, became the model for other mosques in the city. The largest of the mosque is Jami Masjid, which was built in 1424.

The most famous jails are those of the 16th century Sidi Syaid Mosque are known for its architecture and for its latticework. Ahmedabad is also a good place to see the famous wooden havelis of Gujarat. It also has good examples of stepwell architecture like the Dada Harir Vav built in 15th century and the 19th century Isanpur stepwell.

Lothal is one of the most significant sites of the Harappan or Indus Valley Civilization excavated in India. The remarkable feature of this ancient city is the dockyard, which had channels through which ships could sluice from the sea and offload their cargo when gates were locked. The excellent system of sanitary drainage can be seen when touring the site. There is a museum that offers an insight into the town planning and industries and trade of Lothal when it was at its peak from 2400-1600 BC. Shatrunjaya Hill on the outskirts of the town of Palitana is crowned by a complex of about 863 temples that present a magnificent spectacle standing on two ridges of the summit away from any habitation. The site is sacred to Jains who believe Lord Adinath visited it and his disciple attained nirvana here. Noteworthy temples are the Adishwara built in 12th century but renovated twice, the three storeys Vimala Sah Temple built in 14th century and the Motisah Temple of the 19th century.

One of the most historic cities of Gujarat, Junagadh has the 3rd century BC rock inscriptions of Emperor Ashoka. The city and its surrounding hills have Buddhist and Jains caves, most of them dating to the 2nd century AD with interesting methods of retaining water. A short drive to the east of Juangadh is Mt. Girnar which has a hilltop temple complex. The 12th century Jain temples on the hill have exquisite carvings. One of the temple town's most sacred to Hindus, Dwarka is believed to have been the kingdom of lord Krishna. The focal point for pilgrims, the Dwarkadish temple, has a five-storey shikhara tower with a dome. The 12th century Rukmini Temple has a remarkable shikhara and is noted for its exquisite carvings. One of the finest examples of Hindu temple architecture in Gujarat is the Sun Temple at Modhera. The largest of more than 100 stepwells in Gujarat, the Rani-ki-Vav was built in the 11th century when Patan was the capital of the Solanki rulers. Baroda, now called Vadodara, was one of the three premier princely states of India to be awarded a 21 gun salute. The State became prosperous under Sayajirao Gaekwad who is responsible for the building of the Lakshmi Vilas Palace. The work of building the palace was commissioned to Major Mant and the palace is a mix of Indo, Islamic and European architectural elements. Naulakha palace, Gondal, this 18th century palace is part of the older Darbargadh of the princely state of Gondal. The palace is a festival of stone carvings that can be seen on the façade, columns, brackets and balconies. One of India's largest princely states, Kutch had many grand palaces. The most famous is the Aaina Mahal, built in the 18th century in Bhuj. This palace is known for its mirror work, mosaics and other elaborate surface ornamentation. The queen of textiles is the Patola woven by only few families of Patan. About 700 Salvi weavers are said to have come to Patan when it was the capital of the Solanki rulers, their patrons, and today only a few continue their tradition. Jamnagar is one of the best known centers for Bandhini of tie-and-dye, which involves dyeing a fabric in stages to achieve the final pattern. After the fabric is dyed, the areas to be left in the first colour are knotted and covered with resist before it goes back for the dip in the next colour. Resist tie-and-dye stages continue till the fabric is ready for the market.

Kutch is also a centre for block-printing including the intricate "Ajrakh" printing, practiced in villages like Dhamadka and Ajrakhpur near Bhuj. Beadwork is a beautiful craft of Gujarat that is believed to have become popular after trade with the west from the ports in the state brought in top quality beads from overseas in the 19th century. Gujarat's tradition of terra-cotta work is seen in most cities, towns and villages where potters work on making utensils, prayer objects, decorative items and flower pots on their wheels. Gujarat is also known for its ceramics. Morvi, Rajkot and villages of Surendranagar District have thriving cottage industries producing ceramic products. Gujarat has a tradition of woodcarving visible in beautifully sculpted balconies with their perfectly proportioned pavilions of the havells, carved doors, and palace gates. Gujarat is known for its silversmiths who produce beautiful jewellery, utensils and objects. Rajkot, Gondal, Wadhwan and other places of Saurashtra are known for their silverwork and Kutch produces some of India's finest silver ornaments.

Fairs and festivals: Navratri in September-October is probably the world's longest dance festival and is described as a cultural celebration unparalleled in sheer size. Ras is a simple dance based on the Gope culture of Lord Krishna, followed by pastoral groups like the Ahirs and Bharwads. Raasda is performed by men, women or mixed groups set the rhythm by clapping their hands and snapping their fingers, and move their feet to the drumming of *dholaks* or occasionally dance without any music. Uttrayan or Makar Sankranti in January every year is like no other day in Gujarat. This is one of Gujarat's most participatory festivals when countless people throng terraces to fly kites. The kite flown during Uttarayan is internationally called the 'Indian fighter' and it is usually made out of bamboo and tissue paper. The Modhera Dance Festival is held annually at the Sun temple of Modhera in January.

As the name suggests, the 11th century Sun temple of Modhera, a fine Example of architecture, is the backdrop for a range of classical dances. Kutch utsav is a festival that features the folk culture of Kutch district. The Bhavnath Fair is held at the Bhavnath Temple near Damodar Kund on the outskirts of Junagadh during Shivratri in February-March, Chitra Vichitra Fair: About a fortnight after Holi, on the moonless night called Amawas, about ten of thousands of tribals gather to celebrate the Chitra Vichitra Fair at the confluence of three rivers, near the village of Poshina.

Ranging geographically from the desert plains of Kutch which occupies the north-western part of the state to the moist forests of the Dangs in the southeast, Gujarat's variety of habitats makes it an ideal destination for those interested in wildlife viewing and bird watching. Some of the national parks and sanctuaries that have accommodations and other facilities for the eco-traveller are: Nalsarovar bird Sanctuary, this sanctuary comprises the shallow Nalsarovar Lake and its environs, spanning about 13 km, with a checklist of about 250 birds seen over the years. The lake is a paradise for birdwatchers, especially in winter when it attracts more than 100 species of migratory birds. The flooded fields around the lake are the habitat of the threatened Saras Crane and globally-threatened vultures are sometimes seen in the fields. Little Rann of Kutch: Spanning an area of about 4950 sq km of the little Rann of Kutch and its environs, the Wild Ass Sanctuary is the last home of the Indian Wild Ass. The unique geography of the Little Rann of Kutch also makes it a good place to watch birds typical of the desert. The Rann is especially good for larks and wheatears. The Macqueen's Bustard can be seen in winter. The 1412 sq km Gir Wildlife reserve comprises deciduous forests, evergreen and semi-evergreen vegetation, thorn scrub and grasslands. It is well-known as the remaining habitat of the Asiatic Lion. Gir also has a large leopard population. As 359 lions and more than 300 leopards have been counted in Gir during the last census, it may be the best big cat reserve in India with few returning without seeing one over a three of four day stay. The Savannah—like grasslands of Velavadar National Park support one of India's largest populations of the Blackbuck or Indian Antelope.

Gujarat is well-known as the land of Mahatma Gandhi. His great achievements in the state culminated in the Protest March from Ahmedabad to Dandi that is said to have done the maximum damage to the British Empire in India. A tour of Gujarat from Porbandar to Dandi offers an insight into the life and philosophies of the man the world loves to call Mahatma. Gandhiji was born on 2nd October 1869 at Porbandar and the three-storied blue-toned haveli containing 17 rooms with some of the belongings of the Gandhi family has been opened for visitors. Beside the haveli, the Kirti Mandir built in memory of the Mahatma has a museum, picture gallery and library. From Porbandar, Karamchand Gandhi moved to Rajkot to officiate as Diwan of states in central Saurashtra, Wankaner and Rajkot. He studied at Alfred High School from 1881 and was married to Kasturba two years later. Many years later, Gandhiji returned to Rajkot and founded the Rashtriya Shala on February 21, 1921 as an institute working to revive handicrafts including rare weaves like the Patola. After schooling in Rajkot and matriculating from Ahmedabad, Gandhiji went to the Samaldas College at Bhavnagar in 1887, the first arts college of Saurashtra. After leaving India for further studies, Gandhiji returned to Gujarat and made Ahmedabad the base of his struggle for freedom, eradication of untouchability dignity of labour, instilling respect for all religions, creating the spirit of fearlessness and promoting the use of Indian goods. The Gujarat Vidhyapith in Ahmedabad was also conceptualized by Gandhiji. Struggle for *Poorna Swaraj* continued on, under the leadership of Mahatma Gandhiji.

Struggle started with Bardoli Satyagraha (1928). Gandhiji's method was totally non-violent, of high quality and effective. Mahatma Gandhiji correctly apprehended how people of India were becoming victim of exploitation and agonies of the British rule. He was desirous to see that freedom should be obtained as early as possible. In order to achieve objective *Poorna Swaraj* the Congress (Gandhiji) started Civil Disobedience movement. As a part of Civil Disobedience Movement, a march from Sabarmati Harijan Ashram (now Gandhi ashram) to Dandi was started on March 12, 1930, under the leadership of Gandhiji along with 78 supporters including Sarojini Naidu and Mahadev Desai to break the salt law. Two followers joined the march on. On April 5, all of them reached to village Dandi near Navsari. This march was 366 kms long, and Gandhiji completed it on foot at the age of more than 60 years. Women were imparted training to join this *Satyagraha*. Young men and women also joined enthusiastically.

During Dandi March, numerous constructive programmes like boycott of foreign clothes, prohibition of liquor, removal of untouchability, Hindu-Muslim unity, and oath to do social service etc. were given importance. After getting green signal from Gandhiji, salt Satyagraha were held everywhere, among which capital Dharasana and Vadala Satyagraha became well known. The Satyagraha at Dharasana on May 21, 1930 along with 250 agitators, and on next day to Vadala continued up to June. All the agitators had properly digested Gandhiji's Doctrine of non-violence. Gandhiji even brought women of India out of the four walls of the house to participate in the struggle of freedom. Gandhiji became famous in every corner of India and became an architect of the future of India.

Agriculture

The State has accorded a very priority of the farmer's participation in irrigation system management and operation. Perhaps Gujarat is the first state in the country to have such a policy on participatory irrigation management. The number of participatory irrigation management is being increased every time to have better agricultural growth and the farmers will have better benefits. Farmer's movement is not a recent phenomenon in Gujarat. During the last one and a half decades, the farmers organized several struggles with varying degrees. As mentioned Gujarat is one of the developed states of the country. It has a higher rate of urbanization, literacy and per capita income than the all India average. The land distribution in Gujarat is known as skewed 61 per cent of the workers in Gujarat are engaged in agriculture which is the principal source of earning. 38 per cent of them are cultivators and 23 per cent are agricultural labourers 56 per cent of the cultivators (more than 13.5 lakh) over less than 3 hectares of land on the other hand; 1.35 per cent households (thirty thousand) hold more than 20 hectares of land a very negligible number of households own more than 40 per cent of land. The rich and middle farmers have formed up their organization to protect and advance their economic interests like of the Cotton Growers Associations the Tobacco Growers Association, the Vegetables Growers Association, etc. According to the all India debt and investment survey, 40 per cent of the farmers whose income is between 1000 and 2500 rupees, borrowed money for household expenditure and only eight per cent for agricultural purposes. Quite a few of the poor farmers have joined their rank of labourers, as a result, the number of agricultural labourers has increased. Both the agricultural labourers and poor farmers are largely unorganized though some unions of agricultural labourers do exist. Earlier, the poor peasants were taking land as share croppers from the middle and rich farmers and returning a part of the agricultural products the owners, this system has continued, but at the same time the process has been reversed. The rich middle farmers now take land from poor framers as share croppers or on rent as the latter cannot afford to invest in land (Benerjee, 1996: 65). Coming to the soils in Gujarat, there are broadly nine categories yielding various important crops, rich minerals and forest cover. Status of Gujarat soils is fairly high. Declination of micro nutrient deficient areas on the basis of soil analysis of 11,162 samples all over the State has revealed an overall deficiency of Zinc to the tune of 26 per cent of the sample analyses. Zinc deficiency is largely confined of the districts of Banaskantha, Sabarkantha, Surendranagar and Jamnagar.

Industrialization in Gujarat

Gujarat has 202 well-planned industries established by the Gujarat Industrial Development Corporation (GIDC). The existing industries in the State are textiles, engineering, chemicals and Pharmaceutical units. The textile industry in Gujarat contributes about 25 per cent of industrial production in the sector consisting several spinning as well as composite mills generating about 60 per cent man-made fibre. Meanwhile the fast growing industrial structure has given boost to the growth of chemical and petrochemical industries and the engineering industry in the State. The engineering industry in the State encourages iron crushing, steel casting, steel forgings, re-rolling industry and the like. Besides along with alloy and special steel structural fabrication and metal products such as steel furniture, cutlery, hand tools and springs, nuts, tools as well as ball-bearings, bicycle parts, small tolls and big tolls, etc. are also manufactured. In addition the State also has several chemical fertilizer plants. Gujarat's second largest petrochemical complex has taken shape at Kawas near Surat. Gujarat has Asia's largest chemical industrial estate at Ankleshwar that produces salt and soda ash. The pharmaceutical industry in the State accounts for about 33 per cent of the production of drugs and medicines in the country. Further the availability of non-metallic minerals in abundance like limestone, fire clay, manganese, bauxite, lignite, gypsum, flourspan accentuates the process of industrialization. Gujarat leads in agate and salt production and is second in calcite and third in China clay in the country. A multi-processing complex of Oil and Natural Gas Commission (ONGC) with an investment of Rs. 580 crores has been commissioned at Hazira in Surat. Country's first Sponge Iron project costing Rs. 305 crores has been established at Hazira with an installed capacity of 8.80 lakh tones per annum. Manufacturing accounts for the largest employment of manpower across industries. Employment in public sector establishments covered under the Employment Market Information (EMI) scheme was 830,000, whereas in the private sector it was 860,000 (as on March 2005). Out of the total 1.69 million people employed in the organized sector, 234,000 (13.82 per cent) were women, the public sector employed 17.30 per cent of women, while the private sector employed 10.45 per cent. The agriculture sector has provided a strong base for the growth of Gujarat's economy. Rapid strides in agro-technology and food production have played a key role in augmenting the manufacturing and services sectors. Gujarat is India's largest producer of castor, groundnut, cotton, banana and tobacco. The growth of the services sector has been augmented by increasing industrial activity (*Socio-economic Review*, 2006-07).

The manufacturing sector has been the backbone of Gujarat's growth and development. The State's recognition as a manufacturing hub is supported by the presence of more than 312,000 small and 2,200 medium enterprises. Contributing 30 per cent of total manufacturing and exports of Gujarat, the Small and Medium Enterprise (SME) sector has played a key role in shaping the manufacturing industry. The number of factories increased from 12,795 in 2003-04 to 13,603 in 2004-05, showing an increase of 6.31 per cent. The billion in 2003-04 to $9 biliion in 2004-05, an increase of 24.77 per cent. The average daily employment in working factories also increased from 978,000 at the end of 2005 to 1.03 million a year later. Fixed capital employed by the factory sector in Gujarat increased from $21.45 billion in 2004-05, an increased of 1.54 per cent. As per the provisional summary results of the Annual Survey of Industries (ASI, 2004-05), Gujarat ranks second in the country, in terms of the state-wise percentage share in Net Value Added by Manufactured generated by the factory sector. Gujarat's share in the country's industrial aggregate is 9.97 per cent factories, 9.56 per cent employees, 15.59 per cent of value of output, 13.86 per cent Net Value Added (Gujarat State Economic Review, 2007-08). An SEZ is a specifically delineated duty-free enclave, deemed foreign territory for the purpose of trade, operations and duty and tariffs. SEZs have been created as designated industrial areas for establishing units, which would in turn lead to an increase in manufacturing activities, augment exports and generate employment. Currently, with 51 approved, Gujarat has among the highest SEZs in the country and the highest geographical area (over 15,000 hectares) under development for establishing SEZs. Three giant sized units of big national companies, namely Reliance, Larsen & Toubro and Essar Steel, have come at Hazira in Surat. The huge concerns of state sponsored enterprises such as Kribhco, Oil and Natural Gas Corporation and the Indian Oil Corporation are also located in the same area. Big chemical units such as Navin Flourine, Cyanide, Citurgia, Adarsh chemicals etc. are also situated near Surat.

The Reliance is India's largest private sector enterprise, with businesses in the energy and materials value chain. Group's annual revenues are in excess of US $34 billion. Reliance enjoys global leadership in its businesses, being the largest polyester yarn and fibre producer among the top five to ten producers in the world in major petrochemical products. The group exports products in excess of US $ 20 billion to 108 countries in the world. Major group companies are Reliance industries limited (including main subsidiaries, reliance petroleum limited and reliance retail limited) and reliance industrial infrastructure limited. Hazira manufacturing division located near Surat, Gujarat is spread over 700 acres. It comprises of a Naphtha cracker feeding downstream fibre intermediates, plastics and polyester plants (http//www.Reliance.com.). Reliance industries limited operates world class manufacturing facilities across the country at Allahabad, Barabanki, Dahej, Dhenkanal, Gandhar, Hajira, Hoshiarpur, Jamnagar, Kurkumbh, Nagothane, Nagpur, Naroda, Silvassa and Vadodara is spread over 11018 acres, manufacturing polymirazation, black fibre, Dahej manufacturing division located near Bharuch, Gujarat, is spread over 1,778 acres. It comprises of an ethane/propane recovery unit, a gas cracker, a caustic chloride plant and 4 downstream plants, which manufacture polymers and fibre. Staple fibre, a wide range of PSF, PFF, POY and polyester chips. Jamnagar manufacturing division located in Jamnagar, Gujarat, is spread over 7400 acres. Starting as small textile company, reliance has in its journey crossed several milestone to become a fortune 500 company in less than 3 decades. The company's net profits crossed the $ 1 billion over the last 25 years, RIL has seen its sales grow from Rs. 120 crore to Rs. 74418 crore. This remarkable performance was reflected in the stock markets too. Shares of Reliance gave a return of 39 per cent on an annualized basis. Since RIL accounts for 12 per cent of the Sensex's market cap and one out of four investors in Indian equities is a Reliance shareholder, the petrochemicals segment which accounts for 41 per cent of Reliance's revenues and 45 per cent of profits, the upturn in the Indian economy and demand from the rest of Asia. The RIL produced 12.4 MMT (million metric tones) of petrochemicals in the 2006 and 2007 (http//www. Reliance. au)

L&T has its world-class heavy engine facilities at Hazira, Surat, on the coastal belt of western India. The unit is engaged in design and manufacture of hi tech fabricated equipment for core sectors such as oil and gas, refineries, petrochemicals, fertilizers, nuclear, Aerospace and marine in India. Energy consumption at L&T Hazira, primarily Electrical power, high speed diesel, Natural gas and LPG are sources of energy. L&T's output and energy consumption patterns in year 2005 and 2006 production in tonnes is 30384 (http//www.larsentaubro.com).

Essar Steel Complex at Hazira, houses a 5.0 MTPA sponge iron plant, the world's largest gas based HBI producer. The plant provides raw material for state of the art 3.0 MTPA Hot Rolled Coil (HRC) plant, the first and largest of India's new generation still mills. Essar. Essar is India's largest explorer of flat products, selling almost one third of production to the highly demanding US and European markets, and to the growing markets of south East Asia and the Middle East. Essar Global limited is a diversified business corporation with balanced portfolio of assets straddling the manufacturing and services sectors; steel, energy, power, communication, shipping and logistics and construction. Through its six sectoral holding companies, has a firm value of over US $ 50 billion and employs 30,000 people worldwide. Essar oil and gas is an integrated oil company operating in three separate divisions each focusing on one link in the petroleum value chain, exploration and production, refinery, marketing, world class US \$2.14 bn (Rs. 99 billion) 10.5 MTPA refinery. Within place reserves of 500 million barrels of oil and recoverable reserves of 145 million barrels of oil. Essar power's 515 MW power plant at Hazira set up India's first new generation independent power project at Hazira, India in the early 1990s. Vodafone Essar Ltd. is India's 2nd largest GSM telephony provider, with over 46 million customers. Essar shipping is an integrated sea logistic companies with an unblemished track record of over two decades in the transportation of crude and bulk cargo (http//www.corporate.com).

NTPC—National Thermal Power Corporation Limited Kawas. Surat was incorporated in the year 1975 in a span of just over 15 years after commissioning of the first 200 MW unit. NTPC has grown to become the largest utility of the country with a commissioned capacity of 16,795 MW as in April 1998. NTPC has been ninth in thermal generation amongst the world's thermal generation companies. NTPC is a prime player in the power sector; it spearheads the process of accelerated development of power sector by planning and implementing power projects and operating power stations economically and efficiently. Already giant in the field of thermal power, NTPC has also recently diversified into wind and hydropower in their new projects. NTPC has several plants such as National Hydro Electric Power Corporation Ltd., National Thermal Power Corporation Ltd., North Eastern Electric Power Corporation, Nuclear Power Corporation of India Ltd. With authorized capital amounting to Rs. 25,500 crores and investments of Rs. 304.33 crores in 1998-99, this power sector has employee strength of 50,439. NTPC is mainly engaged in the generation and distribution of all forms of power viz, hydro, thermal and nuclear (excluding solar). NTPC has established itself in a leadership position to a great extent because of its phenomenal manpower. The value of the human resource assets has been valued at Rs. 693.55 crores. NTPC has projects across the country in Vindyachal (MP) Auraiya (UP) Gandhar in Gujarat, Talcher (Orrisa) and Kayamkulam (Kerala) to name a few (http//www.ntpc.com).

Krishak Bharti Cooperative Limited (KRIBHCO) has been the world's premier fertilizer producing cooperative under the administrative control of the Department of Fertilizers, Government of India. Incorporated in April 1980 as a national level Cooperative Society to manufacture and desirable Chemical Fertilizers and allied farm inputs, KRIBHCO has fully imbibed the cooperative philosophy and has made sustained efforts towards promoting the cause of modern agriculture and cooperatives in the country. The membership of the Society is 5790 Cooperative Societies spread across the country. KRIBHCO operates two Natural gas based Ammonia plants each of the 1520 MTPD capacity and four urea steams each of 1310 MTPD capacity. The annual installed capacity of Urea plants is 17.29 lakh MT of Urea. The complex is also having facilities to produce 30 MWH power and 550 MTPH HP stream and other utilities. KRIBHCO has achieved an average capacity utilization of 112.52 per cent during the last twenty completed years of service to the Nation. Production levels of 122.11 per cent to 124.35 and 124.41 per cent of its installed capacity of Urea were achieved respectively in the last three financial years (2003-04 to 2005-06). The overall performance of KRIBHCO during the year 2003-2004 has created new records in Urea specific energy and production 1806500 MT, Amonia production 1112892 MT, Urea specific energy 5.891 MT., Bio- fertilizers production 539.2 MT (http// www.kribhco.com).

Tata Motors, the largest automobile company in India in terms of revenues, launched Nano, commercially on March 30, 2009. The car with an ex-factory price tag of Rs. 1,00,000 generated a Tata came to Gujarat to meet Chief Minister Narendra Modi and to see the land offered to them. Lastly, Narendra Modi was successful in this offer. Narendra Modi offered 1100 acres of land to Tata Motors in Sanand in Ahmedabad District. Now Gujarat has raised the head of all people of Gujarat. Tata Group's Nano project plant started in Sanand, 30 kms from the Ahmedabad, on the land of Anand Agriculture University (AAU). Tata Motors will produce 2.5 lakh cars annually in Gujarat; the capacity can go up to 5 lakh cars per annum. The land for the "Nano" project is located within a 2200-acre campus owned by the Anand Agriculture University. The university has already transferred 1,000 acres back to the government. Tata Motors officials had also been looking at sites in Karnataka, Andhra Pradesh and Maharashtra in search of a suitable site for NANO plant. With the Tata Nano project moving to Sanand in Gujarat, local component manufacturers will save about Rs. 16 lakh per month as transportation charges, for nearly 400 tonnes of spare parts that they sent to Singur. Vendors in Gujarat will also benefit from the Tata Nano mother plant shift to Gujarat. The Tata's moving to Gujarat has also made a difference to the investment sentiment in India. Gujarat already has impeccable credentials when it comes to business and industry. A recent study by the RBI has said that in 2007-2008, Gujarat attracted the maximum investment in the country and has 100 projects—worth Rs. 624.42 billion ($13.85 billion)-in the implementation stage. The Tata Nano Project will only strengthen Gujarat's hold on new investments. Currently big business houses like Reliance Industries, Aditya Birla Group, Essars and Adani and global conglomerates, such as Matsushita, ABB, Shell and Bombardier have made their home in the State. Meanwhile, land prices have shot up in Gujarat, in and around Chharodi in Ahmedabad district. The overall spurt in land prices in Ahmedabad district is expected to put an end to the recession in the realty market. Prices in Chharodi have gone up to Rs. 8-10 lakh per bigah, up from Rs. 3-4 lakh per bigah. In Sanand, land prices are Rs. 3000 per sq yard, up from Rs. 2500 per sq yard price before the announcement about the Tatas moving to Gujarat was made. In Sachana and Virochandnagar, agricultural land prices have shot up from Rs. 3-5 lakh per bigha to Rs. 10 lakh per bigha. Gujarat has very good infrastructure for transportation and has large sea shore that can help import/export of raw material and finished goods. In addition, Bombay and Pune is in close proximity which will help setup synergy for suppliers similar too Chennai.

The small industrial enterprises, diamond cutting and polishing industry has rapidly flourished in present times involving imports, exports, manufacturing and processing operations. Major part of this industry has remained confined to a few districts of Gujarat. At one time 90 per cent was from Surat city only, thus Surat attained the name of the Diamond city of India. The world's first diamonds were found in the soft, alluvial plains of South India, along the banks of the rivers Krishna and Godavari. Since then, India has had an undeniably strong connection with the diamond trade. A staggering almost 90 per cent of the diamonds sold all over the world come the expert hands of the diamond cutters of Surat. After the polishing is done, the polished diamonds follow the same mechanism as above to reach to the exporters or the big trading houses which finally export these polished diamonds in the international market. The entire process of polishing the raw diamonds constitutes of several tiers of agents. These imports are managed through big trading houses such as the Diamond Trading Company (DTC) whose primary responsibility is the sale of the raw diamonds produced by the international majors of the likes of DeBeers (of South Africa). The other trading houses involved in the import and sale of the roughs (raw diamonds) are the Hindustan Diamond Company (HDC), Minerals and Metals Trading Corporation of India (MMTC) as well as National Mineral Development Corporation (NMDC). Surat is a popular center, owing to its proximity to Mumbai where all the major trade merchants and houses dealing with diamond exports are situated. Surat accounts for nearly 35 per cent of the volume of trade in cutting and polishing of rough diamonds in the country. The growth of Gujarat as a major diamond centre is generally traced to the initiatives taken by the traders belonging to the Patel community who brought experts from Belgium to train the artisans in the art of diamond cutting and polishing near Palanpur. In the diamond industry of Surat, cutting and processing units range from tiny cottage based artisan job shops to organized factory system. The diamond industry began with a turnover of Rs. 65 crores in 1960, has grown to over Rs. 80,000 crore. There are several reasons why Surat became the chief exporter of polished diamonds, the primary one being labour, which is 80 per cent cheaper. There are 8,00,000 diamond workers in Surat, in almost 10,000 diamond processing units in the region. The polishing and cutting work is being carried in small workshops that are mainly located in one area, called Varachha Road (Surat Development Plan, 2006-2012). A reliable source such as Diamond Association of Surat estimates it around 11000. Most of the owners of these units are 'Patels' and belong to one specific sub region of Gujarat State, Saurashtra. At that point of time, migrant labour, mainly from Saurashtra region entered. The owner of the polishing units of diamond in Surat is mainly from Saurashtra region.

Table 2.4: Work Participation Rate

	2001			*1991*			*Increase/decrease in %*		
	Total	*Male*	*Female*	*Total*	*Male*	*Female*	*Total*	*Male*	*Female*
Total	42.10	55.02	28.03	40.39	53.64	26.20	1.7	1.4	1.8
Rural	47.55	55.59	39.04	45.79	55.03	36.04	1.8	0.6	3.0
Urban	33.07	54.12	9.11	30.22	51.09	7.20	2.9	3.0	1.9

Source: B.K. Bhatt, 2003: 174-175.

The above Table 2.4 reveals that during 1991-2001 1.8 per cent work participation increased in rural area. In 1991 worker's population was 55.03 per cent which in 2001 55.59 per cent rural areas have more male workers 1.47 per cent than the urban areas. While women workers in 1991 were 36.04 per cent than has increased 39.04 per cent in 2001. Compare to 1991 in 2001 women workers rate increased 3.0 per cent.

The above Table 2.4 shows that the work participation rate in 1991 was 34.2 while in 2001 it decreased to 33.7 per cent. Examining the WPR in rural areas, male workers have decreased while in urban areas in 2001 it has increased.

Table 2.5: Population of Main Workers in the State

Urban/Rural total	*Year*	*Total*	*Male*	*Female*
Total	1991	34.2	53.3	13.7
	2001	33.7	51.3	14.5
	Increase	-0.5	-2.0	+0.8
Rural	1991	36.6	54.5	17.7
	2001	35.1	50.4	18.9
	Increase	-1.5	-4.1	+1.2
Urban	1991	29.5	50.9	6.0
	2001	31.3	52.6	7.0
	Increase	+1.8	+1.7	+1.8

Source: B.K. Bhatt, 2003:177.

Surat formerly known as **Suryapur** or **Khubsoorat**, is the eighth largest city in India. The city proper is the seventh most populous city in India and 49th in the world. Surat is the administrative capital of Surat district. The city is situated on the left bank of the Tapti River, 14 miles from its mouth. The population of Surat with its Twin City Navsari is above 6.3 million as of 2009. A moat divides the older parts of the city, with its narrow streets and handsome houses, and the newer suburbs. The city is largely recognized for its textile and diamond businesses. It is also known as the diamond capital of the world and the textile capital of India. 92 per cent of the world's diamonds are cut and polished in Surat. Surat is also the third cleanest city in India after Chandigarh and Gandhinagar. Surat was once the largest city in India. It has one of the highest GDP growth rates in India at 11.5 per cent as of 2008. Surat was the primary port of India during the Mughal period, a distinction it lost to Bombay during the British Raj.

In the early centuries during the reign of the Mughal emperor Jehangir, the port of Surat was used as the gateway to Mecca for pilgrims of the hajj from India's interior regions. Both the Makkai Pool and the Mughal Sarai guesthouse for *hajjis* (pilgrims) are indicators of this historical significance. Surat is mentioned in the Sanskrit epic, the *Mahâbhârata* when Lord Krishna stopped there en route from Mathura to Dwarka. According to other later Sanskrit records, the area was ruled by the Western Châlukyas in 610 CE, and continued to be ruled by Hindu kings until one of Qutubuddîn Aibak's generals captured it. The Parsis started to settle there in the 12th century, and added greatly to its prosperity. Local traditions state that a Brahman named Gopi, who called it Suryapûr, or 'City of the Sun', founded the city in the last years of the fifteenth century. In 1512 and 1530 Surat was burned and ravaged by the Portuguese who were trying to maintain influence in the area. In 1513, the Portuguese traveller, Duarte Barbosa, described Surat as an important seaport, frequented by many ships from Malabar and various parts of the world. By 1520, the name of the city was Surat. During the reigns of the Mughal emperors Akbar, Jahângîr and Shâh Jahân, Surat rose to become a chief commercial city of India and an imperial mint was established there. As the major port on the west coast of India, Surat also served as the port for the Hajj to Mecca. In 1608, ships from the British East India Company started docking in Surat, using it as a trade and transit point. In 1613, the British Captain Best, followed by Captain Downton, overcame Portuguese naval supremacy and obtained an imperial firman establishing a British factory at Surat following the Battle of Swally. The city was made the seat of a presidency under the British East India Company after the success of the embassy of Sir Thomas Roe to the court of Emperor Jahangir. The Dutch also founded a factory.

At its zenith, Surat was popularly viewed as the city of Kubera, the God of Wealth. In 1664 the Maratha King Shivaji attacked Surat, a key Mughal power centre, and a wealthy port town which generated a million rupees in taxes. When Shivaji arrived in Surat, he demanded tribute from the Mughal commander of the army stationed for port security. The tribute was refused and instead of battling the Marathas, the prosperity of Surat received a fatal blow when Bombay was ceded to the British as part of the dowry for Catherine of Braganza's wedding to Charles II in 1662. Shortly afterwards, in 1668, the British East India company established a factory in Bombay (Mumbai) and Surat began its relative decline concurrent with the rise of British interests in Bombay. Surat was sacked again by Shivaji in 1670. By 1689, the British East India Company had moved the presidency to Bombay. At its height, Surat's population reached an estimated 8,00,000, but by the middle of the 19th century the number had fallen to 80,000. The British took control of Surat again in 1759, and assumed all government powers of the city in 1800.

A fire and a flood in 1837 destroyed many of buildings of Surat. By the early 20th century, the population had slowly climbed to 1,19,306 and Surat was a center of trade and manufacturing. There were cotton mills, factories for ginning and pressing cotton, rice-cleaning mills and paper mills. Fine cotton goods were woven on handlooms, and there were special manufactures of silk brocade and gold embroidery (known as *Jari*). The chief trades were organized in guilds. Manufacturing and trading brought an eclectic mix of ethnicity to the city, making Surat's culture unique. In 1992, violent riots took place between Hindus and Muslims, the first and worst of their kind in the modern history of Surat. In 1994, a combination of heavy rains and blocked drains led to flooding of the city. A number of dead street animals and public waste were not removed in time and a plague epidemic spread through the city, which caused a number of countries to impose travel and trade sanctions. The Municipal Commissioner during that time, S.R. Rao and the people of Surat worked hard in the late 1990s to clean the city up, after which it was recognized in many circles as the 'second-cleanest city in India'.

Surat has a Tropical monsoon climate, moderated strongly by the Arabian Sea. The summer begins in early March and lasts till June. April and May are the hottest months, the average temperature being 30°C. Monsoon begins in late June and the city receives about 800 mm of rain by the end of September, with the average temperature being around 28°C during those months. October and November see the retreat of the monsoon and a return of high temperatures till late November. Winter starts in December and ends in late February, with average temperatures of around 22°C, and little rain.

Surat is economic capital of Gujarat and also one of the economic hubs of India. Surat is famous for its diamond industry and textile industry, along with silk and chemicals. It is at the heart of India's thriving diamond-polishing industry, which in 2005 cut 92 per cent of the world's diamond pieces and earned India $15 billion in exports. Gujarati diamond cutters emigrating from East Africa established the industry in 1901 and by the 1970s; Surat-based diamond cutters began exporting stones to the US for the first time. It is a major production centre for synthetic textiles in India. Surat is known for producing world-class synthetic textiles. It is known as the MANCHESTER OF EAST. Surat has excellent roads according to *Business Today Magazine*. The November 18, 2008 issue of the Wall Street Journal had an article about the diamond industry in Surat. It claims that 80 per cent of the world's finished diamonds are cut and polished in this city. However, the wages of the industry's workers remained flat for years and 250,000 workers, or one-third of the city's diamond industry workforce, has left between the years from 2005-2008, leaving about 500,000 workers. Only after a July 2008 strike did the workers obtain a 20 per cent salary raise, their first in a decade.

The textile industry has traditionally formed in Gujarat on the basis of industrial development. However, in the 1970's and 1980's manufacturing of cotton goods grew rapidly. Gujarat has a dominant electronics industry. In 1990-91 Gujarat ranked second after Maharashtra (22.7%) among the States of India in respect of percentage share in gross value of output. Ahmedabad and Atul (Valsad) produces one-third of the national total share in gross value of output. An electronics establishment at Gandhinagar produces components for India's increasingly sophiscated consumer market. The State is major producer of inorganic chemicals such as soda ash and caustic soda as well as chemicals fertilizer. The core industries in the State are Textiles, Engineering, Chemicals, and Pharmaceuticals. The industry in Gujarat contributes about 25 per cent of industrial production in the sector consisting several spinning as well as composite mills. After 1970 State witnessed the use of man-made fibre in a big way. There are approximately 80,000 embroidery units in Surat which makes Surat the embroidery capital too. Surat also has many large industrial units such as Reliance Petrochemical plant, Essar's 10 million tonne steel plant, KRIBHCO fertilizer plant, L&T Engineering unit, gas processing plant of

ONGC, NTPC gas power plant. All at Hazira and ABG Shipyard (Shipbuilding Yard) and Ambuja Cement (Grinding Unit) at Magdalla Port whereas Torrent mega power plant and GIPCL are located at Kamrej.

Demographics

The population of Surat according to new city limits is 53,74,429. Males constitute 56 per cent of the population and females 44 per cent. Surat has an average literacy rate of 83 per cent, higher than the national average of 59.5 per cent, male literacy is 81 per cent, and female literacy is 70 per cent. Gujarati, Marathi and Hindi are the main languages spoken in Surat. In Surat, 13 per cent of the population is under 6 years of age. Around 5 per cent of the total population is Oriya, over 0.6 million people or about 11 per cent hail from Uttar Pradesh and Bihar. Surat also has sizeable Parsee, Jews and Bohra Muslims. It is generally believed that as of 2009 about 5.4 million people live within the Surat City Corporation.

Culture and Festivals

Surat is known for its Surti cuisine, which includes perennial favourites such as Ghari (a type of sweatmeat), Locho, Undhiyu, Rasaawala Khaman, and Surti Chinese. Surti cuisine is not as sweet as other Gujarati food, and is quite spicy. Roadside kiosks, called "laaris" or "rekdis", are popular. In the cooler winter months, Suratis converge at river Tapi's banks to eat Ponk, a roasted cereal that is available only in this part of the world. All major Indian festivals are celebrated in Surat. Navratri, Diwali and Ganesh Chaturthi are celebrated with great enthusiasm. The kite-flying festival of Utrayan which falls on Makar Sankranti — 14 January — is very popular in the city. It is also well known for the celebration of Chandi Padvo which usually occurs around October and is a holiday unique to Surat. This day comes after one of the two biggest full moon days of the Hindu calendar year, "Sharad Purnima". On this day, Surtis buy almost 100 tonnes of Ghari and other Surti delicacies, and then head to the city's seaside beach area, Dumas where they have dinner and a late night snack under the full moonlit sky.

Education

Schools in Surat are either "municipal schools" (run by the SMC) or private schools (run by trusts or individuals), which in some cases receive financial aid from the government. The schools are affiliated either with the Gujarat State Board or the Central Board of Secondary Education (CBSE) and few schools are affiliated under National Institute of Open Schooling (NIOS). Gujarati or English are the usual languages of instruction. The government-run public schools lack many facilities, but are the only option for poorer residents who cannot afford the more expensive private schools. A majority of residents prefer private schools because of better infrastructure and the use of English as a medium of instruction. Surat has the prestigious, Sardar Vallabhbhai National Institute of Technology (SVNIT), commonly known to local people as SVR from its earlier name SVREC (Sardar Vallabhbhai Regional Engineering College). This is one of the NITs, is a premier engineering college, is also located here. It is among the top five of all 20 NIT's in India and top most in Gujarat for technical education. With its festivals throughout the year, the college keeps a very vibrant atmosphere inside as well as outside the campus. The college is favourite destination for morning joggers of the city. The city holds the prestige of providing Medical Education to students. It has two medical colleges namely "Government Medical College and New Civil Hospital" and "SMIMER", both giving the degrees of MBBS and MD, MS. Under the 10+2+3 format, students attend primary and secondary schooling during the first ten years and then may complete two years of higher secondary education, followed by three years at college for commerce, arts or science degrees. Generally, engineering degree courses take four years, while medicine takes about five and half years or more. Most colleges in the city are affiliated to Veer Narmad South Gujarat University.

Media

Gujarat Mitra, one of the oldest and most respected dailies, is the most popular daily newspaper of Surat and South Gujarat. Besides *Gujarat Mitra,* other dailies include *Gujarat Samachar, Sandesh, Divyabhaskar* and

Commodity World. Local editions of these newspapers are published in Gujarati. *Loktej* was the first Hindi daily published in Surat. *Rajasthan Patrika* and *Savera* are now the top Hindi daily newspapers in Surat. The National English dailies such as *The Times of India, Indian Express* and *Mid Day* are the most popular English-language newspapers. *DNA-Daily News and Analysis* is a new addition to the list of English dailies available in Surat. Since the city has the largest synthetic textile manufacturing center in India, there is an exclusive textile newspaper called *Textile Graph*. It is published in Surat, since 1994 both in Gujarati and Hindi. The 'Textile Directory of Surat' (5th edition) comprising business information of textile traders and industry in and around Surat is also published by *Textile Graph*. Most cable service providers have local television channels. Satellite TV DTH services are provided by DISH TV, TATA SKY and BIG TV. Broadband internet connections are also available in the city. Broadband service providers include BSNL, TATA Indicom, Reliance Communication, YOU Broadband and VSNL (ANAR COMMUNICATIONS). Wi-Fi connectivity is available at many cafes. Currently, Surat has four FM Radio stations - Radio City 91.1, Radio Mirchi 98.3, My FM 94.3, Big FM 92.7 along with the National Radio Vividh Bharati.

Sports

Surat has many sports facilities, the majority of them are dedicated to cricket. The Lalbhai Contractor Stadium and the Pithawala Cricket Stadiums have facilities for hosting cricket matches. In addition, Surat has an indoor stadium, used to host events like badminton and table tennis, with modern facilities and seating capacity for 7000. In August 2006, the **3rd Asian Gymnastics Championship** was held in Surat. There are a few sports clubs which provide many types of indoor and outdoor games, including the Surat Tennis Club, Surat City Gymkhana and Rander Islam Gymkhana (RIG). Recently one of the biggest swimming pools in the city has been opened near Palanpur Patiya area. The Rander area also hosts the Royal Cricket Ground.

Places of Interest

The Old Fort — The Old Fort was built by Muhammad bin Tughluq in the 1546 to fortify the defence against the Bhils. It is now used for municipal offices.

The Sardar Patel Museum – Established in 1898, and originally called the Winchester Museum; this museum has a collection of over 10,000 specimens of arts and crafts.

Gaurav Path – A well planned and well-built major road in New Surat area of the city. Surat is a home of multiplexes, shopping malls, show rooms, restaurants and much more.

Chowpati – This is also a very popular place in the city. It has a large garden and provides Indian fast food like 'Paav Bhajee' and 'Pani puri'.

Beaches – There are a number of beaches near Surat. Only 16 km away, Dumas is a popular resort with locals. Suvali is 28 km from the city and Ubhrat is 42 km out, while Tithal is 108 km away and only five km from Valsad on the Mumbai to Vadodara railway line.

Table 2.6: Growth of Population in Surat City (1881 2006)

Year	*Total*	*Population*		*Decadal Variations*	
		Male	*Female*	*Absolute*	*Proportion (%)*
1881	1,09,844			+1,989	+1.81
1891	1,09,229			–545	–0.49
1902	1,29,500	66,215	63,285	+20,201	+18.49
1911	1,25,220	64,477	60,743	–4,280	–3.30
1921	1,27,356	66,448	60,908	+2,136	+1.71
1931	1,10,739	58,767	51,971	–16,617	–13.05
1941	1,85,955	97,483	88,472	+75,216	+67.92
1951	2,37,394	1,23,252	1,14,142	+51,439	+27.66
1961	3,17,519	1,65,250	1,52,269	+80,125	+33.75
1971	4,71,656	2,49,902	2,21,754	+1,54,137	+48.54
1981	7,76,583	4,18,114	3,58,369	+3,04,927	+64.65
1991	14,98,817	8,14,938	6,83,789	+7,22,234	+93.00
2001	24,33,835	13,72,415	10,61,420	+9,35,018	+62.38
2006 (i)	31,00,705	(estimated population within the old city limits)			
2006 (ii)	28,17,235	(estimated population within the city limits extended in 2006)			

Note: The 1931 figures are unreliable, for many people did not co-operate with the census owing to the Non-Co-operation Movement. The figure(s) related to 2006 are estimated by the Surat Municipal Corporation.

Source: District Census Handbooks and 2006 population figure as estimated by the Surat Municipal Corporation.

Data related to population growth within the city show that during the last decade of the nineteenth century, the figures fell considerably. Barring the 1931 figures, which are only partially reliable, one finds a constant growth in its population since 1941. A significant growth, has taken place during the three decadal periods between 1961 and 1991. Proportionate to the growth in the area of city limits, the highest growth of population has taken place during the 1981-1991 decade. For example during the 1961-1971 decade as against a growth of 413 per cent in the city area the absolute increase of population was 48.54 per cent over the 1961 figures, whereas during the 1981-1991 decade the population grew by 9.60 per cent while the city area increased only by 100 per cent. During the 1971-1981 decade to the population growth has been substantial with 64.65 per cent over a city area that was 228 per cent more than the preceding decadal point (Das, 1994).

The spatial distribution of population within the city over the last two decades indicates certain specific patterns. By the end of 1971, the old or the inner city zone housed 77 per cent of its total population within an area of 8.18 sq kms. By 1981 within the same area while an absolute population increase of 64.6 per cent was recorded over the 1971, the area housed 56.8 per cent of the city population. By 1991, the old city had 40 per cent of the population located within the correspondingly comparable area of the city. Since by 1991, the city Corporation limits have increased, the proportion of population distribution too has changed. From the total figure calculated pertaining to the entire Corporation area as of today, the old city houses 28.3 per cent, the inner periphery and Rander zone 42 per cent and the outer suburbs 29.6 per cent of the total population. In terms of trends, the inner city witnessed a high population growth during the 1961-1971 and 1971-1981 decades respectively. However, by 1991 the rate has seemingly fallen in the area indicating at a probable residential mobility from the old city towards its inner or outer peripheries. Data related to the density pattern at the zonal levels show a substantial growth in population density during the 1971-1981 periods, but a significant fall during the 1981-1991 decade within its old city limits. As against this, the figures continued to grow in the peripheral wards progressively. Figure of 4214 persons per sq.km. In the Inner periphery and Rander zones during 1971 the population density reached to a figure of 13.598 persons in 1991. During the corresponding period Rander zone with an area of 55.60 sq kms. Now has a density of 7,739 persons per sq.km. It is however interesting to note that in spite of substantial growth in its total population, the overall density figures in the city during the last three decades have broadly remained uniform. This has been mainly owing to the intermittent but substantial changes in the total area of the city limit after 1963. Figures related to the distribution of population and density by different zones in Surat city. Based on the provisional figures of the 1991 Census, a broad pattern of population density within Surat City has been seen.

Table 2.7: Occupational Composition of Surat City (1921)

Occupation	*No. of Workers and Dependents (Per thousand of population)*
Pasture and Agriculture	28
Industry	467
Transport	24
Trade	202
Public Administration	21
Professions	72
Private Income	17
Domestic Service	53
Insufficiently described	96
Unproductive	13

Source: As quoted in Haynes, *op. cit.*, from Census of India, 1921, Vol. IX, Cities of the Bombay Presidency, p. 298.

The Jari and Kinkhab producing units continued to grow through the early decades of the twentieth century without undergoing any significant institutional or even technological change in its modern sense. This however was not true of the handloom sector, for most of it turned into powerlooms. The dominant character of the sector, especially at the production state remained 'enclosed' for they did not go beyond family enterprises. Weaving skills continued to be passed from one generation to another with the entire sector being linked variously with large number of job working units. It was Gujarat that recorded a continuous growth with the city of Surat having largest share of it in the state. To be precise "from a small number of 4,628 looms in the city in 1942, it increased to 39,000 in 1968". Such a growth also gave an impetus to other subsidiary activities such as engineering units, manufacturing, Jari, silk and art silk machinery and parts, wire drawing and pressing machines, diamond, dying, etc.

That such patterns have largely been caused by the way industries have grown in the district becomes clear after examining the growth, distribution and concentration patterns of industrial workers, factories and industrial centre over the region. For example, the related data on area-wise concentration pattern of the industry types and industrial workers at 1965, 1970, 1975 and 1981 show a high degree of their continued localizations in the city of Surat and its immediate surroundings (Das, 1994). Surat's economy is characterized by large number of small and medium unorganized industries. The industrial base is labour intensive. However, the wages are also lower and the workers are generally deprived of social and other benefits. Surat is known for its textile manufacturing trade, diamond cutting and polishing industries, intricate zari works, chemical industries and the gas based industries at Hazira established by leading industry houses such as ONGC, Reliance, Essar and Shell. The entire industrial sector put together contributed a gross revenue income of Rs. 2975.60 million to SMC in 1997-98. Rs. 18118 million in excise tax, Rs. 2715

Table 2.8: Population and Growth Rates of Urban Centres in Surat District

Status Size	*Class*	*Population (1991)*	*Growth Rate*	*Sex ratio*	
				1941-81	*1981-91*
Surat/U.A	I	15,17,076	87.40	64.21	839
Bardoli/M	III	38,349	46.04	36.32	935
Vyara/M	III	30,861	26.91	28.60	977
Ukai/VP	IV	17,543	52.31	17.18	902
Songadh/NP	IV	16,016	14.24	18.68	955
Madvi/NP	IV	14,297	69.73	31.68	963
Kathor/NP	IV	11,720	25.83	9.25	975
Kosamba/NP	IV	11,655	31.30	15.09	946
Olpad/VP	IV	10,493	—	24.28	912
Kadod/NP	IV	10,493	—	7.17	937
Utran/VP	V	8,669	—	35.46	946
Sayan/VP	V	8,361	—	59.01	881
Chalthan/VP	V	8,665	—	—	813

Source: Census of India 1991, provisional population Total: Rural-Urban Distribution paper-2 [1991], series-1. U.A. = Urban Agglomerants; M = Municipality; VO = Village Panchayat; NP = Nagar Panchayat.

million in income tax and Rs. 4215.4 million in sales tax. As estimated 4 per cent of GDP is contributed from the sector. It adds to about 7 to 8 per cent of the gross import bill. Surat is a dominant player in the textile sector. The traditional handloom weaving industry has given way to powerlooms, printing and dying textiles. Surat is one of the largest centers in the world for production of synthetic fibre fabrics, mainly nylon and polyester. The Indian Government's policy since 1956 of providing incentives and protection to small-scale industries boosted the powerloom industry in the city. Weavers took advantage of the incentives and converted their handlooms into powerlooms. At present, there are about 0.45 million powerlooms (about 45,000 units) in the city region and the sector provides for over 0.7 million jobs in Surat. Mota Varachha and Bharthana-Vesu have the highest number of workers spread as in agriculture and other minor works. Surat Municipal Corporation areas have very little workers as it is public service areas and majority is employers or service class. We find that Palanpur has the highest amount of workers that are related to household industry. Whereas Sachin, Parvat Patiya, Bamroli and Amroli have more workers engaged in industry works or working in factories.

Market is booming in Surat, national retail giants and companies which are competing over one another to buy huge chunks of land in Surat. And real estate in the diamond city is becoming costlier than ever. There seems a growing consumer culture in Surat since recently is reflected in setting up of various in commercial and residential area shopping malls like, lifestyle, Max, Globus, Foot Mart, Adani, Regent Mall, Jolly mall, Iscon, Reliance and Pantaloon Retail India Limited, Big Bazaar, etc. The diamond and textile merchants of Surat spend crores on swanky marts and luxury homes. This has triggered the retail price rise in select areas. With industries growing real estate development in Surat has out spaced demand for housing too has gone up with the continuous influx of migrants, land prices have sky rocketed (*Vishleshan*, Vol. 31 No. 2, April-June 2006). The Surat city is becoming a concrete jungle. This is compounded by a huge number of vehicular traffic raising the levels of pollution constantly.

As mentioned earlier Surat is one of the leading cities of Gujarat and is known to be a major hub for industrial activity in the State. With high economic growth witnessed by the State, the city is also growing rapidly both in terms of economy and population. The growth in population along with the increased urbanization has led to significant straining of civic infrastructure in the city. This also led to surge in the demand for better housing facilities providing modern amenities and livable environment in the city. Accordingly, the proposed township at Surat has to be developed based on the regulations provided in the Gujarat Township Planning and Urban Development Act, 1976. The proposed township can also avail 100 per cent Foreign Direct Investment incentive as permitted by the Government of India.

Surat was at its peak in trade in the sixteenth century which gradually declined, though it took momentum later. The city has been expanding both geographically and demographically. Surat is mainly characterized by household *jari* and art silk industries, diamond cutting and polishing units which operate in unorganized sector. Main occupation of the people in Surat is business of all kinds and forms starting from a petty shop to a giant mechanized textile mill while encompassing innumerable number of several small unorganized industrial units. Today in Gujarat, television is the leading medium reaching 24 per cent of the population, 49 per cent in the urban and 10 per cent in the rural areas. It is estimated that the television households in Gujarat are 4.29 million of which 2.37 per cent million are cable and satellite households. The number of television viewers in the State 22.18 million out of a total population of 50.60 million (*Source*: National Readership Survey 2001). Apart from the terrestrial channel DD 11 Gujarati i.e. DD Ahmedabad, there are other Gujarati satellite channels like ETV Gujarati and Alpha Gujarati. Interestingly, the Gujarati viewers prefer to watch Hindi channels like Star Plus which has the highest viewership ratings among television channels. The reach of the channels is as follows: Star Plus 49 per cent, Sony 441 per cent, Zee TV 39 per cent, DD Gujarati 35 per cent, Alpha Gujarati 17 per cent (*Source*: RK Swamy/BBDO website).

From the above discussion we hold that telecommunication industry, information technology and media in India in general, and Surat in Gujarat in particular is growing at a fast pace. There are reporters that the telecommunications giants are planning as investment of Rs. 14 billion in Gujarat while the telephone connections in the State stand around 6 million, the subscriber base for phones in the country by end March 2004 has gone up to

76.53 million, internet subscriber base to 4.55 million, cafes/ community internet centers to 10,237 and the village telephones up to 522,263 respectively (www.trai.gov.in). Telecommunication is poised for growth. Mass media expansion is also going on with the entry of newspapers chains from the Hindi heartland into Gujarat. Mass media readership and viewership is associated with increasing literacy in Gujarat, providing circulation figures, the growth in industrial sector providing advertising revenue and the general prosperity of the State. On all these parameters, Gujarat has a relatively high score. Thus, within the State, Surat in the past decade has seen a growth in the media industry and media consumption patterns giving rise to a distinct ethos and way of life.

From this brief note on socio-economic dimension of the state and Surat at the macro level we make an attempt to understand the social processes at the micro level through the empirical analysis in the fourth chapter.

3
Mass Media and Gender Stereotypes

Information is power. It is a source of knowledge. Modern age is the age of information. Information plays an important role in each and every sphere of life. It is rightly said that Iraq War was not a war between America and Iraq, but it was a war between two parties, one equipped with information and the other deprived of all information. Hence, the result was a natural outcome. We are living in an age of information revolution. Newspapers, radio and television are all well-known resources for getting information. Although mass-media as a subject of study is not very old but its history is as old as the humanity itself. Mass media and journalism have evoked into a strong force, over the years. Print media was the first phase followed by radio and television and later on internet and websites. In fact in broader sense, media has two different segments. One is print media and the other is electronic media. Electronic media may be more popular than print media, due to its visual power. But, print media has lasting value. Journalism and mass-media deal with a wider range of information comprising collection, writing, editing, proof reading and publication.

With the invention of new communication technologies, the power of mass-media has grown in stature. The mass-media shapes our perceptions and views of social reality by presenting only some aspects of reality and by continuation repetition of images and messages. We can say that the role and content of mass-media has changed dramatically, playing decisive role in reinforcing gender stereotypes and patriarchal culture by constructing new images and meanings by setting agendas for public opinion through selective themes and views. In this chapter, we would like to understand a global picture of representation of women in mass-media—films, television, serials, and advertisements on the basis of available Indian and international research literature on women and mass-media. It argues that women and their concerns are no longer invisible in the mass-media. However, old sex stereotypes have continued by taking new forms. On the other hand, progressive discourse on women's issues often co-opted and re-constructed in the mainstream media to establish the hegemony of dominant social classes. Hence, the task of changing media images of women has become more in the context of market economy.

What is Media

The media is instrumental in defining what we think, how we look and our social place and issues in the society. The term mass-media is defined as a means of communication that operates on a large scale, reaching and involving virtually everyone in the society to a greater or lesser degree. Mass-media has been influencing the social, cultural, economic, spiritual, political and religious aspects of society as well as personal level thinking, feeling and acting. Media feed the people with the latest information and create the need for change in contemporary society. Mass-media have both positive and negative role in the society. Media is all pervasive; its functioning is very subtle. Media plays a vital role in dissemination of information. It is called the fourth pillar of democratic policy. Radio, television, films and the printed word reach all of us in this age of information and each strives to perfect its modes of communications to become more effective as a medium. By gradually shaping public opinion on personal beliefs, and even people's self-perceptions, media influences the process of socialization and shapes ideology and thinking.

The term mass-media denotes various forms of entertainment; television, films, music, newspaper, magazines, internet, advertising, etc. disseminating information and it is used by media organization to target and impact youth. Idealized beauty standards, irrelevant sexualization and domestication are only some of the ways that women in media are portrayed today. Indian Journal of Women and

Development, October 2008:45] The study provides a general overview of how we perceive things and states that these give a negative image to young people. Radio, television, newspaper, magazines and films play a vital role in spreading information, propagating, educating and enlightening, strengthening national integration, creating national identity, etc. Mass communication essentially means dissemination of information, ideas and entertainment by the communication media. If one was to ask what is today's most powerful vehicle in molding of beliefs, attitudes, values and lifestyles, one would say it is media. By becoming more gender aware in content and language, media can present a clearer and more accurate picture of the roles and responsibilities of both men and women in the society. The need for mass-media to cover the entire population is widely admitted. Developing countries give priority to broadcast media, radio and television, even though the people's access is not always equitable and balanced. (Aggarwal, 1994; Rao and Annanta, 2000). Mass-media has been influencing the social, cultural, economic and religious aspects of the society. The impact of mass-media especially the television on the society has been compared with the effect of water dripping steadily on a stone imperceptibly eroding old values and attitudes in favour of new ones. It gives the people latest information and creates the need for change in contemporary society.

The press is not the most important means of communication in a country like India, because of its large illiterate population. Yet because of the existing power structure, which is dominated by the educated people, the written records carry much value. Hence, its capability to influence the attitudes of both ordinary readers and policy-makers are inevitable on large scale. The significance of printed media initiated from the India's struggle for Independence. Only press was the important weapon used by the great leaders of national movement such as Lokmanya Tilak, who founded the Marathi newspaper *Kesari* and Mahatma Gandhi with his *Hind Swaraj, Young India, Harijan* and many more publications. These newspapers were used as a vehicle to communicate their ideas to the rulers as well as to fellow citizens. Repressive press laws during the British Raj gave the indigenous press what M. Chalapathi Rau veteran journalist, terms as "reforming and crusading zeal" (Chalapathi Rau, Press in India, Allied Publications, New Delhi, 1986). After Independence, the crusading anti British nationalist press assumed by, and large, a supportive attitude towards the State. A congenial relationship between the press and the state continued to govern the nature of Indian journalism for several years after independence, continued. A major break in 1975, imposing of Internal Emergency restrictions, including Press censorship, brought revolution for the first time in free India. The imposing of censorship laws, were considered antipathetic during the Independence movement. Yet, the response to censorship was not resistance seen during the British rule, but created some initial protest and brave resistance for a few small publications. It also paved the way for greater courage of human rights issues, and the condition of marginalized social groups. This period also coincided with increased awareness about women's oppression globally and nationally. The years following the emergency witnessed the beginning of nation-wide campaigns by women's groups who protested for the change in laws, of special concern to women, relating to dowry. A number of these campaigns received fairly prominent coverage in the press.

While these changes could be perceived throughout the print media, they were particularly evident in the English language press. According to a readership survey by the operations Research group, just 5 per cent of the adults in India read English language newspaper. For e.g., the highest literacy State of Kerala, 57.8 per cent read Malayalam newspaper and magazines while only 5.8 per cent read English publications. The highest readership for English publications is in four metropolitan cities of Mumbai, Delhi, Calcutta and Madras. But even in these cities the readership of local language publications is at least twice as high (Centre for Media Studies, Media Scene in India: Highlights from ORG-NRS 1989-90, New Delhi, 1990). This is really a legacy on India's colonization experience which made English the language of the ruling class and the elite. The situation remains the same even after nearly six decades after Independence. The important consideration is assessing media coverage of the press, to a large extent, determines what constitutes 'news'. The traditional definition of news conforms to the general liberal, yet elitist, upwardly mobile, university educated, and upper caste urban male. While these newspapers accept that the interest of minorities and other marginalized groups should not be entirely ignored. Similarly, in relation to women's issues, most mainstream newspaper do not pursue an openly anti-women line. This is least partly because the ideal of equality of the sexes is enshrined in the Constitution of India. Measures to ensure equal participation in national life as well as eliminate discrimination and oppression are among the accepted social goals of the country.

However, it does not necessarily follow that the press does not neglect or trivialize women and many women issues.

The Problem

Ever since the human society has developed, people have been communicating with each other through gestures, sound and body language. Later on, sounds were transferred into objects and ideas to develop oral language and for the development of written language, written scripts and symbols were evolved locating ideas and objects. The amazing fact to note is the intense and deep influence of oral tradition over centuries through myths, epics, legends, sagas, folk songs, etc. from one generation to another. Speaking historically, communication developed from simple interpersonal note to globally transmitted phenomenon which is portrayed by sophisticated technology, huge capital investment, vest designed organizations, legal frameworks prepared by professionals and experts to pop up into an unstructured and formless mass of audience, consumers of capitalism.

In the present information period, we have noticed printing technology against a revolution in communication technology. Communication satellites, cable networks, computer systems, and their usages and ideas have become a central feature of modern life. The mass-media always have their basis on the prevailing economic structures comprising specific mode of production at a given point of time, simultaneously the forms of communication in society and the level of development of productive forces are also accompanied. As a part of the socio-cultural reproduction the institutions of mass communication are essential to be analyzed.

The aim of the present study is to understand the impact of electronic medium i.e. television, cable and satellite on young generation under specific economic and geographic conditions. Accordingly, we tried to develop the relationship between the State, media and capital influenced by the multinational capital in the present chapter. Apart from this we also attempt the relation of the state to capital and its significance in sustenance and conservation of capitalism, the priority of the transnational cooperation's and the role of mass-media in the expansion and the authorization of capitalism in its current form of globalization. We can initiate by saying that the state is the push factor and forces in the perpetuation of capitalism. The State does not only acts as an active agent in deciding the economic pattern, but also performs as a neutral arbitrator in the society. The States control the means of production by showing paths and ways for specific classes to perform or act. In this conflict the dominant classes enjoys the supremacy by ensuring its survival and perpetuation. In pre-capitalism the dominant class pervasively sustains unequal distribution by different institutions such as religion, education, family etc. among the institutions that contribute to the makeup of a public sphere in society, the mass-media performs the most critical function. In the society the mass-media legitimizes the *status quo* or innovators of the existing social equilibrium. The neutral relationship between the State and the mass-media is oppositional or complimentary, as such influenced by others. During the last two decades, the media have undergone a sea change, particularly in their intellectual context and cultural ambience. There are two sources from which the transformation draws sustenance and inspiration: one emanating from outside and the other internally generated. The State which seeks to subordinate the media to global control, comes with a variety of promises of development, technology, and extremely appealing to the modernizing quest of the middle class. It leads to an intellectual climate in favour of a mode of development. After eighties, the transnational corporations not only created a stronghold over the economy but also on mass-media, telecommunications and information technology as well as fibre optics and the internet. Their oligopoly propagates capitalist ideology leading to the strengthening of the global capitalist system (Hermen and Machesney, 1977). Capitalism leads by suppressing humanity. Suppression in society can be noticed in race, class or gender, for example, Women labour not considered for equal wage, marginalized castes not given equal standards or rights, etc. Currently, capitalism has found a powerful tool in the mass-media, especially satellite and cable television and advertisements for reinforcing the patriarchal value system and reinforcement of gender and economic inequalities.

Talking of women in society; the male ownership of private property in society transformed women's social labour into labour for an individual and ultimately served capital. The latent maleness that existed in the vicious and brutal stage manifested as control of women's labour, their sexuality, and fertility also, which resulted in the oppression of women. The patriarchal value system itself reveals the truth and oppression of women by class, caste and gender. Media content creates needs primarily and then transforms into consumer needs. Women are treated as consumers and as commodities to be exploited in the advertising television, film and pornographic industry. Women even have faced the marginalization in economic labour force, in the post 1980s globalization women have been regarded as subordinate classes who bears the onslaught of globalization. The media, especially television reinforces the conservative and pathetic role of women as the upholders of a value system by reinforcing consumer culture.

Our prime effort in the present exercise is to comprehend the effect of media, especially cable television, advertisements and satellite televisions on women under globalization. As cable and satellite television broadcasting i.e. media which is closely and formally bound to the state our study concentrates and highlights on the segment. Initially, television in India was a state owned medium project founded by Ford Foundation in 1959 in Delhi. The project was implemented for the development and education purpose, but further it went commercial and advertising including films and film-based programmes and serials. This pattern of commercialization continued till early 1990s and these channels merged with its cable distribution, which brought a revolution in consumerism. Since, 1970s Satellite Instructional Television Experiment (SITE) and their commercial potential was tapped by global conglomerates only in 1990s in the third world. The economic crisis in the United States and Western Europe in the 1980s was the main reasons for this which discovered new forms of organizations which led to production and capital to overcome the crisis of the respective economies. Multinational corporations entered the third world countries in search for the markets comprising convenient laws and tariffs. This new ideological propagation and new form of capitalism was termed as globalization by the World Bank. This gained maximum profit and capital accumulation process made it into a branch of industrial activity for only the sake of maximizing profit in the guise of democratic principles. The idea behind this principle is that multinational corporations and advertisers should be allowed to deal globally without the interruption of the government. Media globalization has tremendously facilitated the globalization of trade and finance. This is characterized by centralization and concentration of the media industry leading to the emergence of giant global operating media conglomerates increased transnational flows of media products and consequent spread and intensification of the commercialization of media output (Herman and Machesney, 1997). International Monetary Fund (IMF) and World Bank loan of 15 billion introduced globalization in the name of economic liberalization. In the 1990s the amalgamation and integration of economy with the global market aroused. This integration of India into the world capitalist system clearly reflects further subjugation and suppression of the economy, media, politics and cultural traditions in the interests of global capital. The print media which includes books, pamphlets, journals, newspapers, etc. facilitated the growth of consciousness based on liberalism particularly among the capitalists. Even the earlier communication technology like the telephone, telegraph, printing and radio broadcasting came to the colonies shortly along with road and railways networks. Cinema is considered as the mass-media of the monopoly phase of industrial capitalism of the 20th century. Currently electronic media and modern communication technologies have become the facilitations of financial markets as international corporations and financial institutions in their bid for monopoly and hegemony. The commercial international media and communication creates the cultural basis for world imperialist system with the help of new and modern economic tools and communications technologies. By promoting and legitimizing the interests of western corporate industry the mass-media leads as chief cultural institution which mediates the culture and the value system. From this we can say that mass-media are the chief agents of cultural colonization of the current modern society and capital in the arms of the state molding people's thoughts and thinking. The major channels of ideological control connected are institutions like the education systems, mass-media, sports and other recreational activities. Globalization with regard to media acts as a powerful arm of corporate houses which results in the possession of big chunks of media and communications systems through direct investment, equity shares, joint ventures, collaborations etc. capitalism needs market to survive and for existence new consumer forums and patterns are reinforced in the society. And in this situation the television media fits perfectly. Cable network invention along with television broadcast through satellite television became a powerful medium for the propagation of corporate capitalism. Daily soap operas, serials and other film based fictions entertainment make up the bulk of popular television fare. Apparently, the current study makes an attempt to comprehend and grasp this form of mass-media content and its subsequent bearings on young generation especially women and culture particularly cultural notions in society. Thus, the exercise aims to survey the impact of T.V. serials and advertisements and cable television on women cutting across different geographical locations and areas and to investigate if serial and advertisements on television reinforce conservative and regressive values among women and encourage consumerism. It also attempts to examine the level of acceptance and awareness of women and college students.

Functionalist Perspective

Functionalism explains social practices and institutions in terms of the structures and functions of society and its institutions. Society and individuals have needs that are fulfilled by institutions. Thus mass-media fulfills needs of individuals regarding information, motivation, adaptation, socialization, continuity, social order, integration, and so on. Relatively, functionalist approach holds that society is system of which media is a sub- system that contributes to the maintenance of continuity. It also uniformly orders the assumption that social life requires social integration, *status quo* maintenance, and harmony, consistent and complete picture of society and of social environment. Lasswell (1948) delineated the main functions of mass communication in society as surveillance of environment, correlation of the parts of society in responding to its environment and transmission of cultural heritage. The functionalist thought also argues that entertainment and mobilization are the other key media functions for the social integration in the society emphasizing social agreement (Wright, 1960). Apart from this, it is also opined that media tend to support the values of not only society as a whole but also its various segments. Several researchers have pointed that the media reinforces the values of the community and the maintenance of a local order (Jackson, 1971; Cox and Urgan, 1973; Murphy, 1976). The fact is institutions are not the product of decisions made by individuals since them prior to these individuals. For it is the people who decide what is functional for them and not few classes or individuals posses the authority. A basic symmetry is seen to exist between media institution and their audiences, since "the relationship is generally entered into voluntary and on apparently equal terms" (McQuail, 1977: 91) and audiences are seen as capable of manipulating the media in an infinite variety of ways according to their prior needs and disposition and having access to the plural values of society enabling them to conform, accommodate and challenge or reject them.

Functionalism points out that social customs, relationships and institutions persist because they have some social function that is an ongoing utility. The utility of social arrangements are taken for granted. Functionalism school of thought is a mere manifestation of the properties in a given system of relation and reduces complex phenomenon into simple description of function of systems. Accordingly, the mass-media becomes the determining part as an element of the system discharging a specific function, denying contradiction and historical processes.

Empiricism

Initially, mass-media research in United States and Western Europe was first established in order to fulfil the needs of the media industries in accordance of improving the influence and potentiality of media which is always regarded as a powerful tool in achieving the commercial objectives. Henceforth, where advertising revenue was very much important it became necessary to consist detailed information about the size, composition, reaction of media audience research, circulation studies, viewer- ship studies, advertising research, public opinion polls and so on. Understanding the media problem, question and methodologies were formulated and functionalized within the narrow media oriented parameters; we can find thousands of projects and piles of data working on it. The issue is that there has been no attempt to relate data to any theoretical approach. Hence, most of the research enhances improving methods to facilitate and promote the achievements of specific goals rather than on clarifying concepts and developing theories. The extract of empiricism seizes upon one juncture in the process of work and allows it to dominate the mind. The approach is bounded to the statistical analysis of social issues by describing them in formulas and structures. Even then not statistical tools are used established relations. Philosophies of natural sciences and canons for work in social science are the two factors which are adopted in abstracted empiricism, and hence the issue of blindness of data without theory ultimately results in psychologism.

Structural Perspective

The structural perspective of media analysis enhances dominance to the ideological role of the media independent of the economic structure. As structural perspective analyses the form and content of cultural artifacts and then it links to the economic base. In this approach emphasis lies on ideas rather than on material structure, analyzing the ideological effects of media in the interest of ruling class. Thus, it proves that mass-media reproduce essentially exploitative relations while sanctioning the dominance of capitalism and the subordination of the working class. Correspondingly, the main contribution of the media is to stimulate and then to satisfy the false needs, leading to the assimilation of groups who have no material interest in general society. Instead of starting from a concrete analysis of economic relations and the ways in which they structure both the processes and results of cultural production, structuralism starts by analyzing the form and content of cultural artifacts and then working backwards to describe their economic base. The characteristic outcome is a top heavy base analysis in which an elaborate autonomy of cultural forms balances insecurely on a schematic account of economic forces shaping their production (Mudock and Golding, 1977). A structuralism emphasize its relative autonomy with cultural sphere and its irrespectively to class interests but tries to be connected power structure capitalist state through its relations. In precise, the emphasis is on semiological analysis and not on the material practices. The concept of hegemony refers to a ubiquitous and internally consistent culture and ideology which are openly and implicitly favourable to a dominant class or elite, although less closely and consciously organized (Gramsci, 1971).

Any sort of analysis in which mass-media operates as ideological agencies, is bound to be partial. Likewise in India, the centre of gravity lays significantly with the communication conglomerates. Structuralists concern with the system reducing media research to a textual analysis; television programme and literary test. Accordingly, structuralism shows a concern to establish the autonomy and effectiveness of film and television form, enhancing (promoting) the idea that ideology embodied in film and television is an important and necessary area of ideological struggle.

Marxist Perspective

Marxist perspective being a theory of history is rather more concerned with the whole of people's social life compared to the above perspectives as it symmetrically discerns the stages in the stages of history and social life. According to this approach, under capitalism media is the ideological tool for propaganda. Thus, transnational corporations use media to serve the interests of the capitalists by circulating their ideas and world-view. The net result is there is a large concentration of media ownership by capitalist entrepreneurs (Bagdikian, 1988). Besides media studies reveal correlative evidence of conservative tendencies in content of media so organized (Hermen and Chomsky, 1988). The larger part of economic infrastructure and power base are controlled by the economic dimensions of media institutions whereas the integral part of culture in capitalism is formed by images, ideas and information circulated by the media. In true words, media is related to the prevailing structure of political and economic power. Simultaneously, media is observed as an effective instrument of power to reinforce and apply influence in various ways. The real potentiality of media can be observed in its context of ideas and values. The Marxist approach emphasizes on control of media and its way media market forces operate because the primary focus is on the relationship between economic structure and the ideological content of media. Concluding, we can state that amongst the rest, media ranks the highest position in the commercial organizations that produce and distribute the commodities within capitalist economic framework. As media is an economic interface between producers of goods and services, they form integral part of the strategy for the circulation of economic commodities within capitalist economy through advertising. Thus, we can conclude that as a whole media is a large scale commercial enterprise in capitalism. Economic interests of multinational corporations are fed by media. Media creates enhancement of structural inequalities in wealth and power for the interest of class which is owned and controlled by media itself. Thus, their central function is, "to maintain the financial equilibrium of a deeply institutionalized social system which is highly integrated with the economic institutions" (Defleus, 1970). The content of media then depends on "the exchange value of different content, under pressure to expand markets and by the underlying economic interests of owners and decision-makers" (Garnham, 1979). Media has its own ideology with regard to profit making business. i.e. low investment in less profitable media tasks and consequently neglects the economically poorer section who is neither subscribers nor advertisers. Never ever media reflects and concentrates the concerns of the marginalized in the society, and if so, they must be profit hidden stunt behind it. Meanwhile media highlights only those celebrities and politicians which return them with crores of profit. Media already establish the position of groups of those whose market is consolidated and exclude those who lack capital base required for the successful entry.

Another perspective highlighted by Smith (1977) is that of the primary product of the media being the audience attention, which is sold to advertisers. People spend hours and all their leisure time watching television, which includes use value and exchange value. Television creates interest and power of an audience is reproduced in the necessary time and surplus watching time of the audience works for capital. Capitalism first creates the dichotomy between work time and leisure time and then it exploits the leisure time. Audience watches advertisements which become an activity for consumer economy that is crucial for the market economy. In the same way attention to advertisements in the print media can not be controlled and measured accurately, while attention of radio and television can be measured and sold to gain profit in advertising. Smith considers the huge advertising industry (in India it was rupees 102.30 billion in the year 2002. Kohli, 2003: 4) as a creation of the exchange value with the audience being one element of the labour that creates it. The attachment of people's time creates advertising value. The manner in which media exploits, traps the audience as the market is very dehumanizing and therefore their world view, lifestyles and need are further manipulated accordingly. The Marxist approach examines the relationship between media and structures of power and dominance, and thus it is necessary to analyze the ownership of multinational media with regard to globalization to study media critically and its impact on the society. Hence, these theoretical base, i.e. functionalism, empiricism and structuralism will help for approaching mass-media in a different way.

Media and Advertising

The relationship between institutions and advertisers is best described as a symbolic one. The central issue raised is about the degree to which the media depends on advertising revenue. There are some of the comments which relate and proves, "Media institutions and finance". Quality newspapers rely on advertising for about two- third of their revenue; the tabloid press for about one-third magazine producers rely on advertising for 50 per cent and more of their income. Broadcasters rely entirely on advertising, excepting a proportion made from programme sales and turnover. Movies vary low budget films rely on box office and T.V. sales for their income, big budget and mainstream movies rely more. But in both the cases box office relies a great deal on the amount spent on promotion, advertising and publicity which adds additional 20 per cent to the production for a low budget movie, and to about 50 per cent for a big movie. Advertising as an activity stands for the ideology of the market place—commercial competition, company expansion, promotion of product, pleasing consumers, and maximizing benefits at any price. It effectively underwrites the tendency of media owners to support the dominant ideology, the security of the *status quo* and conservative values (Garnham, 2000:19).

Soap Operas

The essence of soaps is the reflection of personal problems and the emphasis is on talks not actions, on slow development rather than the immediate response, on delayed retribution rather than immediate effect (Geragthy, 1996-(b), 253). Soap operas are real life but not real: soaps invoke a reality experience through elements such as naturalistic sets, probable situations and the authentic appearance of characters. And for commercial television the crucial factor is that the pulling power makes the advertisers happy. Gauntlett and Hill (1999) ask whether we should still classify soap operas as women's programme. In the survey, students in the 1990s reject these gender divided approaches completely, finding them laughable. They say that it is questionable how far gender differences are significant in terms of understanding audiences and their responses to soaps (Cited from Media and Society by Graeme Burton, 252). Issues rose about female viewing and pleasures are held in soap operas.

Characteristics of Soap Operas

According to Brown (1994) (Soap opera and Women's talk) and Allen (1995) (Soap operas around the world) one may summarize the characteristics of soaps, stories are mainly dominated by the female characters, some of them are strong women such as "The Matriarch or the bitch", male characters who are 'sensitive men' or 'who are weak or lacking in social skills and articulacy; a large cast of characters polarized round a few core families, stories located in places which allow for social interactions and which include occupations which positively require conversation, e.g. homes, pubs, cafes, garden, etc. Soaps are all about the present and have multiple storyline rapidly cross out through parallel editing, stories which implicitly recognize a class system and are often located within working class culture. A serial form in which the narrative resists closure: indeed encourages continuity and viewer anticipation from episode to episode and week to week. Soap operas have the capacity for reversing events. It refers most obviously to instances where dead characters have been brought back to life through some plot device (*ibid.*, 253-254). Hobson (2003, soap operas) says that "The concept of a strong women who copes with problems, brings up her family, supports and enjoys life with her friends, survives when men betray her and sometimes lives happily with a male partner, has become a major tenet of the soap operas since its inception". In terms of audience identification, Geraghty (1996 women in soap opera, in J. Corner and S. Harvey, Television times) refers to the centrality of mother as characters, as a property for others in the face emotional or practical crises. These characters often have close female friends who also acts as props to them in the times of crises, not least problems which involve weak men. If there is a pleasure of identification for the female viewers, then from this point of view it is one that is ideologically naturalized. Soap operas never reveal women's work, nor the final meal is ever cooked, the floor never stays clean. It is no part of women's genetic inheritance to become cleaners and cooks. If such gendered roles are part of the social realism of soaps, then the realism is also an expression of ideology.

Role of Mass Media in New World Order

In 1989, the National Front Government came out first with a cabinet paper and then introduced the 'Prasar Bharti Bill' in December 1989. The death of Rajiv Gandhi and the advent of Congress rule in June 1991, under P.V. Narasimha Rao put an end to many hopes about the issues, meanwhile, the question of broadcasting autonomy has become irrelevant as other sources of information and entertainment viz. Star Television, CNN and BBC have burst into view in the wake of the Gulf War. The invasion from the sky has begun. Today the rapid expansion of television in India in terms of availability 7 channels and the sheer expansion 545 Television stations speaks of unqualified success by any standards. Television has often reached a high degree of professional excellence in its new coverage. The 32 hour continuous election telecast in May-June 1991 involving on the spot reporting from the counting booths even in the remote corners of the country and the swift shutting between the national network and the local centre was a refreshing dramatic experience for the viewers. But the barring and isolated instance, it has steadily developed an urban bias an elitist approach, popularizing, in the process, an alien lifestyle and culture far removed from the realities of Indian life.

The Doordarshan has always suffered from the dichotomy between policy pronouncements (which emphasize the use of mass-media for social progress) and the continuous drift and departure from them in actual practice. In a developing and democratic country like India, access to television and social benefit accruing from it, is a crucial test of the social relevance of such an expensive medium. The reason to the establishment of the Doordarshans in India, according to official statements, is to create a sense of participation in own efforts to usher in a new social order. As early as February 1973, a seminar on software objectives sponsored by the government recommended, "Television must be used in the development process as an instrument of social change and national cohesion by unhesitatingly upholding progressive values and involving the community in a free dialogue. Indian Television has to shun an elitist approach and consumer value system and evolve a truly national model". Mrs. Indira Gandhi, who played a leading role in the growth of Television in India, saw its role primarily as affirmed the national importance of utilizing. Television not just for the idle entertainment of the elite but for the uplift of the poor, especially in the inaccessible.

Mass-Media: Types and Influences

Mass media has become an integral part of our lives and cannot be separated from our lives. Particularly for the urban people, the need for information is more important than ever. Our values and way of life in the society in this information era are strongly influenced by mass-media like newspaper, Television, radio, video, and the internet. Mass-media's influence on people's lives is even greater and deeper than many kinds of state indoctrination or priest's sermons from the pulpit in the church. The full range of unfiltered is now available to most of us by using a parabola and satellite transmission. We can buy many kinds of videos freely and access to the internet is easy and inexpensive almost everywhere. We can find many kinds of information using the internet technology. It is worth remembering that there have been three recent revolutions in the history, i.e. agrarian revolution in farming, industry revolution and mass production and information revolution that provides global access. We are now in the midst of information revolution. Due to continuing developments in media technology, we are flooded by a huge volume of non-stop information. Most of this information comes to us without a filter or censor. The information can be positive or negative. It is important for all of us and particularly teenagers, to be able to look critically at the information and the sources and make positive choices. Having a critical attitude means that we can distinguish between positive and negative information and make choices that will give us information that will benefit us and our society.

The research from the US tells us how many teenagers' lives are troubled. The results of the research show that 43 per cent of teens in the US have used drugs and alcohol at least once. Around 1 million teens have left their homes and half of them live as delinquent (naughty) boys and girls and other half users are drug users. About 2000 teenagers from the age of 10 to 19 years old commit suicide each year. Most of them come from wealthy families that are not harmonious. There is no love, care and acceptance in those families. Many make their all of their own choices about the media they use. No one guides them or restricts them from accessing any type of information that they choose. Everything is allowed and then the kids grow up and become people who are out of control. They feel mature enough to make decisions on their own. Many forms of authority, rules and norms are seen as an obstacle to their freedom and so on, should not be followed. Ethics and morality are not really important for them. For many of them violence, crimes and sex are their daily life and concern. The research from 1980s in the US shows us that teenagers between 16 and 18 years old are wasting up to 16,000 hours of their time per year watching Television. In the same period, the violence and crime in US grew by 293 per cent. *Times* weekly magazine reported that the frequency of crimes committed by students in New York per month was the same as that committed by Japanese teenagers of the same age in a year. Here are some positive and negative influences of mass-media in our lives.

Media technology reduces the distance between human beings. The world is smaller due to increased communication and access to information. It makes human being closer to each other in terms of space and thinking. We are exposed to a broad range of ideas and thoughts from across the world. Media technologies allow us to take part 'virtually' in occasions and activities in other parts of the world. Information is power and those who control the media empires have great power and a great responsibility to use that power positively. Those who have power over the media have real power in the modern world. Media could create new cultures which change the old and original ones from the community. This could be both either good or bad. Media is business and in order to exist, media providers must make a profit. The owners and sponsors tend to create a media environment that is driven by materialism, consumerism, and hedonism. Media can create the wrong perception of prosperity. Prosperity is made out to be having an excess of material goods (cars, houses, jewelleries, etc.) men are not measured by their character and dedication but by what things they have in life. It is promoted by advertising in most kinds of media. Media can create stereotypes of beauty and which is then imitated by citizens, like fashion and hairstyles, for instance. Media can create a sensation of sex, violence, and horror which may be popular with the audience. The owner, ruler and media sponsor can make up any trick for their own business and politics interest. People's daily schedules and work schedules can be interrupted if most of our time is used by listening to music or watching Television shows, movies and chatting *via* internet or HP. The trend towards urbanization creates a constant flow of people coming from the villages to the city and is at least partly caused by the unrealistic glamour of urban life as shown on Television.

News

Dominant perceptions of what constitutes news are among the most important determinants of coverage. According to general accepted definitions, events rather than processes make "News". The activities of the wealthy and powerful rate more highly than those of the poor and marginalized, including women. Most of the issues are special concern to women do not fit into the traditional concepts of what constitutes news. First most women in India are neither affluent, influential nor in position of authority and dominance. The invisibility and inaudibility of women in society is thus further perpetuated and enhanced by the media. (Gaye Tuchman, 'The Symbolic Annihilation of women by the mass-media' in *ibid*.) A number of serious women's issues are not overtly violent or dramatic although often involving large numbers. The affected persons are not necessarily part of a readily identifiable group or concentrated in a particular geographical area. Further, many aspects of women's oppression are not so common place and widely accepted that they are not considered sufficiently extra- ordinary to merit coverage (Joseph, 1994: 19, Whose news).

Issues related to women's work, health, position in society and experiences within the family—the everyday conditions of their lives and the degradation and autocracy they are routinely subjected to prompted less far coverage. When such issues are infrequently made in media, it is because they are referred by the government, the Police, Parliament, the courts, well-known personalities, specially politicians, conferences etc. Dowry deaths, rape and *sati* also happen to be the issues on which some of the most active campaigns by women's groups were based. Events and issues involving politics, economics, law, religion, in that order are invariably at the top of the ladder of newspaper. The reach of mass-media among women is much less due to reasons like illiteracy, inaccessibility, inconvenient programme timing etc. which restricts their movements. Last few decades the government has taken special campaigns against illiteracy, ill-health and expression of exploited through Radio and Television. In spite of granting equality of status as freedom to enter diverse walks of life, more so among women in the lower stratum is invisible. Despite the many positive developments in securing women's rights patriarchy continues to be embedded in the social system in India. Thus media play an extremely significant role in spreading awareness, promoting alternative-empowered images of women, breaking down stereotypes and shaping mindset. Women entering the labour market are at its peak, there is increase in the number of educated women, and heightened awareness of their mobilization to fight against the unjust and discrimination. The role of women in the family has undergone significant changes. As an educated housewife or as a working woman she has acquired a respectable place in society. Today's women are increasingly conscious of the change in the civil society and magazines especially women's issue carry a lot of information on social issues and personal family issues. Mass-media now plays an important role in affecting, changing, molding and shaping the lifestyle and patterns of behaviours of women. It also helps interest in acquiring knowledge, sports, national and international politics and engaging them towards more effective participation in national affairs. Some of the gender issues that have been highlighted by the media, off late, are human rights violations against women, domestic violence and reservation of seats for women in the Parliament and State Legislative Assemblies.

The role and status of women in relation to men have gradually changed since the beginning of this country. The mass-media have played a efficient role in perpetuating gender stereotypes and in maintaining the *status quo*. In the 1960's and 1970's the mass-media in developing countries were assigned the role of modernizing traditional societies. Exposure to mass-media was perceived as an important indicator of modernity. The mass-media continuously worked and is engaged in redefinition on modernity and individuals. The influence of mass-media on society is in two ways. On one hand, the mass-media provide a large population of society with the dominant leisure time activity. On the other hand, the mass-media in contemporary society are increasingly responsible for the construction and consumption of social knowledge and meanings which people draw on to make sense of their world and act upon their social reality (Patel, 1995: 1).

Earlier communication research argued that the way in which men and women are portrayed in the mass-media represents reality. The media, however, does not represent as it is lived. It draws upon social reality but selectively picks up certain existing values, behaviours and images, while censoring the others. By highlighting only selected aspects of reality in a particular context, by projecting them as larger than life, and by continuation of repeated media images and messages, the media influences reality (*ibid.* 2). The mass-media function in the larger system of patriarchy and capitalism that controls media structures and organizations which represents women as dependent and subordinates. The recent debate of mass-media *vis-à-vis* gender produces much more complex understandings of the cultural dimensions of power and equality, and more specifically feminist analyses of the media, culture and society (Gallager, 1992: 1-15). With the proliferation of "women's genres" soap operas, melodramas, women's magazines and so on women has emerged as an important consumers of mass entertainment. The mass-media also set the agenda for public opinion by selecting themes, items and points of views that tend to reinforce the patriarchal culture. But media does not reveal the real picture of the cultural society, but it shows only one side of the construction of women's marginality in culture.

The relationship between media and reality is logical and argumentative. Culture is not static system, but an ever-evolving process that constantly changes to accommodate emergent, alternative and oppositional meanings, values and practices (Williams Raymond, 1977) Marxism and literature. The mass-media, particularly print and broadcasting media i.e. television and radio also provides some space for construction of new meanings and images. Although the progressive discourse is often co-opted in the mass-media and reconstructed again to create the hegemony of dominant social classes and reproduces gender relations. The larger system of patriarchy and capitalism that controls the mass-media and subordinate women challenges women's groups often. Many of the feminist activists and academicians who are concerned regarding the women's issues have also critically analyzed negative portrayal of women in media. This is even found in the developing countries across regions. Indian scholarship has been given far more attention than any other country. Some research is reported from Asian countries, but scholarship from Latin America and Africa is hardly represented. This is partly due to in availability of international research literature on women and mass-media in India. It is assumed that despite apparent in societal context with which the media function, there are notable similarities in the portrayal of women in mass-media across divergent media systems in developing countries. Although the images of women and types of messages transmitted through various mass-media, such as print media i.e. newspaper and magazines, electronic media i.e. television and films are not very different, it would be necessary to examine the specificity of media in reinforcing existing gender ideology. Discussion in this chapter is divided into four sessions. The first section highlights feminist approaches to the study of media content. Continuity and changes in the portrayal of women in the mass-media are examined in the second section. The third section highlights strategies for changing the images of women in the mass-media. The final section summarizes emerging trends in the portrayal of women in the context of current media developments.

Feminism

The word 'feminism' itself originated from the French word feminism in the nineteenth century, either as a medical term to describe the feminization of a male body, or to describe with masculine traits. When it was used in the United States in the early part of twentieth century it was only used to refer to one group of women: namely that group which asserted the uniqueness of women, the mystical experience of motherhood and women's special purity (Jaggar, 1983: 5) it soon came to denote as a political stance of someone committed to changing the social position of women. Since, then the term has taken on the sense of one who believes that women are subjugated because of their sex and that women deserve at least formal equality in the eyes of law. Feminist writers and activists, even those who were in existence long before the term feminism came into popular usage, shared the will to imagine a world where women were able to realize their potential as individuals. In doing this, they had to conceptualize ideas that were, when women had no legal identity as individuals, literally knowledgeable. And when feminist knowledge was introduced then it became important to make feminist ideas legitimate by circulating own ideas and inviting their contributions and responses.

Since the 1980's it has become common to use the plural form when talking about feminism in order to signify that although all feminists may share a basic commitment to end female oppression. We can say that all feminists agree that women suffer or material inequities simply because of their biological identity and are committed to challenge this. But the means by which such challenges are made are many and various. This inevitably means that feminism as a term becomes rather over burdened with meaning. Even all feminists agree on the central fact of women's subordination, but some feel feminism's heterogeneity as a sign of healthy debate and many feminist try to see it as a sign of feminism's inbuilt weakness. Although some critics are associated with fragmentation with modern feminism, but feminism have always emerged from diverse cultural and political perspectives and hence focused on issues germane to the time and location they inhabit.

Liberal feminism draws on the diversity of liberal thought dominant in western society since the enlightenment, and affirms that existing political processes under democracy can address women's subordinate social position. For liberals the key battle is access to education, following Mary Wollstonecraft, it is argued that they will get equal access to society (Pilcher and Imelda, 2005: 49). Radical would favour liberal feminists and socialist, as democracy itself is naturally adaptable to equality for both sexes. This liberal feminism is broadly dominant and applicable to majority of women who identify as feminist in some way, but don't want to overturn the social *status quo* on order to achieve better social condition for women. In addition, liberal feminists would be more likely to accept in limited terms that women and men might be shifted to separate spheres of home and workplace and simply lobby for greater reorganization of housework and caring. Whelhem 1995 has given a good detail in changes in women's social condition with the overthrow of industrial capitalism and changing relations of the worker to the means of production. Nonetheless socialist and Marxist feminist are always mindful of the ways society is driven by class and race distinctions as well as those of gender and that it is more useful to consider oppression as multi-pronged and inert-related rather arguing that one form is more destructive than others. In common, with liberal feminism, socialist feminism, because of its links to Marxist thought, suggests a necessary link with men and an acceptance perhaps that men are part of any movement for change.

Feminism is thus a term that emerged long after women started questioning their inferior status and demanding an amelioration in their social position. Even many of the women's rights organization in the late 1960s and early 1970s did not call themselves feminist. The term feminism had a restricted use in relation to specific concerns and specific groups (Delmar, 1986: 1). There are those sociologists who argue for a much stronger definition of feminism and as per Delmar (1986: 13) points out, "There are those who claim that feminism does have a complex of ideas about women, specific to or emanating from feminists". This means that it should be possible to separate out feminism and feminist from the multiplicity of those concerned with women's issues. It is by no means absurd to suggest that you don't have to be feminist to support women's right to equal treatment and that not all those supportive of women's demands are feminists. In this feminism can claim its own history, its own practices, its own ideas, but feminist can make no claim to an exclusive interest in or copyright over problems affecting women. Feminism can thus be established as a field (and even is skepticism is still needed in the face of claim or demands for a unified feminism) but cannot claim women as its domain. In an attempt at some kind of classification, histories of feminism have talked about the historical appearance of strong feminists movements at different moments as a series of 'waves'. Thus first wave feminism is used to refer to the late nineteenth century and early twentieth century feminist movements that were concerned with gaining equal rights for women particularly the right of suffrage. 'Second-wave feminism refers to the resurgence of feminist activity in the late 1960s and 1970s, when protest again centered around women's inequality, although this time not only in terms of women's lack of equal political rights but in the areas of family, sexuality and work.

A basic version of this categorization would divide feminism and feminist into three loose groups: Liberal feminism, Marxist or Socialist feminism and Radical feminism. A brief and rough summary of this typology could be stated as follows, liberal feminist include all those who campaign for equal rights for women within the framework of liberal state, arguing that the theoretical basis on which this state is built is sound but that the rights and privileges if confers must be extended to women to give them equal citizenship with men. Marxist and socialist feminist link gender inequality and women's oppression to the capitalist system of production and the division of labour consistent with this system; and radical feminist see men's domination on women as the result of the patriarchy, which is independent of all other social structures—that is, it is not a product of capitalism.

Liberal feminism draws on the diversity of liberal thought dominant in western society since the enlightenment, and affirms that existing political processes under democracy can address women subordinate social position. For liberals, the key battle is access to education, following Mary Wollstonecraft, it is argued that if men and women are educated equally, than it follows that they will get equal access to society. This liberal position is broadly held to be the dominant, common stance which is applicable to majority of women, who identify themselves as feminist, but they do not want to overturn the social *status quo* in order to achieve better social condition for women. Liberal feminists would be more likely to accept in limited terms that women and men might be well suited to separate spheres of home and the workplace. Socialist/Marxist feminists are always mindful of the ways society is driven by class and race distinction as well as those of gender and that it is more useful to consider oppression as multi-pronged and inter-related rather than arguing that one form is more destructive than others. In common liberal feminism and socialist feminism links to Marxist thought, suggest a necessary link with men and an acceptance perhaps that men are part of any movement for change. Even though radical feminism is usually associated with separatism and man-hating, the assumption that man as part of the problem should be part of the solution was a theme in early radical feminism. Radical feminist from USA emerged from new left and civil rights political groupings. Their politics was broadly radical left, but they became hugely disenchanted with the male dominated power, which resulted and formed the Women's liberation. This movement aroused in order to allow a space for the consideration of women's oppression outside of the confines of male-oriented knowledge and politics. There conviction, that a woman-centered politics could only be devised in a woman' space, resulted in a policy of separation. This politics of radicalism wanted a political formation freed from the taint of maleness, evoked in leaderless groupings, job sharing and structurelessness, well beyond the parameters of contemporary democracy. Many of their aspirations have been misunderstood by others and so radical feminists are all too often sent up as man-hating lesbians, totally obsessed with the correct politically part in order to shape their own movement that smacked of the male political imperative.

Equal or Different

The idea between equality and difference may seem to be attractive in that it promises to rid feminism of on its perennial conflicts. However, some feminist believe that to stay here in any practical discussion of women's position in society equality and difference has to be there, there is no escaping the divide in discussion on how to treat women's claims maternity rights for example, feminists are divided between those who think that maternity benefits should be special rights granted to women on the basis of their specific biological capacity to have children and the particular social role of maternity that they have been assigned, whereas others argue that maternity benefits should be subsumed under general category of sickness benefits so that pregnant women are treated the same as men who have an illness which prevents them from working for a period of time (Bacchi, 1991; Bock and Thane, 1991: 43). As per Segal (1987: VII) contends, "There has always been a danger that in re-valuing our notions of the female and appealing to the experiences of women, we are reinforcing the ideas of sexual polarity which feminism originally aimed to challenge". So what do we mean by sexual difference? Many feminist have struggled hard and stated a natural difference between men and women was assumed and also have analyzed the ways in which this difference was given various social, political and economic meanings in different societies and civilizations. And because of this assumed sexual difference, women have been given an inferior or secondary status in societies.

As Sherry Ortner (1998: 21) argues, "the secondary status of woman in society is one of the true universals, a pan-cultural fact." And as she goes on to explain, this secondary status of women can be explained by the fact that within the multiplicity of cultural conceptions and symbolizations of women that exist in society, there is constant that women are seen as being 'closer to nature' in their physiology. And men have been 'closure to culture', which are more suited for public roles and political association'. And this is the reason why women are neglected to secondary status in society, i.e. roles in the home rather than able to accede to powerful public positions. A key problem that feminists identify in this continuing perception of difference is that it is almost impossible to escape the formation of social hierarchies based on these perceptions and representations of difference. Although some people argue that men and women are equal but difference it seems impossible to argue for difference without creating some kind of hierarchy. This debate over equality and difference has been couched in various terms over the history of feminist activism. Ann Snitow poses the questions as a tension between needing an identity not over determined by gender (1990: 9). She further describes this tension as a divide between minimizers and maximizers, where the minimizers are those who wish to reclaim the category of women and revalue it in order to empower women; between radical and cultural feminists, between essentialists and social constructionists; between cultural feminists and poststructuralists; and between modernists and feminist" (Freedman, 2002: 12). Women were judged to be less reasonable than men, more ruled by emotion and thus incapable of political decision-making, for example, these types of assertions by philosophers and political theorists were supported by anatomists and biologists who, who as scientific of the knowledge of human body advanced in the nineteenth centuries, began to use such data for measurements of brain size to establish a difference in intelligence between men and women.

As Lynne Segal (1999) points out the late 1980s and 1990s saw a resurgence out social Darwinism, scientific theories that seek to explain male and female behaviour in terms of demand of human evolution and survival and that therefore dismiss the idea that masculinity and femininity are social constructs in favour of purely biological explanations. This has led to a distinction in much feminist theory between physiological 'sex' and social 'gender'. This distinction we can express by the terms 'female' and 'feminine', female being the biological category to which women belong and feminine behaviour and roles being the social constructions based on this biological category. (cited in feminisms: 13). One of the difficulties has been that although as Delphy (1996: 16-17) argued the concept of gender opens up the possibility of an analysis of hierarchy, gender analysis may lead to the neglect of the power inequalities that exist between men and women. Gender is seen as the content with sex as the container (Delphy, 1996: 33) and although gender is perceived as variable, the container of sex is perceived to be universal and unchanging because it is natural. Sex is seen as a primary division on which gender is predicted. The distinction between sex and gender was first used by feminists to move the focus away from 'natural' and universal differences between men and women and to put the emphasis on the way in which society created so. We find these differences whether to minimize the relevance of difference and to claim that men and women should be treated alike, or to insist that differences do matter and even to valorize these differences. This chapter has highlighted some of the ways in which feminists have talked about difference and the means with which they have tried to overcome traditional views of sexual difference in order to promote women's emancipation.

Feminists Approaches to Media Content

Contemporary women's movements in North America and Western Europe have played an important role in shaping the academic agenda of feminist communication research. An important part of feminist cultural politics is a feminist critique of media content and its implications in the construction of gender. The first international review of research and action, initiated by the UNESCO, drew our attention to the striking similarities in the negative portrayal of women in mass-media (Ceulemans and Fauconnier, 1979, reports and papers on mass com. No-84, Gallagher, 1983) and women's lack of decision- making power in media organizations throughout the world (Gallagher, 1981: The case of women and the Media). In the developing countries, feminist communication research on media content, images and representation has grown since the early 1980s. It was the United Nations International Decade for Women (1975-85) that provided political impetus worldwide to initiate research and action for changing women's portrayal and participation in the mass-media. Comparatively to the Western feminist scholarship communication research in the Third World Women has communication remained fragmentary and descriptive. Despite proliferation of women in development literature in the last two decades, gender in the field of mass communication has remained a marginal area of inquiry among feminist scholars (Sleeves, 1993, *Journal of Communication*, 43: 3, Summer, 218-229). Hence, empirical and theoretical work in the area of women and mass-media in developing countries is limited and uneven across region. As a result, media research on women in developing countries has relied heavily on the West.

Gallagher (1992: 4-7) highlights three stands in feminist research on media content, images and representation. The focus of feminist scholarship in the 1970s conducted mostly in North America and Asia (Japan, Korea and Philippines) was quantitative content analyses of sex roles media stereotypes. This research documented invisibility of women in various media forms and highlighted how media images reinforce negative portrayal of women in terms of behaviours, aspirations, physiological traits and so on. Gallagher argues that such juxtaposition of 'positive' and 'negative' media images of men and women is problematic. It is difficult to approach to define positive image of women in masculine terms, such as showing women as authoritative, autonomous, self-fulfilled and successful, etc, while ignoring the ways in which the audience read and reinterpret media content. In 1980s, feminist film criticism based on qualitative European perspectives and methodology which use psychoanalytical, semiotic, and post-cultural frameworks in analysis, contributed to broadening our understanding "representation of women through the study of text and textual mechanisms" (Patel, 1995: 5). The question is not to examine whether media reflect or distort images of women, but to explore how this images and meaning of femininity and masculinity in media are socially constructed within the context of patriarchal social relations. Gallagher argues that in the recent years feminist media criticism, heavily influenced by post-structural it and post modern theory, places far more emphasis on autonomy of audience reading of the text and validating audience "pleasures and ignores the fact that women as audience are positioned within a cultural system which reproduces particular representation of "femininity" and "masculinity" In summary, Gallagher (1992, *ibid*. 1-15) concludes that the recent feminist media research and criticism gives us very useful insights in understanding cultural dimension of power and equality. However, she expresses caution against the apolitical trend in current feminist media studies that focuses on the micro-level while ignoring the issue of power and broader political and economic concerns. She argues that feminist action and politics is important to situate micro-level work in political economic concerns of media development. We all are aware of some commonalities of women's oppression around the world and women's position in cultural and communication, adaption of analytical frameworks of Western feminist can be useful to some extent. However, recent discourse of feminist media criticism, based on "post-modern" view of society is conceptually ethnocentric and inappropriate for most of the Third World women, who have not yet experienced the modern life (Gallagher, 1992: 14). Furthermore, in the changing global context of new communication technologies and rapid commercialization of mass-media, it is far more important to explore the issue of power and critically examine political-economic forces that impinge on media development and media content in the developing countries.

Portrayal of Women in Mass Media

The reach of mass-media among a majority of the Third World War is much less due to the factors such as illiteracy, inaccessibility, lack of respite from household chores, inconvenient programme timings, and traditional restrictions that inhabit their mobility to go out to the theatre or cinema hall. The ways in which women are portrayed in media has emerged as an important area of research and action among feminist researchers and activists in developing countries since the 1980s. It was the comprehensive study of Gallagher 1983 on the portrayal of women in the mass-media that drew our attention to demeaning and derogatory media images of women across the world. (The study was conducted in several developed countries such as Australia, Austria, Canada, the Federal Republic of Germany, Denmark, Finland, Japan, New Zealand, Norway, Sweden, Switzerland, United Kingdom, and developing countries of China, Columbia, Brazil, Iran, Jamaica, Philippines, Puerto, Rico, Senegal and Venezuela). The study concluded that except in the case of government controlled media in "socialist" countries (for e.g. China) media under represent or misrepresent women and their concerns use them in advertising as a commodity and present traditional stereotyped images of women as passive, dependent and subordinate to men. Subsequently, how media in different countries portray women have been discussed by women's group and researchers in various forms in the 1980s. Although periodically efforts are made to highlight the existing trends in the portrayal in media, most of the countries have remained fragmentary and essentially descriptive in nature. After Gallagher's study, probably no systematic review of literature on media portrayal of women has been undertaken in a large number of developing countries. It is against the gap in systematic and critical media research in developing countries that this session attempts to highlight continuity and changes in the portrayal of women in films, television and print media (newspaper and magazines). In spite of shortage of media content in divergent societal context, the Indian situation throws light on how media reinforces gender and social relations, while at times challenging them.

Television Research in India

Television expansion, both in magnitude and multiplicity, seems to be phenomenal in the eighties by any stretch on imagination. Earlier, it reflected a sad saga of extremes caution and was considered a luxury. Mid-seventies saw the Satellite Television experimentation which opened the flood gate of an operational

Satellite Television system capable of covering the entire country. In less than seven years, there is a conscious effort at all levels within the government for rapid and large scale expansion of Television research on the one hand and towards having a multi-channel television system for the selected urban viewers on the other. The entire effort is towards providing Television signals in the technical sense to a large number of potential Television viewers. Also in this scheme, as of now, little effort seems to have been devoted to provide messages and programmes relevant to a given region or linguistic group, leaving aside special target groups like the poor, women and children. Somehow technological expansion of television has followed the creation of audience research units and production facilities. Experience is that communication research production planning should follow the technological expansion of Television (Chitnis, 1977). Within the audience research units of Doordarshan, one observes two kind of communication research approaches being followed, one for rural viewers and the other for urban viewers, in which the urban Television research has an upper hand. At present administratively and academically the research in Doordarshan *id* replica of audience research unit of All India Radio except the Research and Evaluation Cells located in Cuttack, Delhi and Hyderabad. Major research planning and execution is conducted from its headquarters and suggestion for its research in most cases is initiated by the production of the administrative staff. Such audience research plays the 'audit' and 'faultfinding' with little positive function towards improving the quality of programme production of enhancing the media utilization. The communication research which is turned from "sender oriented" to "receiver oriented" makes significant organizational change and arguments with the audience research unit both by money and manpower.

Television Research on Women

A research was enhanced during Satellite Industrial Television Experiment (SITE) both women and children were treated as separate social categories for measuring the impact of effect of Television viewing on them. After the completion of SITE, social impact on survey on adult, it became evident that the difference between men and women were so significant in a variety of areas that separate analysis for men and women should be essential (Agrawal, *et al.* 1977). Results of the study indicated that women's participation in Television viewing was significantly smaller than men (Agrawal, *et al.*, 1977: 45). But the research revealed that those women who viewed Television gained more than men in areas like family planning, health and nutrition. Another significant finding of the study was that illiterate women, more than literate women gained knowledge from Television viewing in the same areas thereby indicating that literacy was no barrier for learning from Television (Agrawal, 1981). A detailed and in depth study conducted during the same period indicated that information needs and the viewing behaviour of women were different from men (Agrawal and Rai, 1980). In a recent paper Chandiram and Agrawal (1982) indicated that the proportion of telecast time for women had been not more than 5 per cent. What emerges from these analyses is in general very little effort have been made to understand how best a medium of television can be utilized for the development. The few studies conducted so far clearly indicate that television as a medium of communication breaks the barrier of literacy and in certain social situations can act as a catalyst of the development of the women. "Telecast language was a single most important factor that affected the comprehension of the programme in spite of the fact that four languages were used in the programmes" (Agrawal, 1981: 27). Some of these observations as also research studies are indicative of the need for communication research if Television is to be used meaningfully for the development of women.

India is one of the few countries in the world where female species has had a declining sex ratio over the century—only marginally reversed in the last decade. This has been the result of higher male mortality at practically all ages including from birth to the age of 9, and unconsciously high rate of maternal mortality, regards to a pervasive neglection of the female child and female necessities. The factors such as poorer nutrition, lesser health care, despite higher levels of morbidity, lower education and skill formation are some aspects which women are deprived of. The problem of universal education has been long identified as one mainly of women, scheduled castes and tribes. The progress in female education literacy has reached only in 1 in 4 women as against 1 in 2 men and absolute numbers are 100 million more illiterate women and girls today that there were in fifties. The planning process has finally come to recognize that the enormous economic contribution of women both within the family and to society has remained largely submerged. Hence, government is providing support services to women to be more productive in fulfilling their multiple roles. Even more heartbreaking than the low priority television seems to have attached to the subject of women's status and betterment, is completely impunity which uses itself for the detriment of women. A seminar on Doordarshan's role in Women's Equality and Development conducted in the year 1988 by, Centre for Women's Development Studies and the committee for the portrayal of women in media made two major points:

(1) A very wide distance existed between the national policy objectives *vis-à-vis* women's equality and development and Doordaarshan's present role and programming.
(2) The general tenor of Doordaarshan's programme counters to its stray efforts to be purposive on women's behalf (Media Utilization for Development of Women and Children. (Thakur & Agrawal, 1989: 72).

In any case films and film-based material continue to constitute substantial chunks of Doordaarshan's output and as the report on Doordaarshan's Role in Women's Equality and Development highlighted, "These programmes are loaded with derogatory images of women and are usually explicitly or implicitly exist. They play a significant role in reinforcing negative stereotypes" (*Ibid.*, 73). These stereotypes are nothing but basically drawn from a middle class vision of women that sees her and glorifies her solely in the role of wife, mother and home-maker. Stereotypes fail to expose the richness of women's total dimension and her critical larger role within the community and the country. Thus, the medium instead of widening the women's horizon and taking her further up the road of partnership is now carrying women into a narrow niche and makes it more difficult, indeed dangerous.

In India, there is "Unity in Diversity" in terms of languages, religion, climate, people and its cultural entity. Nevertheless, women in our country, seldom enjoy equality with men. The ancient law givers like Manu and Kautilya assigned a lower status of women to so much that women were often grouped with dogs and *chandals* (i.e. the lowest caste). According to Jawaharlal Nehru,

"If our nation is to rise, how can it do so if half of the nation i.e. our woman lag behind and remain ignorant and uneducated? Our civilizations, our customs, our laws have all been made by men and he was taken good care to keep himself in a superior position to treat women as the chattel and a play thing to be exploited for his own advantage and amusement. Under this continuous pressure woman has been unable to grow and develop her capacities to her fullest and then man has blamed her for her backwardness". "The women of India have to free themselves from the tyranny of man-made customs and laws. They will have to carry on his second struggle (along with their participation in the first struggle for freedom) by themselves, for man is not likely to help them. There is a significant section of social scientists and media researchers engaged in studies related to women in mass-media. These studies cover all continents and show how media have been biased against women. The International Association for Mass Communication Research has a separate work which deals with this subject. The first meeting of this working group was held in Paris 1992. The focus on women implies identifying the structural constraints which inhibit their fullest growth and development. There are major issues related to women in media and the other about the image of women projected through these media. Worldwide feminist's movement of women has pointed out that the employment of women in media is low and particularly so in decision-making levels. The worlds are dominated by men, who not only lead women but also constitute the bulk of the management on top editorial ranks. We can hardly avoid the obvious male domination from their earliest history to the present time. It does not require much logic to prove that women have been and continue to be victims of poverty and under-developed on one hand and socio-economic injustice and exploitation on the other hand. As the MacBride Commission p. 18 has pointed out, "journalists dealing with serious issues and political events are seldom women, and few women become editors or holds directing positions. In the USA, out of 3000 films directors, only 23 are women. Although extensively employed as production and continuity assistants, women rarely have the responsibility for taking broad decisions." In India, the dominant stereotype images of women and girls are that of:

(1) Less competent human being,

(2) Key to commercial success in this age of advertising,
(3) Instruments for exploitation by men.

To break the vicious circle of existing undesirable images and project the reality of the lives of women and girls would need an overhaul of the content of existing communication message through a well thought out National Communication policy on women. A number of studies conclude that the overall effect of the portrayal of women in media is to reinforce rather than reduce prejudices and stereotypes. This distortion tends to justify and perpetuate existing inequalities. The exploitation of the women's image for commercial purposes has been noted and criticized varies widely. But the emancipation of women poses the most formidable problems in such values and practices of social, economic and cultural oppression and domination of women which evade attention. This is because there values and practices are a part of the "normal" social life of millions and millions of Indian people in day-to-day interaction between husband and wives, mother and children, brothers and sisters, parents and daughters, wives and their in laws, employers and their women employees and so on. In these very ordinary relations, men and women are constantly violating in practices which they profess in words. Men are more often unconscious of what is being done to them. Whether in matters relating to distribution of food or other items of consumption, or of work or leisure, of property or income, women are subjected to discrimination and oppression which assume in numerable forms. Far from bringing these to light, the media, specially the feature films, are all the time idealizing and rationalizing them. In fact, myths, legends, images and symbols are derived from the vast treasures of Indian mythology and folklore which are injurious to women's personality and antagonistic to their emancipation and equality. Women constitute half of the population in India, as indeed in most other countries of the world. Women are also among the most under-developed, illiterate and exploited segments of the society. The role of women is ignored not just in India but even in developed and advanced countries. Women remain backward educationally and socially. However, women are slowly emerging out of their centuries old darkness, shaking off their traditions and man-imposed roles and are increasingly raising their voice to demand their rightful place in society and their due from it in economic, political and social. Television, the most pervasive medium and master of image and illusion, results that both programmes and commercials are highly biased against women. In India the situation as seen by feminist organizations has been summarized by the Joshi Working Group, on software for Doordarshan, "Middle class ideologies of women's roles as wives and mother's provide the underlying basis for most programmes. In a country where 36 per cent of the agricultural workforce is female, women continue to be projected as predominantly non-producers and as playing a limited role outside the home." The plural nature of Indian culture and diverse role that women play is neither acknowledged for communication. This results in a reinforcing of the stereotyped images and role specifications of women in unidimensional projections of their reality. The negative stereotypes have been identified as:

- A women's place is in the home,
- The most important and valuable asset of a women is physical beauty,
- A woman's energies and intellect must be directed to finding the right man in "keeping" him,
- Women are dependent, coy, and submissive; they are masochistic in their indignities, humiliations and even to physical violence inflicted on them,
- A good woman is the traditional housewife, long suffering pious and submissive, the modern woman who asserts herself and her independence is undesirable and can never bring happiness to anybody nor find happiness herself,
- Woman are woman's worst enemies, and
- The working woman is the undesirable exception who must be brought into the marriage fold and made to conform to social norms, etc.

In this new age children are born into homes with Television and viewing as infants. Most of the stories they hear are not told by the parents, the school, the church or neighbours. Today they are told by a handful of conglomerates that have something to sell which has a powerful effect. Gerbener's comment reflects the concern of many media experts in western countries who continue to be deeply related about the commercial context of television programming and the impact of television advertising on society.

Many advertisement broadcast on television are masterpieces. They are the creations of brilliant minds and wonderful talented people who have nothing but only one mission in life that is to persuade us to buy and only buy their products. However, advertisers argue that consumption is limited, always exciting and is also the key to happiness. Over the last decade television in India has undergone a complete transformation moving from a single channel, government controlled service to a multi-channel, multi-optioned and transnational programming. In this process, advertising on television has blossomed and became fragmented adapting itself to diktas in market.

In this Television study we have concentrated upon the impact of Television advertising and serials on college students. Accordingly, they included some of the important questions in the Interview Schedule such as:

- Do Television serials and advertisements make college students want to look and live in a certain way image shaping;
- If so, does it suggest how they can achieve that certain image and lifestyle;
- Does it enforce a social responsibility;
- Does it evoke and give rise to gender stereotypes;
- Does it create a true picture of adult world; and
- In the other words, does it influence the college student's values, attitudes and aspirations; etc.

Any study of the impact of Television advertising on college girls or women, must take into account the relationship between the women and television, which in India, is still evolving. After all the success of ads. and serials shown on Television depends on who catches them, i.e. audiences, how often they are watched (by the women) and whether their messages are indeed absorbed and utilize sufficiently to attract the audience to eventually purchase a product. Eric Barnouw in The Sponsor says, "Television clearly represents one form of communication which is tied up with a world-view that promotes a material culture the basis, relevance and future of which needs to be debated". Television and advertising together present a lethal combination. Television offers the advertiser the most effective way of reaching the consumer's mind. Advertising, on the other hand, exerts on influence on Television which is no less significant—it plays a vital role in shaping the priorities and quality of television programming. Advertising has affected the fortunes of the media the world over. Today we cannot imagine television without advertising, it seems unrealistic. But few of the exceptions are BBC News and once it was Doordaarshan. Jerry Mander in the case of U.S. says, 'Since virtually all media in this country depend upon advertising for survival, it ought to be obvious that these one hundred corporations, themselves dominated by a handful of wealthy people, can largely determined by magazines, newspapers, radio stations and television stations can continue to exist and which cannot.'

It is not difficult for a regular Television watcher in India to identify the major competitors for Doordaarshan's commercial time. The list includes the companies which produce brands such as Aerial, Pepsi, Nirma, Surf Excel, Nescafe, Titan, Colgate, Pepsodent and many more. According to the best brand equity in 1992, out of 34 hair oils, only three made it to the national network and in washing powder i.e. detergent five out of 34 made it to big time. The really successful brands which were included were Nirma detergent, Rasna and Colgate toothpaste. Television advertising came to be dominated by the war between detergent ads. such as Rin, Nirma, Wheel, Surf; later on Aerial competed vigorously as highest and spending on television. Television companies stand to gain more advertisement the huge revenues they earn off it. The broadcasting suggests that advertising support to Television, while benefiting the advertising industry and it does not encourage an improvement in the content or quality of programming. A former secretary of the Information and Broadcasting Ministry, S.S. Gill, wrote in *The Times of India* (7th March 1994) "It is a sad commentary on our times that instead of establishing our benchmarks of good taste and excellence, Doordarshan is aping those who should be emulating its high standards." He further argues that good films like '*Padosi, Devdas*, and others did exceedingly well at the box office while retaining high aesthetic standards.' Then we corrupted the people's taste by exposing them to excessive violence, crime and sex. And now we argue that is what the viewers want.'

Commercialization paves the way for longer hours of broadcasting. Advertising costs skyrocket and commercials expensive to make strive to be technologically superior to regular

Television programming. And the reason for this is in order to stand out from all other forms of programming; television advertising must be qualitatively different so as to catch viewer attention and to make lasting impact. With so much shown on television, advertisements should be able to successfully squeeze its way through audio-visual fare. And if it fails to do so, advertising would not be able to survive or exist and would not have proper justification for the vast amounts of money which they have invested in Television. Advertisers than have to withdraw support to television and hence the survival of television would be at stake. We see that advertising is cluttered and unrelated ads. have to compete for viewer attention in high density clusters, advertisers have to work more harder to ensure that their advertisements stands out in a crowd. Advertisements merely act as a bait to attract viewer attention for a few seconds during which they implant their message in people's minds. A Television network's loft aims are educating, informing and generating social awareness, but these all are easily pushed aside by aggressive players in the selling games. In this context television advertising comes to represent future investments, a process aimed at changing attitude and altering mass perceptions. Indeed, one might ask, is the choice between drinking Bournvita and Horlicks really fundamental? Likewise, is Television advertising democratic when it represents a set of options to all Indians although only a segment can afford them? And what about the alternative options which never get advertised? We feel that the society is leasing to accept the ideals imposed on them by television and advertising codes which are not capable enough to evaluate the real worth of products and their priorities. One example of this can be from nutritional learning acquired from Television ads. by children an issue that has astonished parents and researchers, concerned with what children learn from Television advertisements.

Charles K. Aktin from National Institute of Mental Health and Neurological Sciences (NIMHANS) reports that not only does food advertising influence food preferences, but also can shape the basic nutritional beliefs and attitudes of the child. In India, a large number of Television viewers are becoming visually literate although being illiterate they cannot have access to vast amounts of important information that could be vital to their personal and social development. Mass-media plays an important role in affecting, changing, molding and shaping the lifestyle and pattern of behaviours of the women. They also help in generating interest in acquiring knowledge, sports, national and international politics and engaging them towards more effective participation in national affairs. Gender issues are being given increasingly importance in the media, especially after the UN Fourth World Conference on Women (Beijing)." The strategic objectives of the Beijing platform are—Increase the participation and access of women to expression and decision-making in and through the media and new technologies of communication; promote a balanced and non-stereotyped portrayal of women in media. (Cited in *Indian Journal of Women and Development*, Oct, 2008: 50, p. 12). The Central Board of Film Certification has also been previewing films for public release and permits over three thousand Indian and foreign feature films for certification for public release. The film preview consists of themes and picturization, especially dance sequences, which continue to be strongly sex oriented "Commercial Cinema" also, has presentation of violence and horror which seems to be an inevitable formula.

Portrayal of Women in Mass Media

The main highlight of media critics in the present times is the subject of portrayal of women in Indian media. Women are shown and portrayed according to male desires like beautiful creatures, submissive mothers of children, efficient housekeepers, cruel and deceptive vamps but nothing else. The positive roles of women's progress and their contribution for national development have a largely been neglected in the media of communication. The emphasis on stories about women about their struggle for recognition is only the surface trimming.

Electronic Media

The film industry is one that has a major effect on how young women has viewed in society. Young women often have roles as passive and vulnerable characters, which tend to leave the tough, strong and assertive roles to men. Women's roles are written with irrelevant sexualization their characters primary function is to please men, dance and sing in skimpy costumes. The music industry is very similar to the film industry, which exhibits the use of irrelevant sexualization, and their aim is to attract an audience of young people. Music videos showcase behaviour is just as promiscuous as shown in the films. Women's bodies are constantly displayed in a sexual way and this behaviour is imitated by young girls in and across the country who idolize them. Another negative portrayal of women depicted in media is domestication. The majority of commercials about house products or childcare are still aimed at women. This reinforces the sexist and outdated stereotypes of women only working inside the home, whereas, men are never shown contributing to housework or childcare. It is very true that images of young women in the media have a tremendous impact on young people everywhere. Whether it is through film, music, Television serials, advertisements or any other mass-media format, the public is constantly pressured to fit into today of what beauty is. Young people and even children are interested to act like the characters they watch on Television. There is no better way to describe what really matters than with the age old saying's sells.' The ads. for a certain shampoo on the television portraying two of the most sensuous and physically attractive star models, (who also are on off-screen pair) as an indicator of how sex roles have changed in Indian advertising. Many advertisements which are cinematographed in monochrome with the right shades of darkness and mood lighting, and are very hot ad, but have no direct relationship with the product being advertise. Such kind of ads. in media raises relevant questions about perspectives on gender in media representations of men and women. Ads. for instance, underscore how men in Indian ads. are being presented in a much more macho dominant manner than they were before. Another ads. for male underwear shows a number of females with pseudo-coy expressions on their faces coming out of a toilet. The camera cuts to a shot inside the toilet where a handsome male model prostate lies with telltale lipstick marks across his body. Again the product advertised does not really have a direct relationship with the message on the script. Secondly, few Indian males would be caught dead before females catch them in their underwear and in a public toilet. These all are Western concepts which are imposed on Indian ads. scripts and prove that visuals need not necessarily represent the social norms of a society.

On the other hand, while sports and athletics are concerned

more man is sported than women in the past India and in the West. But today real achievers like Sania Mirza and Sania Nihaal have changed all that. We may find Mahendra Singh Dhoni and Sachin Tendulkar more often compared to them no matter the product they are advertising for. Women in Indian advertisements are being presented in less dependent roles then they were before. An advertisement for a leading women's fortnightly recently carried a delightful image of an aging woman in bridal attire. It later transpires that her daughter is getting her married again. This is an example of positive advertising that subtly carries a social message. Many mother and daughter advertisements in recent times bear out female bonding and marginalizing the role of men by cutting them out completely from such advertisements. Yet, women do not appear in ads. for 'solid' products such as steel and cement and even if they do, they all side-tracked within the script.

Print Media

The lack of gender sensitivity in the media is evidenced in the failure to eliminate gender based stereotyping. Generally, the media do not provide a balanced portrayal of women's diverse lives and their contributions to society in a changing world, often reinforcing stereotyped images of women and their roles in the society. It is a common practice to assess the professional success of a woman through questions and claims about her related to being a good mother and a wife. The prevailing portrayal of women in mainstream daily newspapers has the following characteristics (Cited in *Indian Journal of Women and Development*, Oct, 2008: 54). Positive images of women have a narrow scope and are based on new stereotypes of women's success: a popstar, a beauty queen, and a sports woman with an outstanding result. There is an absence of image of an active, assertive working woman, or a successful; businesswoman, or a positive image of a woman politician. Average women are nearly always portrayed as victims of poverty, social injustice, domestic violence and organized crime.

Popular magazines with large circulations like the '*Sunday*' and '*India Today*' flash vulgar and obscene glossy photographs on their cover pages. The advertising world continues to use women to peddle its products and to present women as sexual objects. Advertising also reinforces housework as the sole responsibility of the women, with household equipments ads. addressed only to women. The passivity of female characters in film and television is a major cause of concern. Barring few prime time serials like *Adhikar, Udaan, Humrahi* and *Aur bhi hain rahein* which focused on issues concerning women and have women as their central character, rarely women is shown as capable of solving her problems, standing up to dignities or violence, facing challenges on her own, or taking decisions. Even many serials and ads. telecasted at present i.e. *Bidai, Balika Vadhu, Jyoti* and so on reveals the dependency of women. The image of educated women is typecast as insensitive, self-centered and uncaring. The economically independent woman is shown as domineering and ruthless. Women are considered ideal only when she is in her nurturing roles and as a supportive supplement to man. Women specific programmes on radio and television perpetuate sex stereotypes and cater to women as housewives and mothers, rather than provide knowledge and skills for their role as economic contributors. Several systematic research studies reveal that the mass-media so far have not been effective instrument to inform and prepare society about women's new roles in national development. This is largely due to the very limited reach of mass-media among women and girls, especially in rural areas. Even the limited exposure is mainly in the form of entertainment films or film based programmes providing little opportunity for education about new values, tasks or skills. The expansion of media facilities especially of electronic mass-media like television is both an opportunity and a risk in the case of women and girls. Widely basis, of a well thought of communication policy for women and girls, mass-media like television can be a great instrument for social transformation towards women's greater participation and equality. The National Plan of Action for Women draw up in 1976 was the first major step towards fixing communication priorities and providing sufficient direction for subsequent media planning. The Sixth Plan focused on employment, economic dependence, education and health, whereas the Seventh Plan moves on to an essential intangible of the desired change. The long term objective of the development programmes for women would be to raise their economic and social status in order to bring them into the mainstream of national development" (Media Image of Women, J.S. Yadava/Pradeep Mathur, 2008: 300-301).

It is an established fact that virtually throughout the world;

women are portrayed in the media either in terms of their sexual appeals to males. This two dimensional image is not sufficiently counteracted by alternative contribution to contemporary society. This is in part the result of women's lack of access to and control over the communication media. On the other hand, Gallagher has shown that the depiction of women in the mass-media is remarkably consistent throughout the world. Baring media controlled by governments with a strong commitment to social change, the overall picture highlighted the negative features of media under representation of women and women's concern; the use of women as a commodity in advertising; an ambivalent attitude to women evident in certain stereotyped images in which women were exclusively and unalterably "good" and "pure" or definitely and unchangeably "bad" and "immortal" (Gallagher, 1983). *The Portrayal and participation of women in the media, Paris, UNESCO, cited in Prabha Krishnan and Anita Dighe*). An annotated bibliography brought out by Signorelli (1986) Role Portrayal and Stereotyping on Television, London, and Greenwood Press revealed that as far as media content was concerned, men outnumbered women by two or three to one, in addition, women were generally younger than the men and were cast in very traditional and stereotypical roles. Less than half the countries surveyed have carried out any research on women and media content, while globally, very little was known about women's employment in media industries. As a response to the drastic growth of criticism shown on television programmes with respect to women's concern, many countries have set-up committees to intervene on behalf of women's citizens. For example, the Canadian Radio Television and Telecommunications Commission (CRTC) established a task force on sex role stereotyping in the broadcast media. Williams research on sex roles on Canadian and US television was designed to reveal this," that although there were some minor changes in the portrayal of women, the Canadian and US television networks were still fundamentally conservative and traditional with regard to sex role portrayals. Males still pre-dominated on all networks and almost all the people portrayed as powerful, authoritative and knowledgeable were male (Tannis Williams, 1986). The portrayal of sex role on Canadian and US television, paper presented at the conference of the International Association for mass communication research, New Delhi, showed that although in the fictional world of television, men still hold the better professional positions. On the Indian scene we found a multiple of articles and papers on the relationship between women and media. The working group on Software for Doordarshan's set up in 1982, published its report in 1985, popularly known as Joshi Committee Report, it condemns television heavy reliance on feature films and film related programmes, emphasizing the middle class orientation of the programmes output and the near eclipse of working class women (*ibid*: 14).

Chandiram and Agrawal (1982) noted that in general, women characters continue to be portrayed in an inferior position relative to men. In this, asymmetrical relationship, the 'wife and the other' image is predominant. They further add that there seems to be a tendency to construct a pan Indian character of women, which is difficult to identify with any one region of India. (Chandiram, Jai and Agrawal, Binod, 1982. "Towards Equality, Women in Indian Television", June, 161-164).

A study of women viewers in Madras city (Krishnaswamy, 1986) pointed out that respondents felt women's programmes to be superficial in their treatment of various issues. Some respondents appreciated the inclusion of male concerns in women's programmes, like the one on male impotency. Others felt that women were aware of their own plight and that such programmes should be addressed to men. (Krishnaswamy, Chitra, 1986, Indian Women and Television Viewers of Madras, paper presented at the International Television Studies Conference, London (cited in Prabha Krishnan and Anita Dighe) Joshi 1986, who studied the participation of women at the higher decision-making levels of Doordarshan's, reported that of his respondents, a large number of women felt that increasing the proportion of women employees in the structure would improve programme quality and bring about a more balanced perspective. Hence, the area is wide open to both empirical and theoretical work.

Researches generally found that women are expressed as occupational roles mostly on television. Even middle class women are almost invariably shown as reveling in housework. Many researchers have voiced their anguish over the inclusion of violence and sex in programmes and their effects on child viewers. Especially for children, television plays an important role in their socialization it determines in the matter of attitudes, values, culture, ethics, etc. children cannot restrict to watch the programmes related to them;

and so it becomes necessary to examine the stereotypical notions of gender roles presented to children in programmes. In order to establish how women are projected through the television programmes, it is not important to critically look at only special programmes related to them but also general programmes which are presumed to of marginal interest of women. Unfortunately, when descriptive analyses of television programme have been attempted on a limited basis, no systematic quantitative study of this aspect of television programmes has been undertaken. The present study therefore aims to provide a systematic understanding about the manner in which women and their concerns are projected through television programmes, advertisements, media, television serials.

The initial approach to communication was based on simple pattern of the transfer of a message from the source to the receiver. According to White Robert A. (1983) 33(3) 279-301 'Mass Communication and Culture, Transition to a New Paradigm believes this marked the early phase of mass-media studies during which there was an initiative belief that the media could shape opinion, mould behaviour and even serve as a panacea for a host of individual and social problems. Culture was regarded as an important intervening, variable between the source and individual effects. During the 1960s the importance of structural factors was underscored as American and European researches started questioning the supposedly benign (beneficial) intention of mass-media and began interpreting media, messages as exploitative ideologies of elites. "For them" patterns of communication and media organization were inherent in a given social structure and thus change could not be effected simply by changing the messages of powerful media but required a more equitable distribution of social power (Colute, 1983).

The traditional method of media analysis is that of content analysis, wherein the noticeable content of the message is regarded as the most important era for scientific social analysis. While content analysis is very helpful for a systematic investigation of a wide range of material, its shortcoming is that it is not concerned with questions of quality, of responses or of interaction (Janus, 1977) notes and feels that the result of content analysis need to be interpreted with care, elsewhere they may lead to the 'males versus female' perspective in which all males are counted together as general category, which is than contrasted with all female category without reference to class, race or cultural divisions. Janus, Noreen (1977) Research on Sex Roles in the Mass Media. Towards a critical Approach, Insurgent Sociologists, and Summer: 19-32.

Semiotics or semilogy, the science of signs, is concerned primarily with how meaning is generated in 'texts' (films, television programmes and other works of art). It deals with what signs are and how they function. (Berger, 1982) Media Analysis Techniques, Beverly Hills, Sage Publications). Studies of gender in the field of mass communication have been done mainly from feminist liberal and Marxist feminist perspectives (Janus, 1977 and Sayers, 1982) According to these perspectives; society organizes itself according to expectations about the place men and women should occupy in keeping with their biological functions. The social regulation of these functions has restricted women to domestic sphere whereas it has facilitated men's participation in the public sphere. Socialist feminists assume that media and popular culture perpetuate and develop cultural ideology, and if women's status is to improve, these structures must change. They further argue that transforming mass-media and popular culture can make difference even in absence of socialist revolution. In this they differ from Marxist feminists who believe that change in women's status is predicted on changes in the economic structure of the state (Steeves, 1986 Feminism, Communication and Development. Complementary Goals in the Context of East Africa).

The feminine self-consciousness sees the female body as the object of another's attention. As Berger (1972) puts in, "men look at women. Women watch themselves at. The surveyor of women in herself is male: the surveyed female. Thus she turns herself into an object and most particularly, an object of vision, a sight." The women holding this consciousness of herself is defined by the male gaze, construct and desire. She is typically the sex object of masculinity pornography (*ibid*. pg. 32 cited in Prabha Krishnan and Anita Dighe).

Mayne (1985) quoted Laura Mulvey (1975) on the power of male gaze." In a world ordered by sexual imbalance, pleasure in looking has been split between active/male and passive/female.

In Indian context, the feminine and the female categories as distinguished by Keohane and Gelphi blur and merge. For though the dutiful wife and mother earth archetype belong to the female category, yet in addition to their nurturing services, they have to provide visual pleasure (Keohane-Gelphi (1982) *ibid.* pg.41 cited in P. Kridhnan).

The female self-consciousness is less inanimate, but still at the service of patriarchy giving and preserving life, nurturing and sustaining. She is either politically powerless and emotionally passive or imbued with mythic powers. But she is never self-defined. On the other hand, the feminist self-consciousness reflects the asymmetries of power, opportunity and situations in women's experience. The consciousness reveals omnipresence patterns of women's subordination, limitation and confinement in society. This results in non-oppressive ways of living. This is because women's experiences have neither provided the grounding for any of these, nor generated problems which these theories attempt to resolve, nor have they served as a test of adequacy for any of them.

Cinema has been considered together with television fiction rather as a separate category. A visual pictorial can be seen in both commercials and fiction, a sharp polarization of roles along gender lines is noticed. For instance, a serial that depicted women exclusively within the home, with men controlling the action all the commercials and advertisements preceded it (for soap, detergent, refrigerators, and after shave lotion) reflected the same polarization. Toilet soap commercials featuring glamorous, light-skinned women sponsored a serial for depicting women as a desirable princess. Advertisements for health and energy drinks featured mothers serving young sons and appreciating the reflected glory of their son's achievements. Majorly most of the advertisements of energy drinks and malts the child depicted are boys only. This also goes with the serial that contrasted with 'feminine' girls engaged in household activity and boys and 'boyish' girls exploring the world and engaging in action. "In several commercials films and fiction programmes women were presented as being home-bound, serving man and children and seeking male approval, while men were located in the world outside. Thus, commercials served to underscore and emphasize the message contained in the fiction programmes" (*ibid.* 49).

In the 27 programmes that covered Television fiction and cinema, men were principal characters in much larger numbers than women (105 principal male characters as opposed to 55 female characters). In terms of occupation 34 women were depicted as housewives. The rest comprised stray cases of a dress designer, school teacher, flight attendant and office workers occupations that are basically female-oriented and extensions of female roles. In the male characters, however, the range of occupations represented was very wide. They were industrialists, bureaucrats, businessman, journalists, executives, police officers, farmers, scientists and defense personnel. There appeared to be a distinct preference for 'white collar' jobs and 'blue collar' workers were seldom principal characters (*ibid.* 50).

Hence, though both men and women appeared to seek peer group approval in large numbers, men acknowledged as peer figures from the larger world, while women drew theirs from within the home. An analysis surveyed by Prabha Krishnan and Anita Dighe (1990) on fictional programmes and cinema television serials depicted the most common attributes that could be ascribed to the male and female characters were:

Most Common Attributes found in Male characters were self centered, decisive, self-confident, seeking a place in larger world, convincing, dignified, dominant, ruthless, ambitious, unprincipled, assertive, Loyal.

Female characters were shown sacrificing, dependent, emotional, sentimental, anxious to please, defining the world through family relations.

Several studies have indicated that women are stereotyped on television. R. Stephen Craig (1992) took this line of inquiry one step further to examine the portrayal of both men and women during different periods of television programming. To study gender stereotyping in television, commercials, Craig selected a sample of 2,209 network commercials during several periods between January 6 and 14, 1990. The weekday part (in this sample, Monday-Friday, 2-4 pm) consisted exclusively of soap operas and was chosen for its high percentage of women viewers. The weekend part (two Saturday and Sunday afternoon during sports telecasts) was selected for its high percentage of men viewers. Evening "prime time" (Monday-Friday, 9-11 pm) was chosen as a basis for comparison with past studies and the other day parts (1992-1999) each of the commercials was coded in several ways. "Characters" were coded as:

- All male adults

- All female adults
- All adults, mixed gender
- Male adults with children or teens (no women)
- Female adults with children or teens (no men)
- Mixtures of ages and gender

In addition, Craig's coders noted which character was the longest during the commercial—the "primary visual character" as well as the roles played by the characters (such as spouse, celebrity, parents) the type of product advertised (such as body product, alcohol) the selling (such as kitchen, school, business) and the voice over narrator.

Table 3.1: Percentage of Adult Primary Visual Characters by Sex appearing in Commercials in Three Day Parts

	Daytime	*Evening*	*Weekend*
Adult Male	40	52	80
Adult Female	60	48	20

Source: R. Stephen Craig, "The Effect of Television Day part on Gender Portrayals in Television Commercials: A Content Analysis" Sex Roles 26, nos 5/6 (1992) 204.

Table 3.1 indicates the differences in the times when men and women appeared in commercials. Women appeared most during the daytime (with its soap operas) men predominated during the weekend commercials (with its sports programming) and men and women were equally represented during evening prime time. Craig found other differences in the ways men and women were portrayed. Further analysis indicated that male primary characters were proportionately more likely than females to be portrayed as celebrities and professionals in everyday part, while women were proportionately more likely to be portrayed as interviewer/ demonstrators, parent/spouses, or sex object/model in everyday part.... Women were proportionately more likely to appear as sex object/models during the weekend than during the day (1992: 204).

The research also showed that different products were advertised during different time periods. As we know, almost all the daytime commercials dealt with body, food or home products. These products accounted for only one in three on the weekends. Instead, weekend commercials stressed automotive products 29 per cent, business products or services 27 per cent, or alcohol 10 per cent. There were virtually no alcohol ads during evenings and daytime. As we might suspect, women were most likely to be portrayed in home settings, men most likely to be shown away from home. Other findings dealt with the different roles played by men and women. The women who appeared in weekend ads were almost never portrayed without men and seldom as the commercial's primary character. They were generally seen in roles subservient to men e.g. hotel receptionist, secretary, or stewardess or as sex objects or models in which their only function seemed to be to lend an aspect of eroticism to the add (Craig, 1992: 208).

Women activities and concerned citizens have been rightly clamouring for a National media policy to curb the portrayal of women, to set right the historic distribution of the fair sex and to highlight women's proper role in the society. Any action plan to have the desired effect should combine both defence and aggression, while on the one hand, attempts should be made to introduce statutory regulations to curb negative portrayal of women, positive reporting and coverage of women and their achievements should be promoted. This also will help change the existing archetypes in portraying women. In International scenario Asia is in the grip of a media revolution. Transitional media co-operations and barons are busy rewriting the communication system and broadcast norms in Asia. But the tragedy is that the problems of women have been only confounded as they care no longer take out effective protest against biased media projections. Women can now only pity the biased media portrayals in a male prejudice society. Only concerted action of international level can put breaks on the unlimited freedom of the skies. Government should come together to ensure that due respect is given to the fair sex by the entertainment industry in the global village.

Role of women as mothers, as sisters and as wives is regarded as secondary as they are meant only to serve men and family and fulfil their material needs. This aspect is so much ingrained in our day-to-day life that a woman does not reach her real role as a citizen until she comes across a particular situation in her life. When she is distress or exploited, her plight is decided by the community or the court of law. This might lead her to cutter isolation and hence being rejected by her family and the society thereby forcing her to land up in a rescue home or a brothel. The overall scenario of the present state about women in amply clear from the date of atrocities against women and girls in the first six months of 1992 and 1993 in the Union Territory of Delhi alone. They are:

	Jan-June (1992)	Jan-June (1993)
(1) Rape of women and minor girls	172	154
(2) Rape of minor girls	100	122
(3) Rape of women	72	32
(4) Molestation of women	134	107
(5) Cruelty by husband and in-laws	350	285
(6) Cases of dowry	155	86
(7) Eve-teasing	1050	1086

The above-mentioned figures would show that women and girls are not safe even in the Union Territory of Delhi, because of abnormal conduct of men and boys who play a positive role in harassment and sexual assault on women in Indian society.

To quote Dr. Upendra Baxi, (then the Vice-Chancellor of the University of Delhi), who gave guidelines to Research Scholars some years back: "Action must begin with an end of the crime of silence. We cannot be built on the administration of dignified silences concerning raped bodies of women. Aggression against women should not just become raw empirical data for Ph.D. in women's studies. I know of a number of young social scientists, men and women, who have been able to pursue their dissertation on aggression against women in India without being moved to articulate a gesture of even simple protest. Such mere scientific pursuit generates no capabilities for the comprehension of patriarchal structures let alone for effective intervention or social action". The distance between women and media not only deprives the women of their right to information and knowledge but also keeps the women in the dark regarding the blatant misuse of the female and the distortion of the truth. Although the images of women as reflected by the different mass-media in the country are not very different, it will be an interesting exercise to study how these images feed and reinforce the stereotypes propagated by these media (Craig, 25).

According to Feroze Rangoonwala, there was little effort on the part of popular cinema to show women in a little more liberated, assertive, independent and progressive form. If she did anything unconventional, it was within the bounds of a moralizing drama, bringing her round finally to the second class status, or worse still, what was ordained by fate? The mass-media in India not only tend to reflect the prevailing and well entrenched, attitudes towards; women strengthen and reinforce the stereotypes but also destruct the image. The channels of communication do not generally portray the reality about labouring women in poverty. The fact that works for these women is a permanent necessity as they are the sole breadwinners, but that truth is not brought out. Neither their hard realities are exposed, i.e. long hours of work, low nor discriminatory wages and total lack of social support services is given much attention. The distortion of realities by the media has increased the gap of understanding between the different sections of society. Yet communication is one of the most important channels for the growth and development of women in the informal sector, as without information regarding services and benefits available through legislation, government schemes, banks and voluntary organizations, women can hardly take advantage of them. Most development programmes, which visualize the self-employed women as the potential beneficiary would need to accord a broader orientation to communication support systems. Overall, the reach of mass-media in India is rather limited especially in rural areas, among women and slum dwellers. This is mainly due to four mutually reinforcing factors. These are: Low literacy rate (35%); Low purchasing power (about 40 per cent of the population lives below poverty line); Poor means of transportation for timely delivery of newspaper, or maintenance of Radio/Television sets; Lack of relevant information, if purposive communication is the aim of mass-media (*ibid.* 25).

The oppression which limits their capabilities, both in the conventional roles of home-maker, wife and mother and in the wider roles of productive resources and responsible citizens of a free nation, poor access to knowledge, social and cultural barriers to a choice of option and a low level of confidence in seeking and using knowledge have continue to inhibit, women's potential to overcome these limitations.

Television

"The Joshi Committee report (report of the working group on software for Doordarshan) has condemned Doordarshan for its failure in furthering the stated national objective of women's equality and the lack of proper perspectives of the issues concerning women on the part of the policy-makers, programmers and producers." With its reach extended to rural areas, television can play a crucial role in instilling confidence and self-respect in rural women (and urban women) and help them in securing their dignified and rightful place in the society. The mass-media are guilty of promoting the *status quo* of women; they have taken on the role of fundamentalist. There is singular lack of social consciousness. Media have to change and play a positive role. The media has the capability to restore the self-esteem to women and go a long way in promoting the cause of women by the gross misuse and exploitation of the much glorified sacrificing wife/ mother/sister.

Since the Sixth plan there is a definite move on the part of the government to give higher findings to the communication sector. Now the question arises has the higher allocation to this sector been achieved at the cost of other basic sectors, such as health, education, water and sanitation? The fundamental issue is whether the government is morally justifies in diverting huge funds to the communication sector in the face of growing poverty in the country. The Seventh Plan clearly states that over 300 million people in India lie below the poverty line. It is very sad that over Rs. 12,000 crore have earmarked to develop a network, which benefits less than 25 per cent of the population thus depriving hundreds of millions of people of their basic right to food clothing and shelter (Government of India, pp. 36 and 82).

The bias against women now getting jobs in media is increased but perhaps not to the satisfaction of the feminists. But the ratio of number of jobs given to women looking for such jobs is still small compared to men. The problem is itself the society, not just with media alone. The media are not the fundamental cause of the subordinate status of women nor can it be remedied by the media alone. There are many other factors which are responsible for this situation and should not be ignored while considering these issues. Saida Bano, who was the first women armour at the Lucknow station of AIR and who compared the children's programmes in the early forties, recalls the strong opposition of her orthodox family to her working at a place where she might come into contact with 'immortal professional singing girls'. She was able to get her way only when she assured them that such persons used separate entrance to the studies. She later became the first women newspaper of AIR. The national policies would still require considerable affirmative and special attention to the special needs of girls and women; without contradicting the fundamental point of equality in development and thus in motivation of development. Nor does it ignore the social challenges posed by culture, religion and the allocation of duties and activities to one or the other sex. In other words, mass-media has not any concerted efforts to discuss serious issues that concern women and prepare the women to play their rightful and equal role in the society. To change the situation, we will have to regularly monitor the media and point out the merit as well as the demerits on continuous basis. Perhaps the women's organizations could create a media-monitoring cell for the purpose.

Thus, to conclude we believe that as a shaper of ideology and public opinion, media influences all sections of society in a major way. As has been shown, it affects all aspects of women's lives including their self-image and influences most decisions regarding women's development. Thus, it would be nothing short of tragic if women and men activists concentrated only on economic and political issues and neglected to grapple with such a powerful and insidious force such as media. It is important to note the manipulative role and the class and gender bias of media and it is therefore essential to challenge it. Women must create alternatives in different media and use them to inform and empower women, to get women out of their isolation. We must make ourselves more visible and audible so that our concerns do not remain unarticulated and unattended. Not only must women create alternative methods of working together; methods which are more democratic and participatory and which break the divide between 'media makers' and 'media takers'. It is heartening to see many women making feminist films, publishing magazines, writing plays, songs, children's poems, etc., to express themselves and to initiate a dialogue with other women, to challenge stereotypes and myths. The struggle is long and complex as the patriarchal society is very strong. But according to me there is no alternative but to struggle.

4

Empirical Analysis: A Socio-Economic Overview of Media Impact on College Students

In this chapter, an attempt has been made to understand the level of media impact on college students, specially women in Surat city in the present socio-economic context. In the earlier chapters we have discussed the sociology of gender in which we studied existing gender stereotypes, perceptions and its consequences on the society. In the second chapter, we deliberated on the relation between gender stereotypes and mass-media with the outline of socio-political profile of Gujarat state specially with reference to media industries, telecommunication and information technology. In the present study, we have observed that how the Gujarat state is significantly growing in the maintenance and continuation of capital flow in the form of multinational capital. The transnational corporation under the semblance of globalization has become instruments of capitalism as the media reinforces and propagates the consumer culture of capitalism for the market expansion. The media justifies the patriarchal value system prevalent in the society and its dimensions on women's sexuality, submissiveness as well as their total liability for household chores.

In the second chapter, we have studied the existing socio-economic profile of the Gujarat state to understand the research problem from macro perspective. In the third chapter, an attempt was made to examine the influence of mass-media on society, social institutions and values. Therefore, an analysis of the impact of mass-media and gender stereotypes in society is pertinent to reveal the underlying forces that give a definite shape and direction to it. It is very essential to study the historical depth of materialist methods that help us to understand the process to establish the link with different stages in economic growth and the ideology that is used to reinforce the *status quo*. We all are aware of the usage of mass-media by the dominant class for greater subordination and exploitation of the working class, creating its hegemony along with their ideological dominance and social control within the society.

We live in the mediated world. Even remote geographical areas are influenced by advertising, magazines, newspaper, radio, television, music, films, and other print and electronic media. The broader academic study of media has burgeoned over the last century but especially so in the last few years, when media research finally took its own roomy place in the newly recognized discipline of communication (Miller, 2002). This dynamic discipline has evolved quickly and voluminously, particularly with regard to research on gender, race, ethnicity, sexual and national identity, etc. on the construction and consumption of media messages. Also in question are the implications that such messages hold for the political realities of those they represent. These areas of media research have emerged by feminist, gay and lesbian, racial justice, and postcolonial social movements in the 1970s in Europe, the United States, South Asia, Africa, Latin America, and other parts of the world respectively.

Research on women's portrayal by mainstream media has been a continuing preoccupation for many scholars in communication studies over the past decades. Sadly, most contemporary studies suggest that despite the incursions which women have made into media industry and the success of the women's movement challenging some of the wider gender inequalities in society, the media seem to stuck in a very traditional and stereotypical groove. As we will see in the following chapter, women have made and continue to make a difference to what we see, read, and hear in the media, but still there exist too many examples of the sexist reporting in the news media, and of stereotypical and sexualized characterizations in entertainment media, for the claim that we are 'post equality' to be seen as anything other than decidedly hollow. The rapid rise and nature of media attention to the sexiest reporting speak volumes about gender power and media practices, as men may have greater authority and practical/cultural resources as media resources. Men also hold more positions of power within media organizations and sometimes clearly identify with the accused fathers (Kitzinger, 1998). Perhaps more significant is the way in which a masculine ethos permeates news-room culture. Media coverage can be informed by subtle processes such as the selective privileging of "masculine" over "feminine" discourses and "ways of knowing" (logic versus emotion, science versus intuition), asymmetrical judgments about men's and women's emotions and credibility (such as through the "notion of hysteria") and the gendered operation of media formats and genres ("hard versus soft news") (Kitzinger, 1998).

In this sociological endeavour an attempt is made to reveal the impact of television serials and advertisements among the college students in Surat city through individual interviews in various educational institutes. The areas covered are S.P.B. College (South West Zone) i.e. Parle point, Surat Zillah Sahkari Spinning Vidya Sankul (West Zone) i.e. Olpad and Veer Narmad South Gujarat University (South Zone) (P.G.) students. We have particularly interviewed U.G. and P.G. students from different sectors of Surat city to study their own perceptions based on their environment and level of educational qualifications. The study noticed differences in colleges situated in urban and rural areas revealing remarkable differences in the mind set. The total number of respondents in the sample are 300 students, 100 from S.P.B. (50 males and 50 females), 100 from Olpad college (50 males and 50 females), and 100 from VNSG University (50 males and 50 females) respectively.

Various statistical techniques have been used to analyze the empirical data. Some questions in the personal interview schedule have elicited a multiple response. For instance it is assumed that people's reasons for watching television are due to variety of reasons such as habit, for leisure time, to gain some knowledge, pass time, for refreshment and entertainment, for advertisement and so on. These factors have been elicited through multiple response questions using a structured interview schedule. Multiple responses shows a set defined as categories of variables, representing multiple answers, recorded for a single question. The set includes as many variables as the number of responses recorded. The response that is chosen by the maximum number of respondents is ranked first and the response that is choice of the second largest number of respondents is ranked second and so on.

We have discussed and drawn a number of statements from the respondents pertaining to concerned issues in the study which further is weighted and added to produce a single score on the related topic. For this, an item analysis has been done to test each item if it really belongs to the scale. As mentioned earlier we have developed different composite indices to analyze gender concerns, consumerism, impact and so on.

General Background

In an attempt to understand the impact of Television serials and advertisements in the present socio-economic and political context, we interviewed college students from the different areas, ages, educational backgrounds and communities. In a total there are 150 males and 150 females in the sample including U.G. and P.G. courses. The age criterion is from 18-29 years, the maximum number of students were between 19 and 20 years of age, in which 36 males and 45 females of 19 years and 36 males and 34 females of 20 years respectively. The number of males of 21 years was 27 and 15 females of 21 years of age and of the age 22 were 18 males and 19 females respectively.

The S.P.B. College under study is, situated in Parle point, comprising elite group residing in the urban area. The second college that was Surat Zillah Sahkari Spinning Vidya Sankul, Arts and Commerce College situated in Olpad district in rural area constituting middle and lower middle class categories. In university, we found the combination of diverse groups hailing from rural and urban areas as well.

Table 4.1: Age of Respondent's according to Gender

Age	*Male*	*Female*	*Total*
18 to 21	112 (74.67)	110 (73.34)	222 (74.00)
22 to 25	34 (22.67)	39 (26.00)	73 (24.34)
26 to 30	4 (2.67)	1 (0.006)	5 (1.67)

Note: Figures in parenthesis indicate percentage.

Our sample reveals the study of all religions amongst them Hindus form a majority of 94.7 per cent (142 males) and 98 per cent (147 females). The next religion is Islam 4.7 per cent (7 males), 7 per cent (1 female) followed by one Christian (male) and two Parsi females respectively.

The sample reveals that 86.7 per cent of males, 82 per cent of females spoke Gujarati language whereas 7 per cent males spoke Urdu language and 6 per cent males and 10 per cent females spoke Hindi language. The rest of the respondents spoke Sindhi, Malayalam, Marathi, Marwari, English, Oriya and Bhojpuri as their mother tongues. In the sample the largest community found in the rural areas was the Patel community which included 38 males (30.6%) and 27 females (20%). During data collection we also stressed upon the medium of education as it plays a vital role in their perception and decision-making. The male ratio from English medium was 62.9 per cent and the female ratio was 72.6 per cent. The English medium students were located in urban areas while the students from Gujarati medium live mostly in rural areas. Thus the Gujarati medium respondent's ratio was 37.1 per cent males and 27.4 per cent females and these respondents were mainly in the rural areas i.e., Olpad College.

The sample was divided into two categories i.e. Under Graduate (UG) and Post Graduate (PG). The under graduate students hailed from the faculties of arts, science and commerce, whereas the post graduate students from the faculties of arts and science. Many of them are pursuing professional courses such as MSW, Mass communication, Journalism, Bachelor of Interior Designing (BID), etc. The sample consisted of 300 students out of which 200 were from U.G. courses i.e. 100 males and 100 females and 100 from the P.G. courses i.e. 50 males and 50 females respectively.

Table 4.2: Respondent's Distribution according to Medium of Education

Medium of Education	*Gender*		*Total*
	Male	*Female*	
English	92 (62.9)	108 (72.6)	200 (67.8)
Gujarati	55 (37.1)	45 (27.4)	100 (32.2)
Total	147 (100)	153 (100)	300 (100)

Note: Figures in parenthesis indicate percentage.

To understand the basic economic status of the respondents, we took monthly income as one of the variables which was further divided into six groups. There is a huge variation in the monthly income slab of the family as it was noticed that the maximum number of students were found in less than rupees 10,000 category i.e. 59 males and 26 females leading to a total of 85 respondents and another slab totally contrasted was above 30,000 which included 30 males and 25 females leading to a total of 55 persons (Table 4.3).

We found that the numbers of respondents with above rupees 30,001 monthly income were from S.P.B College (urban). While those with the monthly income of Rs. 10,001 hail from the Olpad College (rural). This gives a clear picture of the economic status of the respondents which further reflects in their social environment in terms of socialization, attitudes and perception. We observed that some of the respondents hesitated to disclose their monthly income.

Table 4.3: Monthly Family Income of the Respondents

Monthly Income of the family	*Gender*		*Total*
	Male	*Female*	
Less than Rs. 10,000	59 (43.1)	26 (20.5)	85 (32.2)
10,000 to 15,000	17 (12.4)	29 (22.8)	46 (17.4)
15,000 to 20,000	9 (6.6)	19 (15.0)	28 (10.6)
20,000 to 25000	14 (10.2)	15 (11.8)	28 (11.0)
25,000 to 30,000	8 (5.8)	13 (10.2)	21 (8.0)
Above 30,000	30 (21.9)	25 (19.7)	55 (20.8)
Total	137 (100)	127 (100)	264 (100)

Note: 1. Thirteen Male respondents and twenty three female respondents did not disclose their monthly income.
2. Figures in parenthesis indicate percentage.

Media Exposure: The Role of Television

In the previous chapter we have discussed about the media profile in Surat city, and now we will analyze the impact of television through serials and advertisements. Television is the wholesale distributor of images resulting in popular culture as it contributes greatly to popular culture. It also brings into homes images and messages that once were restricted to certain age groups of relationships. It is observed that television has a greater influence than newspapers, magazines, or radio and also strongly influence cultural change. These include "the bypassing of elites in the flow of information, the cathecting of consumption as an appropriate orientation, legitimization of urban, metropolitan and cosmopolitan models of living and working; the authoritative advocacy of established scientific and state ideologies; and the privileging of certain languages, dialects, concepts and terms" (Salzmann, 1993: 7). Print media did not support a lot to the freedom movement. Hence, its institutional framework was a private enterprise including professional ethics which were relatively free from the state and commercial control.

The emergence of radio started with a view to strengthen the colonial empire. When India was politically free from the British Empire, the new government and bureaucrats took control of it and aimed to propagate elite culture as well as socially relevant programmes. In course of time film music and advertisements found place in radio though the institutional framework did not change. Initially television as a medium of luxury the country could not afford, but at the same time its potential for education and development was recognized. The objective behind the genesis of Doordarshan, was "to act as a catalyst for social change, to create national integration, to stimulate scientific temper among the people, to disseminate the message of family planning as a means of population control and family welfare, to stimulate greater agricultural production by providing essential information and knowledge, to promote and help preservation of environmental ecological balance, to highlight the need for social welfare measures including welfare of women, children and the less privileged to promote interest in games and sports, to stimulate appreciation of our artistic and cultural heritage and to educate the masses" (Pokharapurkar, 1993: 16-17).

Television is the only medium which has high potentiality to fight against other media i.e. radio; because of its moving images and capability for drama which makes it more attractive compared to radio. The first and oldest mass-media in India, the newspapers, began with the fierce independence of control from the state, advertisers and circulation figures. Doordarshan has turned commercial and entertainment oriented due to lack of ideological commitment, lack of political interest, and the enforced opening of the economy by the international monetary fund and the World Bank. Transnational television was introduced in the year 1991 highlighting the images of Gulf war by CNN. This was only available in the elite' locales like hotels, and for this they had to connect antenna to get this channel. Later on Star Television took a new venture with the bright images into India, which was actually meant for China. With the coordination of the cable operators with CNN and Star Television the audience were able to watch the telecast and the programmes at home. With the emergence of satellite broadcasting of foreign and controlled channels in India gave rise to culture of globalization, consumerism and individualism. To cope with the competition Doordarshan also started becoming a commercialized channel, introduced DD Metro from metro cities to compete with the satellite channels for audience, and advertising budget. Today more than 250 privately owned channels are being broadcasted in India. Amongst them Sony, Star, ESPN, Cartoon network, NDTV, Zee TV, Colours, BBC, etc. and others are part of global media. In the past decade, the capital has gained control over the world's economic system which includes mass-media and its technologically related segments such as telecommunication and information technology. The monopoly of entire communication sectors (telecom, IT and media) controls and propagates the capitalist ideology leading to the strengthening of global capitalism and this has become a dominant ideological tool of capitalism. Capitalism produces the conditions of productions for its own existence and all this includes the production of the material and theoretical forces with the education system, religion, family and society. In this period, mass-media especially Television is used as a vital tool for reinforcement, conceptualization, authorization and externalization in the present society. Television acts as a dominating medium and leads over the other media on every parameter whether advertising, print, etc. The number of channels is steadily rising (more than estimated 220) as are the homes that have Television's (79 million). It attracted an estimated 100 million in revenues in 2002, and of the top 10 media companies, six are into Television broadcasting (Kohli, 2003: 5).

In the current era of globalization television sustains the world view compatible with capitalism and creates a consciousness that the conditions of the capitalist mode of production are laws of nature. The powerful media justifies and perpetuates the *status quo* through its various software programmes. The elite use television to win over the approval of the rich, by propagating their order that is, ideology and value system of class and patriarchy. The patriarchal system ordains secondary position to women regardless of age, status, or experience. Women are expected by the society to be subtle, submissive, holding responsibility of the household chores and young siblings, care of the old and ill people, biological reproducer, and if the economic situation of the family so demands, enter wage labour market; in brief as fully responsible for the domestic arena while men take care of the external world. Television enhances patriarchy ideology and obstructs equality of women. This is depicted and visualized through the serials and general entertainment channels leading to the topmost rating across programmes and channels. News, Sports, religious and spiritual i.e. mythological, business, film, music, health, animation, comedy and natural history and wildlife are the some of the Indian programmes which are shown. There is another broad genre that we term entertainment channels whose software includes ideas from wide range of mixture of entertainment package comprising music, film and film based programmes, reality shows, game shows, quiz shows/competitions, comedy shows, standby mimicry etc. It also includes serials of comedy, mythology, daily soaps, family shows, horror and detective serials. Besides various channels also addresses various programmes—religious address, health programmes, kid's programmes, cookery shows, talent shows, animated films, and special programmes for women, travel related programmes, etc. are a mixed package of entertainment for the viewers. The popular entertainment channels are STAR PLUS, Zee TV, Colours, NDTV Imagine, SAB TV, Sahara, MTV, etc. in Hindi while many are in regional languages. Amongst all these programmes television serials get the maximum ratings as family serials grab the maximum points. These serials reveal the lives of people who spend lavishly and have status by acquisition and consumption, displayed in surroundings of wealth. In the serial the plots which are been showed are always family-oriented and the atmosphere itself depicts the main intention of advertising and even the stories which are been framed are in accordance with the audience demands as well as to fulfil the needs of the advertiser. Almost all family serials depict joint family especially business tycoons and their norms, living rooms and lifestyles. These daily soap operas run more than three or even four years. These serials mainly highlight the character, appearance, ethics and values of the women in the family. The leading person in the family is mostly women, who play the different characters such as daughter, daughter-in-law, sister-in-law, mother-in-law etc in a large joint business family. The character of the women portrayed in the serial is either positive or negative. On one hand a woman is shown playing a positive character solving the problems of the family and on the other hand, the negative character is an economically independent woman who disrupts the peace and unity of the family. Even though the woman character is very strong and bold, her sexuality and fertility is controlled by men and they are generally economically dependent on men. They have to remain within the patriarchal value system. In spite of her bold character she follows the rituals associated with marriage carrying all the symbols and accessories of married women. She accepts her subordination to the male and believes in the family values.

The free time of watching television makes the viewers attracted by its imaginary world of happiness. Advertisements increase production of goods and services accordingly to consumer demands. Advertising awakens this demand by creating needs and desires constantly. Mass media bridges pool between consumer and consumerism. Advertising projects that material wealth is needed to lead a happy and luxurious life. In this process woman who is depicted as care-takers of the family are exploited by the advertising industry by making them as consumers and using them as commodities to fulfil the market needs. Advertisements brains wash the mindset of the people by pursuing them to purchase certain typical like food products, detergents, processed foods etc. to maintain the status. Women use the advertised products to improve the status and also get appreciated by husband, family, guests, friends, and so on. Women feel strengthened and accepted as best caretaker when they use the advertised products. Women characters in the serials act as protagonists by the viewer's affectionate and responsible housewife and all these characters reflect the patriarchal value systems. Advertisements create a perception in women's mind by imposing that if they are beautiful and attractive they will be accepted and admired in the family as well as society. Thus in order to maintain the identity, beauty and appearance, cosmetic usage and branded clothing and jewellery become a requirement. A study on responses of women to beauty advertisements on television reveals that women get most of their information about products from television advertisements (Centre for Advocacy and Research, 2003). Even popular women's magazines such as Femina and Cosmopolitan and many others in Indian languages focus on beauty, fashion and trend which create an atmosphere for consumption.

In the 21st century, television sets have acquired a universal position which cannot be detached and holds a prime space in our lifestyles. Whether it is service or business categories, television is placed in the main room of the family. During the survey we found that only five respondents (1.67%) out of 300 respondents were not possessing Television sets in their homes. This gives a clear picture and importance of the Television sets in our day-to-day life. Television accommodates all family members to view the programmes together whether it may be soap operas, children's serials, dance sequences, commercial films or any reality shows. As mentioned earlier we have selected television from among the media to analyze the impact on the college going youngsters of the present generation.

Table 4.4: Entertainment Channel Preference of Respondents

Sr. No.	*Channel*	*OLPAD College (Rural)*	*S.P.B. College (City)*	*University (Both)*	*Total*
1.	Colours	30	24	25	79 (26.33%)
2.	NDTV Imagine	25	25	22	72 (24.00%)
3.	Star Plus	16	05	20	41 (13.69%)
4.	Sab TV	12	29	19	60 (20.00%)
5.	Zee TV	10	07	08	25 (08.35%)
6.	Star One	07	10	06	24 (07.06%)
	Total	100	100	100	300

Channel Preference

Table 4.4 reveals that colours is the most popular channel watched by 79 respondents (26.33%), while NDTV and Star plus by 72 (24%) and 41 (13.69%) respectively. (Table 4.4) Rest of the respondents are interested in watching SAB TV, Zee TV and Star One i.e. 50 (20%), 25 (8.35%), 23 (7.67%) respectively. Our sample in the study shows that the taste and preference among the male and female respondents vary to a large extent. Male respondents were less interested in Television serials compared to the female respondents. Male respondents were basically interested in channels such as MTV, Zee Business, Discovery, News channel, Sports channel, etc. whereas, the female respondents were close almost addicted to Television serials and were found to be the maximum viewers of the serials. Thus, the women watch NDTV Imagine, Colours, Star Plus, Zee TV, SAB TV, etc. During the analysis we studied that only (1.67%) female respondent's i.e. one female amongst 150 respondents was interested in the Discovery channel. It was really shocking that not a single respondent from 150 samples was interested in sports or news channel. This helped us to segregate the areas of interest based on gender. The sample reveals the strong preference among respondents for channels that

Table 4.5: Most Preferred Programmes of the Respondents

Sr. No.	*Serials*	*OLPAD College*	*S.P.B College*	*University*	*Total*
1.	Balika Vadhu	36	25	19	80 (26.99)
2.	Yeh Rishta Kya Kehlata Hai	24	8	19	51 (17.00)
3.	Miley Jab Hum Tum	11	38	5	54 (18.00)
4.	Bandini	19	16	33	68 (22.66)
5.	Choti Bahu	10	10	22	42 (14.00)
6.	Others	0	3	2	05 (01.66)
	Total	100	100	100	300 (100)

Note: Figures in parenthesis indicate percentage.

offer a variety of entertainment that includes music, sports, film and film based programmes, stage shows, game shows, reality shows, serials based on horror, supernatural phenomenon, comedy, religious discourse and daily family soaps as compared to news and educational channels.

In our observation, we could not decide the most viewed Television serial as it was difficult to analyze because of wide range of taste of the respondents. Due to the introduction of new subjects such as reality shows, the daily soaps have lost their number of viewers comparatively. Our data shows that the respondents both male and female watch Television serials such as 'Miley Jab hum tum' (18%), 'Choti Bahu' (14%), 'Yeh Rishta kya kehlata Hain' (17%), 'Balika Vadhu' (26.66%) and 'Bandini' (22.66%) (Table 4.5). Balika Vadhu and Bandini are the longest running Television serials that will complete the second consecutive year of telecast shortly. The serials have similar story line portraying upper class and upper caste, Hindu, Rajasthan Marwari business family. In the serial Balika Vadhu, the surname 'Rajput' and the rituals followed suggest that the family belongs to feudal social set up with trading and agricultural land owing class from the state of Rajasthan. While in the serial Bandini, the surname 'Mahyavanshi' and the rituals followed suggest that the family belongs to a Gujarati caste which stays in Dharampur district situated in Saurashtra. Both the serials reflect feudal values and patriarchal ideology especially with regard to women. The character of the serial i.e. Dharamraj Mahyavanshi is depicted as the central figure of the serial, which holds the main and topmost position in the family as well in society. He is the only sole decision-maker of the society with which each and every villager including the family members have to respect and obey his decisions. This shows the importance of the male patriarchy not only in the past but also in 'Modern' India. He marries a young girl equivalent to his daughter's age, but the female character 'Santu' does not enjoy all the rights of a wife and a daughter-in-law in her husband's family. The female character is shown always struggling and fighting against the injustice and insults she experiences. In the family the lead character shown invariably is male whereas the female character is generally depicted as subordinate and submissive. Women do not assert their rights of and once they get married they leave their parental family far behind. The family structure of the male character is a joint family enjoying all the joys and sharing sorrows, whether festivals or personal problems, knitted from the external world whose problems are not reflected in the serial. In both the serials the family has a high degree of unity and integrity. The other family members revolt if the protagonist tries to disturb the family. Similarly, the family members get united against the female character in case of dissatisfaction. The plots in the episode are highly elitist and that there are no doubt the serials incur a lot of expenditure to make it extraordinary realistic family environment. The plots in the episode are telecasted 4 to 5 days a week for 30 minutes each, which rotating around solving the family problems arising from the personal conflicts, unfavourable circumstances, unexpected influences of some outsiders and so on.

The families in the serial follow strict rules and regulations where incision of importance of family's pride and honour and family's rites and rituals are given prime importance. This gives a clear picture of the patrilocal and patrilineal system existing in the family serials. The main expectation towards the family of the daughter-in-law is to uphold the unity and integrity of the joint family and actively work to maintain the *status quo*. Women characters are exploited and forced to keep their interest secondary before the family interest, as think in of utmost importance. In Balika Vadhu and Bandini serials female characters are not economically independent and their sexuality and fertility is controlled by men. In both the serials the negative character is a woman. In Balika Vadhu serial the negative role is played by mother-in-law i.e. Dadisa, whereas in Bandini the woman who is sister-in-law plays the negative character. The protagonist in both the serials is a house-wife whose world revolves around her family and who always keep the family interest above her own.

In Balika Vadhu the leading character is a protagonist, who is shown a widow. She loses her husband at a very young age and starts to take up the responsibility, care of the young siblings in absence of her husband. The female character called 'Dadisa' in the serial is shown as a strong female who not only manages but also expands the family business. Dadisa has two sons; both of them are very obedient and helpful to her mother. The younger son is married in his community and has two siblings namely Suguna and Jagdish. Her elder son marries a very young girl and this is his second marriage with Gehna for the birth of a male child, as it was encouraged by Dadisa. Dadisa got her elder son married to her daughter's age only because to have an heir from her. Being young Gehana was conceived and when they consulted the doctor who advised not to go for pregnancy further due to her young age. However, dadisa wanted the child and that too, a male child from her. In the serials, the woman characters are shown playing roles positive as well as negative. The women in the serials are apparently dressed like a 'suhagan' with all its outward signs such as "sindoor", a long mangalsutra, bangles, earrings, and colourful and bright sarees. Women are projected very beautiful, attractive, admirable, and adorable but they don't have decision-making power and are being projected as mere show piece. The irony is that, in the social context of business communities shown in the serial, the villainous are apparently strong women. They do wear ghunghat, but they carry the potential of problem solving and taking decisions, besides speaking openly in presence of the males. In fact in the two serials, the villainous part of the female character enjoys seniority order and has a dominant position in the house. Even though the women who are projected as modern, bold, initiative taking, decision-maker accepts the patriarchal value system and reinforces male dominance in Indian culture, besides accepting willingly the dominance of male supremacy. In these serials women are portrayed and perfectly presented as gorgeous commodity to attract maximum female viewers but within the paradigm of male subordination.

Table 4.6: Frequency of Reinforcement of Gender Stereotypes

Name of College	*No*		*Yes*		*Total*
	Male	*Female*	*Male*	*Female*	
S.P.B.	35	47	15	3	100
OLPAD	39	40	11	10	100
University	40	31	10	19	100
Total	114	118	36	32	300

To a question in our schedule "Does reinforcement of gender stereotype" reflected in the Television serial, we had a quite combination of answers as majority of the respondents did not believe that stereotypes are reflected in the Television serials. However, when analyzed the answer area-wise and we found that women respondents were more than the male respondents, who did not believe that reinforcement of gender stereotype is created or initiated by media (Television serials and advertisements). Male and female characters are presented in highly stylist and idealistic form in the Television serials. In Television serials women are shown as ideal consorts of powerful men, whom they have to treat Shakti incarnate [pati parmeshwar, swami, nath]. Society has accepted and glorified the ideal behaviour in men and women depicted in the Television serials. Even though, the female character plays the central role in 'daily soap operas' they are always depicted from the masculine perspective.

The women character is shown in the serials are essentially feminine i.e. as beautiful, idealistic and illusionary women. Women in the Television serials are always projected as sheltered and non-productive, passionate and patient idealized as lovers. As couples these women characters are always under male control. The existence of female characters is pondered through male desire, so separation from their beloved or lover is presented as a human condition which creates a special problem for these women. In this situation the women has only two solutions to this problem i.e. either tolerating or adjusting with patience and acceptance until the lover returns or cheat the other women and win back the lover. Bonding with the male is projected as perfect and positive end. Under these crucial circumstances only male is depicted as an ultimate problem solver which clearly convey the message that women without men are incomplete. Therefore, the woman has to strive and struggle hard in every possible way to retain their men lover be it husband.

Table 4.7: Media Portrayal of Women: Response of the Respondents

Portray Women as Sexual Objects	*Gender*		*Total*
	Male	*Female*	
Agree	74	70	144
Disagree	45	47	92
Neutral	31	33	64
Total	150	150	300

Table 4.7 surely conveys that women are portrayed as sexual objects in Television serials. Majority of the males find this statement true and necessary whereas females differ with the answers. Beauty and passiveness is promoted as desirable values

for women as they are necessary, though non-productive even than women strive long hours in maintaining their beauty remain as into illusionary beings.

Table 4.8: Depiction of Women as Secondary Individuals

Response	*Gender*		*Total*
	Male	*Female*	
No	26	40	66
Yes	124	110	234
Total	150	150	300

To a question "if you do feel that women are shown as secondary objects or individuals" in Television serials in the schedule-124 male respondents and 110 female respondents argued that women are shown as secondary to men which clearly shows the awareness of the self and also the perpetuation of gender inequality in the entertainment industry (Table 4.8). We noted the polarities of male and female behaviour i.e. men were largely shown as aggressive and confident while women were shown as shy and responsive. Women were even shown worshipping their husbands, being dependent on them and competing with each other for male favours. Young girls are shown dreaming of their future as brides and wives; while male children dream of professional roles in the future. In some exceptions women are shown economically independent and they hold the secondary position in the family.

Table 4.9: Promotion of Consumerism and Profit by the Media (Advertising Industry)

Response	*Frequency*	*Per cent*	*Valid*	*Cumulative*
Agree	233	77.07.	79.03%	79.03%
Disagree	22	05.04	05.04%	84.07%
Neutral	45	17.00	17.00%	100%
Total	300	100	100	

Television and advertisement along with cinema are considered a fiction rather than a separate category. Our analysis shows that both in fiction and commercials there is a sharp polarization of roles along gender lines. For, example, serials such as Balika Vadhu and

Bandini depicts women within four walls of home, with male domination and control and all the advertisements and commercials that precede the serial (soaps, detergents, after shave lotion etc) reflect the same polarization like beauty soaps, toilet soaps and fairness cream commercials featuring glamorous, light skinned women sponsors a serial which depicts women as a desirable princess. Advertisements for energy drinks and health products feature mothers serving the young sons and dreaming in their glory of their bright and prosperous future achievements. In several commercials, films and advertisements women are depicted as home bound, serving men and children and seeking male approval, whereas men are located outside. In case of male characters the range of occupation presented is very wide. They are industrialists, bureaucrats, businessmen, journalists, executives, police officers, etc. this shows a distinct preference for "white collar" jobs.

Advertisements

Advertisements play a tremendous role in our everyday life. Even though we may sometimes resist its direct appeal, it will often capture us in the end. If the appeal is repeated often enough it will usually achieve its object of leaving us emotionally uneasy, wondering whether we, the consumers oughtn't for the sake of looking like other decent people, for the sake of scoring someone else, and so on. (Messers Leavis and Thompson, Culture and Environment). "Advertisers do not spend millions a year on advertisement for nothing ....We must therefore try to understand how advertisements get at us," so that we can intelligently resist when desirable. It is not surprising; therefore, the skilled creator of advertisements when appealing to the general public, as opposed to members of the trade who want simple statements of fact, frequently bases his plan of campaign on an emotional appeal. Thus if we look through any representative advertising medium, whether newspaper or periodical or television, you will find that there is scarcely a human emotion in the whole gamut which is not plucked at, adroitly, by one or the other of the advertisers. "Fear, for instance, is a great salesman. If you die tomorrow suggest the insurance advertisement, appealing to everyman's concern for his family's security. A great mass of advertising which sells soaps and toilet creams uses it to the exclusion of all other appeals.

Furniture makers, shoe manufacturers and makers of heating appliances often base their appeal on the love of comfort. The growing regard for hygiene in the past few years has caused a great increase in the number of advertisers who base their appeal on love of health rather than on fear of illness. The appeal to the desire for more leisure is another which has grown in popularity with the changing times. It is exemplified principally in the advertisements for washing powder, vacuum cleaners and modern cooking apparatus.

Humour in advertising is another form of emotional appeal, but one which needs to be used with discretion. Its advantages are that it quickly establishes a warm contact between the advertiser and the reader or viewer and that it lends itself to the making of unusually attractive, advertisements. Its disadvantage is that, unless very carefully handled, the impression of the humour which remains in the reader's mind obliterates any recollection of the product advertised (*ibid*).

Advertising and Gender Stereotypes

Advertising agencies reap huge profits by making sexist advertisements featuring women. Largely speaking a sexist advertisement is the one that depicts women as inferior; it is discriminatory, degrading and humiliating women in relation to men. This form of advertising has become an important tool of the perpetuation of male dominance, which exploits women's sexuality and their physical appearance. Many studies have observed that 'men regard women primarily as sex objects' by the plethora of decorative roles assigned to women more than men. The effect is also highlighted by showing equally men and women sharing recreational activities but not work. More often than not, women are relatively shown very less in working roles. Triver Milieu (1999) in his study regarding advertising and women notes that 'most women were captured in pictures which intended to emphasize "mannequin" and "dummy" expression while men more often demonstrated a "thoughtful" expression implying some intellectual processes. In advertisements local media depict women as vein and seductive, sex commodities, dull witted, in constant need of approval by men and ultimately they are shown in home or kitchen.

Our prime effort through this study is to reveal the fact that how women are being portrayed in media especially in advertisements and Television serials. As we have previously discussed about the Television serials, we now examine this assumption of gender stereotyping in advertisements. As mentioned earlier media always depicts women in two major roles i.e. prime caretakers of the family and sex symbols.

Accordingly advertisements promote only women as the main and leading caretaker especially in health and hygiene sector of the family. During our sample collection we came to know the fact that not only men but women also have accepted the fact that the responsibility of the children, sick, husband, in-laws, home maintenance, etc. is fully women's responsibility. However, the respondents also agreed that women have stepped out of the threshold of the house in pursuit in their future. Nonetheless, the basic notion is our social norms invariably argued that whether a woman is financially independent or not, domestic chore is the ultimate job profile of woman eventually. So it goes without saying that she has to manage both house and job equally. In our interview schedule, we included a question regarding advertisements and gender stereotyping with special reference to health drinks (Bournvita, Complan, Horlicks), etc. soaps, detergents, oil, etc. such (dettol, savlon), and food items such as (Saffola oil, Tata salt, snacks, etc).

Table 4.10: Gender Stereotyping

Women as Prime Caretakers	*No. of Respondents*	*Percent*
Agree	146	48.67
Disagree	90	30.00
Neutral	64	21.33
Total	300	100.00

While men are portrayed as successful professionals and important decision-makers, women in advertisements are invariably casted as housewives who engage themselves and are happy with the rice cookers, washing machines, sewing machines, microwaves, mixers, juicers, other household items etc. But if men are shown sharing household chores in advertisements women are shown beam with pride and happiness at the latest household appliance being advertised. This clearly reinforces that housework is the sole concern of women. Such advertisements deny the fact that, increasing number of women is participating in various professions outside the home. The growing acceptance of the idea that men should share in the task of housework is also largely absent. Since, women are generally shown in the context of household, children tend to associate their mother with these secondary chores while fathers are usually seen driving car to work and depicted as main breadwinners and heads of the house while women are shown making a healthy meal (advertising of a particular wheat flour or saffola oil). Children are not exempt either from such stereotyping where boys are always soiling their clothes, camping or engaged in outdoor activities whereas girls are often shown as playing piano, dancing, dressing up dolls, etc. This socialization of the young through advertisements has far reaching effects that on their personhood. No wonder boys identify themselves with their fathers who have done everything for them and one who is strong, dependable, clever, while girls, identify with their mother who is loving, self-sacrificing and devoted 'servant' of the home and the family. Media only highlights multifaceted roles of women as home makers; cooks, mothers' consumers etc, but fail to reveal the other qualities of women such as intelligence, resourcefulness, independent and decision-makers, strong persons, etc. Modern advertising industry always projects women as obsessed with their beauty maintenance on their faces and bodies are indeed sickening. These advertisements and commercials define the characteristics of "femaleness" in terms of glamour, modesty, fashion and so on.

In the present study we have tried to comprehend the perceptions of the young college students with regard to the factors necessary for success in life. The question was classified into five options—intelligence, personality, beauty and smartness. It is gratifying to note that the girls selected all four options except beauty, whereas a large portion of boys (95) considered beauty also as an essential element along with other factors for success. Furthermore, the boys hold, that beauty is also equally important for success. Meanwhile this trend also emulsifies that only girls depend on 'beauty' for success as our data reveal the contrary perception that is boys stressing the need for beauty for success. This clearly point out the impact of advertisement, commercials with reference 'whitening' creams and the like. Besides the growing number of men's 'beauty parlours' strongly supports our argument as how the advertising industry expands.

We now try to analyze the perception of respondents on the influence of Television in general on society and here we found that it's largely perceived as positive (Table 4.11). Especially a majority of the respondents as a medium that gives information and brings awareness in the society predominantly believes it as a window to the world. In a study in Ahmedabad of 245 households from seven economically and socially diverse areas of the city, 78 per cent of the sample agreed that Television has increased people's political awareness (Trivedi, 1986). Studies suggest that people know significant historical events only through the media. During the periods of change and uncertainty, it is also highly probable that people are more dependent on media as source of information and guidance (Ball-Rokeach and De Fluer, 1976; Ball Rokeach, 1985). The second important influence of Television is a source of entertainment and information. However, the poor and uneducated people use television only for entertainment. Thus, the poor class is satisfied with Television as a source of entertainment from the long hours of both physical and mental work and exertion and hence uses this medium as a temporary reliever through films, serials, songs, cricket matches, etc. Besides that the respondents also observed that the Television is a source of entertainment. Cinema offers only entertainment and that too of only one kind; while

Table 4.11: Positive Influence of Television

Sr. No.	*Economic Position*	*World Exposure*	*Entertainment*	*Awareness*	*Relaxation and Stress Relief*
1.	Less than 10,000	39 (81.7)	75 (33.2)	21 (26.9)	27 (25.0)
2.	10,001 to 20,000	36 (29.3)	62 (27.4)	21 (26.9)	30 (27.8)
3.	20,001 to 30,000	15 (12.2)	40 (17.7)	14 (17.9)	18 (16.7)
4.	30,001 and above	30 (24.4)	48 (21.2)	20 (25.6)	30 (27.8)
	Total	120 (97.6)	225 (99.6)	76 (97.4)	105 (97.2)

Note: Figures in parenthesis indicate percentage.

Television offers a cafeteria choice of news, educational programmes, movies, music, serials, film songs, religious programmes, etc. Thus it is natural for the respondents as they affirm that television not only provides relaxation but also relieves them from stress and also a diversion from the monotonous schedule like attending college, tuition, exams. etc. as in all 97 per cent of the respondents gave positive view of television medium.

During the data collection we found that in almost all the houses the Television set was in the main living room while more than half of the respondents were having additional Television sets in their individual bedrooms. Television is a medium which beams out moving objects and its occurrence is brief on the screen which needs a constant supply of images and words continuously speaking. These words and images (illusionary) roll on in the minds of viewers like an ongoing process for 24 hours a day, 30 days a month, and sometimes even 365 days in a year. These constantly jabbing of images and words do not lead to decrease the stress levels. Several studies point out that excess or constant television viewing would result in aggregated tension and insomnia. Meanwhile, our respondents which were college students also expressed that Television has negative and positive effects on the society as it affects the culture and children negatively as belief in super natural and fantasies will invariably impact children negatively like reducing interest in books and reading, making them inactive, and perhaps even affects culture negatively. Besides during the interaction we came to know its negative effect of diverting people from the real issues, reducing interaction amongst the family members and it also results in a huge a waste of time. Thus, the emerging issue out of this small study reflects the enslavement of the audience (viewers) to the television unconsciously which reduces and numbs the thought process ultimately. We are aware of the negative impact of Television is especially on children in the western culture who are diverted to violence and its impact of the medium on attention spans and witting skills has been extensively studied. Passively, it is sure that Television takes children away from the other family members. Television is reported to encourage and influence early sexual activity, drug and alcohol abuse in those countries. The families which do not posses Television sets are seen engaged in variety of activities such as family talks, playing with the young children, sharing their views and ideas, doing productive work's etc. As per some study Television viewing also 'reduced the number of loci at which activities occurred, since the set was usually located in the living room and most activities revolve around it' (Kent, 1985:124). Comstock *et al.* argue that "Television reduces involvement in other activities when it is a normality, and there is a possibility of a lasting decrease in involvement in more frequently engaged in activities." (1978-154). In addition heavy Television viewing is also associated with a higher degree of impatience and restlessness (Marks Granfiels, 1984) Winn (1977) and others have quoted numerous studies to suggest Television affects children's reading and writing skills and brings out a decline in recallable memory. Unnikrishnan Bajpai (1996) in their study on advertising on children found that every child in Delhi is a regular Television viewer; children spend a good deal of their fulltime in front of the Television sets; most Indian children watch adult programming; Television viewing is adversely affecting their reading, writing and concentration skills; and is bringing a major change in familial relationships by creating greater segregation between generations and individuals (1996). Innumerable studies show a strong correlation between Television violence and aggression levels in children. There are various studies on the impact of television on teenagers. Experiment in college campuses by Bandwa and Berkouitz showed that aggressive behaviour could be learnt viewing violent media content and that a stimulation effect was more probable than a cathartic effect (Comstock, 1975).

As has been mentioned earlier in this chapter, few respondents view news channels and none of the respondents in the sample watch education oriented channels like Discovery and National Geographic, especially amongst the females. Thus, we can state there exists mesmerizing effect of Television serials which eclipses all other educative or news channels. A large number of the respondents (81%) discuss with their friends, peer groups and neighbours about acting, storyline, dressing, ornaments, or fashion in the serials. Only few respondents discuss the news or information or the problems of society (9%). This clearly reflects the apparent growth of consumerism and individualism and social concern. During the data cllection we observed the keen interest of the respondents in fashion and makeup of the characters in the serials rather than on current issues.

Table 4.12: Negative Impact of Television across Income

Sr. No.	Income	Affects children	Affects culture	Sets fashion	Identify with characters
1.	Less than 10,000	22 (25.9)	23 (31.1)	36 (29.9)	23 (34.3)
2.	10,001 to 20,000	33 (38.8)	26 (35.1)	35 (27.1)	11 (16.4)
3.	20,001 to 30,000	12 (14.1)	12 (16.2)	23 (17.8)	14 (20.9)
4.	30,001 and above	15 (17.6)	12 (16.2)	33 (25.6)	17 (25.4)
	Total	87 (96.5)	73 (98.6)	121 (98.9)	65 (97.0)

Note: Figures in parenthesis indicate percentage.

Impact of Television on Consumerism

Several researches on advertising in India suggest the cascading effect of television on behavioural pattern of consumers. For instance Singhal and Rogers observe that the brand Maggie 2-Minute Noodles in diets as a consequence of television advertising, "the success story of Maggie 2-Minute in India demonstrates how rapid diffusion of television, the great popularity an indigenous soap opera, and organizational innovations in marketing and advertising can launch an alien product in a Third World country. In fact the Maggie noodles story is considered to be the most successful use of advertising in India during the 1980s" (1989: 76-77). Another study referring to the effects of television advertising states that, "Doctors who work in villages of Mexico report that it is not uncommon... For a family to sell the few eggs and chickens it raises to buy a Coke for the family while the children suffer from lack of protein" (Vilanilam, 1989: 490). Our data reveals that as much as 94 per cent of the respondents watch advertisements on Television (Table 4.12). However, those who watch advertisements are not really interested to watch but they do not have any choice, as they are forced to do so, as the advertisements are flicking in between serials. In other words the general mass is trapped in the advertising network and the myth and glamour associated with it. Besides, this way the advertising industry shaped the taste of the viewers and creates a kind of consumer mass culture.

Table 4.13: Social Impact of Advertisements on Respondents

	Responses		
	Nos.	Per cent	Per cent of Cases
Leads to status competition	160	11.9	53.3
Promote Consumerısm and Profit	233	17.3	77.7
Reinforces gender roles	89	6.6	29.7
Glamorizes life	188	14.0	62.7
Promote unnecessary wants	156	11.6	52.0
Forcibly set the taste	91	6.8	30.3
Portray women as sexual objects	130	9.7	43.3
Humorous and entertaining	181	13.4	60.3
Enables to watch celebrities	119	8.8	39.7
Total	1347	100.0	449.0

The above Table 4.13 shows that a considerable number of the respondents also said that they get information on new and latest products through advertisements. Manufacturers reinforce the desire for existing products and television is the medium which helps to introduce and perpetuate new brands and products as well as services to the consumers. Television as mentioned earlier attracts a large chunk of advertising overtaking even print media over the last decades. The best part of the electronic medium is that it reaches to a widespread audience in the rural hinter land, urban slums and also the elites of the society; at the same time its hypnotizing power, despite with the heterogeneity of its viewers and literacy barrier, through different channels and programmes. Advertising is an excellent medium for repetitive and recalling of products, as the selling products need demonstration and attributes (characters) are visually displayable on the screen. Television acts as a mass and heterogeneous medium in every sense of the word. Television advertisements successfully reinforce the consumerism on the respondents. Market economy has harnessed the medium economy between the producers and consumers. Advertising on television is used to maintain the economic system which creates a demand among consumers for excellent services, status, lifestyles and other fashionable commodities. Advertisements couple with programmes to attract and capture a number of viewers, which pervasively promotes and forces the viewers to watch along with the regular programmes. While the international norm is five minute of advertising for thirty minute of programming, it is very normal for

Indian channels that stretch advertising seconds for popular programmes.

An analysis of advertising time and serial time for the two popular serials (Balika Vadhu and Bandini) reveals that in half an hour of the serial time the advertising time is between eight to ten minutes distributed over three to four brakes showing about 20-22 advertisements. Out of these 15-17 are of consumer products or services while the rest are of regarding the other programmes and serials telecasted on the channel. Some advertisements are of the new Television serials which are to be telecasted in the coming days. Majority of the advertisements shown in the brake during these serials are of consumer non-durable household products such as washing powder, toothpaste, mosquito repellent, soap, toilet cleaners, cosmetic products, health drinks, shampoo, hair oil, fairness creams, etc. while the other advertisements displayed are of suiting, wall paints, and electronics such as Television, refrigerator, washing machine, mobile phones and even their services. Women are not featured in all advertisements like in tooth paste, soaps, mosquito repellents, etc. Significantly advertisements of most consumer durables feature women as consumers of the products, mothers, housewives, daughters, and so on. And the rest few advertisements show women as sex symbol where the woman does not use the product, but it adds glamour to the product. Many celebrities advertise for diamond and gold jewellery, only to raise and attract the consumers. Thus, we can say that advertisement target women as consumers and also as housewives and mothers who are prime users of products of consumer goods as well as services. Many respondents in our study have also said that they watch advertisements because they are entertaining and humorous (60.3%). While (39.7%) of them watch the advertisements for the sake of celebrities like film stars, cricketers, and Television stars respectively. The media strategy is to position advertisements with celebrities with those programmes which feature the same celebrities whether it may be cricket match, film or serial. We developed a composite index on consumerism as promoted through the advertisements and noted the opinion of the women on the following issues namely (Table 4.13). Advertisements on Television "promote consumerism and profit", "unnecessary wants," "status competition", portray women as "sexual objects" and "glamorizes life" respectively (Table 13).

Table 4.14: Advertisements Promote Patriarchy as Reflected in Insurance Policy Advertisements across Gender

Gender	*Promote Patriarchy*		
	Yes	*No*	*Total*
Male	111 (76.6%)	34 (23.4%)	145 (100.0%)
Female	110 (77.5%)	32 (22.5%)	142 (100.0%)
Total	221 (77.0%)	66 (23.0%)	287 (100.0%)

As per our study the vast difference in the opinions of the respondents belonging from the different educational segments of the society, we found and observed that students across educational fields are aware of the impact of television advertisements and its effects. One question which was asked during the interview schedule that do they find advertisements promoting patriarchy as reflected in insurance policy advertisements. We had a combined opinion of the respondents. The question was further interpreted with the variable of education. Taking particularly insurance policy advertisements on television majority of the respondents agreed to the fact and accepted that insurance policy advertisements do reflect patriarchy, as mainly men are portrayed as main breadwinner of the family as their depiction in insurance advertisements is more compared to women. This shows less important of women in the family as well as society by showing them submissive and subtle. It needs to be mentioned that students from English medium College 139 (73.2%) respondents believed to the fact that advertisements promote patriarchy and 72 (83.7%) from Gujarati medium also agreed to the fact. The difference op opinions between the two Colleges can be easily understand as per their medium of education plays a vital role in their upbringing and socialization with regard to exposure of thinking wide. Our field experiences show that the respondents from S.P.B. College and VNSG University which is English medium have a broad exposure of thinking and wide vision as they all were aware of the existing patriarchy in the Television serials, advertisements and even society. On the contrary Gujarati medium respondents belonging from the Olpad College are also aware of the fact but they have digested the system and adapted the patrilineal and patrilocal system. We bifurcated them gender wise, male respondents were more conscious than the female respondents. They too agree to the fact that general public is trapped in the patriarchal system prevalent in the society.

We found that students across economic lines are aware of the impact of Television advertisements and its effects. They too agree to the fact that advertisements on Television promote consumerism and profit, unnecessary wants, which leads to status competition and glamorizes lifestyles. They even agree (43.3%) that women in advertisements are portrayed as sex symbols and are just used for marketing purposes (Table 4.14). As we all are aware that women take up the responsibility of buying goods and services for the family and this is across economic categories and educational levels and this initiates consumerism and becomes further emphasized when images of women in advertisements depicting as a "satisfied consumer" who fulfills the needs of her family as appear on television screen.

Table 4.15: Stereotyping of Women by Media

Medium of Instruction	*Whether or not media stereotypes women*		
	Yes	*No*	*Total*
English	147 (76.2%)	46 (23.8%)	193 (100.0%)
Gujarati	70 (76.9%)	21 (23.1%)	91 (100.0%)
Total	217 (76.4%)	67 (23.6%)	284 (100.0%)

Table 4.16: Stereotyping of Women by Media: Perception according to Gender

Gender	*Whether or not media stereotypes women*		
	Yes	*No*	*Total*
Male	97 (64.7%)	53 (35.3%)	150 (100.0%)
Female	127 (87.6%)	18 (12.4%)	145 (100.0%)
Total	224 (75.9%)	71 (24.1%)	295 (100.0%)

Advertisements and Gender Stereotypes

We tried to understand the gender concerns *vis-à-vis* the market forces in our sample of study broadly based on two views such as 'Advertisements on Television portray women as sexual objects' and 'Advertisements on Television reinforce gender roles.' Thus, we found that students across all economic categories hold that patriarchal value system is packaged in advertisements. Not surprisingly the students from urban are more aware of patriarchal implications and consumerism portrayed through television advertisements than from their counterparts of rural area. The rural area students are the least aware and the university students are between the two as this is an equal combination of rural and urban students. Thus, the urban college students (S.P.B. English Medium College) stand out as the most aware group on gender perception and consumerism in advertisements. This is due to higher exposure and educational level of their families and also corresponding economic status that eventually results in higher degree of awareness. Statistical analysis reveals that this difference in the perception and conceptualization of the respondents in the sample reflects real differences in the population.

As mentioned Television is the wholesale distributor of images as it contributes to popular culture. It also brings into homes images and messages that once were restricted to certain age group or relationships. Hence, the college students are exposed to the struggles, joys, and conflicts, patterns of behaviour of men and women and their reflection.

Thus, it can be mentioned that they learn without much effort and at early age what took many years for their parents to learn.

Table 4.17: Media Stereotypes Restrict Progress and Control Women

Gender	*Whether or not stereotypes restrict progress and control women*		
	Yes	*No*	*Total*
Male	83 (55.3%)	67 (44.7%)	150 (100.0%)
Female	90 (62.9%)	53 (37.1%)	143 (100.0%)
Total	173 (59.0%)	120 (41.0%)	293 (100.0%)

Be that as it may there are many positive aspects of Television as it also promotes of desirable social behaviour, such as sharing, mannerisms, co-operation, ethical values, cultural experiences, sexual understanding, etc. However, constant exposure of advertisements that portray masculine and feminine stereotypes directly influences role expectation. Such socially learned gender roles form attitudes and become the guide to behaviour patterns in society. Since, advertising is so pervasive, people absorb its messages without necessarily analyzing its hidden meanings. As said earlier advertisers target all sections of society and with regard to our study they reach out to college students i.e. consumers successfully cultivate a favourable attitude towards their brands and products. Further, the advertisers hope that such a favourable attitude could be converted into profit once these students and children grow up as the consumers (i.e. students) acquainted well to decide on the brands and products the family purchases, which is a direct influence of advertising. Television has been a subject of discussion ever since it was introduced in India as an experimenting educational service in 1959. Students across language, educational background, economic status and local inhabitants watch almost the same serials and the same advertisements on Television and the duration of viewing is also the same averaging around two hours a day and we tried to understand the perception of the values reflected in the serials they watched in our research. Accordingly, we have tried to understand the reinforcement of patriarchal value system through the popular family serials i.e. Balika Vadhu and Bandini shown on the general entertainment channels.

One interesting question which was asked to the respondents that do they feel that stereotypes restrict progress and control women; the answer to this question was a little shocking as 130 female respondents (86%) did not accept to the fact that stereotypes restrict women from progress whereas 75 male respondents (50%) agreed to the fact. Empowerment has brought a vast advancement in women by struggling through several years and fighting for their justice, women have now learnt to overcome hurdles. So it is interesting to note that the female respondents that they are positive and ready to face challenges coming in their path. We have cross tabulated the question with medium of instruction to get an opinion of how medium plays a role in shaping and moulding their views and thoughts. But we found a similar ratio related to the fact of stereotypes restricting progress. Our data reveals 108 (55.7%) respondents from English medium and 57 (64.8%) respondents from Gujarati medium agreed to the fact.

We observed that characters of married women are portrayed in a similar flamboyance, pretentious, extravagant and easily recognizable fashion in the serials. They carry all the external appearance of marital status, i.e. central parting of hair with 'sindoor' in a neatly tied up bun, all jewellery and ornaments that represent a married woman in Hindu culture, 'mangalsutra', earrings, toe rings, necklace, a systematic wrapped sari and neat and clean attitude and appearance. Married women usually carry a heavy and fashionable style of apparel. Most of the married women in the serials are housewives performing domestic works and apparently do not earn financially. Their prime and sole responsibility is domestic household chores, while the men of the family look after the external world i.e. business and earning money. On rare occasions they are shown as working outside through negative character and not the central character. And in any circumstance if the protagonist does pay labour it is because she is forced by certain situations to do so.

Table 4.18: Television Serials (Balika Vadhu and Bandini) and men's Dominance

Gender	*Do you agree as men's dominance in the serials*		
	Yes	*No*	*Total*
Male	90 (61.6%)	56 (38.4%)	146 (100.0%)
Female	116 (78.4%)	32 (21.6%)	148 (100.0%)
Total	206 (70.1%)	88 (29.9%)	294 (100.0%)

Women depicted in Television serials are always shown contended being housewives as they never show their frustration or regret. Apparently, in order to show appearance of her external modernity and boldness she drives a car, speaks English occasionally, fights for her rights, etc. but she remains a typical Indian woman "Bhartiya Nari", submissive and secondary to her husband. Reinforcement of patriarchal value system is reflected generally more in the Television serials specifying their code for married women, emphasis on rituals, household unity, depiction of women as secondary individuals and sexual objects, importance of joint family, etc. which are all characteristics perceived and accepted as a universal truth by all the respondents in our study across the educational medium of instruction i.e. Gujarati and English respectively.

Our study indicates that 140 (72.2%) respondents from the English medium and 56 (62.9%) agreed and accepted the reinforcement of patriarchal value system reflected in Television serials. As patriarchy is deep-rooted in our society it is very difficult to eradicate it, but only education is a medium which helps to make their view and vision broader and wider to enhance equality in the society. This we can say from our study which clearly distinguishes the fact that education uplifts not only a person but also its views, thoughts and standard of living. According to our study we can understand that even age plays an important part to manifest the society. This we can say by the difference in the mindsets of the respondents from under graduate section and post graduate department. As mentioned earlier that as students proceed from graduation level i.e. college to PG departments their mindsets and thoughts also broadens and upgrades in their actions. The respondents from the VNSGU University were far more matured and open-minded than rest of the two College respondents i.e. SPB and Olpad College. When the question arises of equality and patrilocal value system VNSGU respondents showed more concern related to the issue of women degradation and submissiveness compared to male domination.

Table 4.19: Impact of Television Serials on the Respondents

	Responses		
	Nos.	*Per cent*	*Per cent of Cases*
Household Unity	122	21.9	48.2
Culture code for married woman	87	15.6	34.4
Emphasis on rituals	76	13.6	30.0
Depiction of women as sexual objects	79	14.2	31.2
Depiction of women as secondary individuals	66	11.8	26.1
Serials help to handle interpersonal relations	127	22.8	50.2
Total	557	100.0	220.2

Gender Inequalities in the serials is felt more by the respondents of rural area college (Olpad) as compared to urban area college (SPB) and the VNSGU university students. This clear difference across classes in the perception of gender equality as reflected in Television serials also reveals different levels of perception based on exposure, economic and educational status. As much as 90 per cent of the respondents from SPB and VNSGU opine that, 'women should fight against the injustice and similarly a large group believed that career is important for women to lead an independent life. Awareness regarding future planning was also found amongst the Olpad college students but they had to face a lot of personal and family problems. Due to lack of education and ignorance their parents do not allow especially girls to study more and earn to be independent. These students (rural-Olpad) they believe that they belong to an economically sound family so they need not worry for their future. Our study shows that SPB and VNSGU students were more career-oriented compared to Olpad and has a strong impact on the awareness regarding gender equality. The respondents from the Olpad college i.e. girls are more aware of the need for women to fight for justice as portrayed in Television serials. While for SPB College and (VNSGU) University students earning money, achieving success through education and to be independent are very essential for their lives. The respondents from the (VNSGU) University belong to a mixed category of working, business and service group. Therefore, for them acquiring education and success take top priority as well as a necessity. All these factors make them more aware of the need to fight for justice and that they try to locate their aspiration on television. The respondents from the service category who are more educated to a large extent feel that women must fight for the justice compared to the respondents from the business category. On the other side respondents from the business category have internalized their fashion, beauty and luxurious life so much that they do not think that career is important for women.

In our empirical analysis we tried to evaluate the level of perception of women on patriarchy and its implications on women through Television serials and advertisements. We looked patriarchy broadly as the economic and sexual control of women by men. Thus patriarchy is the control of men over women's domestic and paid labour, their fertility and their sexuality

Patriarchy upholds men by giving them the power and authority differentiating the women by allotting secondary position. Patriarchy reinforces the gender division of labour and control of their fertility and their sexuality through the institution of society called 'marriage'. The data show that female respondents across economic categories legitimizes' patriarchal value system and do not raise their voices as patriarchy is deep rooted within the society the women have accepted women's subordination to men. However, there was a silver lining that the new generation is becoming conscious and only supports certain dimensions of patriarchy and not entirely. For instance the respondents in the present sample do not entirely agree with the total perceptions like control of women's labour, men have more power in sexual relationships than women, child care is women's work, women should support men, main breadwinner of the family is men etc. Majority of the female respondents did not agreed and accepted the patriarchal value system totally by showing liberal views on aspects related to the position of women in society. This we can hold because of the argument of the topic the female respondents stated that women may have extra marital affair under certain circumstances. Whereas all the male respondents did not agree to the point and further argued that only men can have extra marital affair but women should not. The male respondents believed that all this Television serials and programmes should be banned as they create a nuisance in the society. They felt that it spoils all women including their mother, sister and girl friends. They even denied about the gender difference as male respondents believed that nowhere in the world a single space or field is left where women held behind men. They accepted that working women are stepping one step ahead than men in all the spheres of the society. The differences in the perception males across economic categories on the manifestation of patriarchy can be extended to their own education, locality and environment they stay. Thus, male respondents from Olpad College had very rigid and typical view against women. As they have the narrow thinking and pathetic nature and environment which plays a critical role in developing their mentality. The data lead us to conclude that women believe in the value of their labour and do not perceive that it is in any way less compared to men's labour. The opening avenues in the field of education and employment to women and the rise of women in varied professions has brought the awareness in their economic potential and the value of their labour. We may argue that on the whole somewhere media has contributed in raising social consciousness especially in this context the electronic medium's vital role.

Table 4.20: Perception of Serials and its Impacts on Women's Lifestyle and Social Context

Medium of Education	*Do serials impacts women's lifestyle and social context*		
	Yes	*No*	*Total*
English	140 (72.2%)	54 (27.8%)	194 (100.0%)
Gujarati	60 (65.2%)	32 (34.8%)	92 (100.0%)
Total	200 (69.9%)	86 (30.1%)	286 (100.0%)

Table 4.21: Impact of Serials on Women's Lifestyle and Social Context across Gender

Gender	*Do serials such as Balika Vadhu and Bandini have impacts Women's Lifestyle and social context?*		
	Yes	*No*	*Total*
Male	109 (73.6%)	39 (26.4%)	148 (100.0%)
Female	98 (65.8%)	51 (34.2%)	149 (100.0%)
Total	207 (69.7%)	90 (30.3%)	297 (100.0%)

An analysis of the perception of women across under-graduates and post-graduates regarding patriarchal value system existing in the present economic era depicts that the respondents with higher education i.e. post-graduates are more understanding and can easily point out critical views. Except the respondents from comparative study the students from the other departments hailing under university are more aware of the oppression of women in society compared to respondents of graduation i.e. S.P.B. College and Olpad College. Our study reveals that the impact of serials on women's lifestyle is far more observed on under graduates from the university. As per study we even observed that age is an important factor in creating and building awareness amongst the youngsters. Our study depicts no noticeable difference in the perception of women's role as consumer and their secondary role across graduates and post-graduate levels. This helps us to understand the degree of internalization of patriarchal system and its impact amongst the respondents despite economic and different educational backgrounds. From the above discussion we can hold that the role of patriarchy in capitalism is strong, especially regard to women it restricts through various means and mass-media particularly television as a whole.

In the analysis of relationship between the perception of television and patriarchal value system, it was observed that all respondents irrespective of the kind of programmes they watch legitimize the patriarchal value system. However, it is noticed that respondents who view news and serials and other channels too, do not accept patriarchy totally. Not surprisingly respondents who view only serials score higher on the perception of patriarchy stressing stronger patriarchal values. From this we can conclude the impact of Television on the present generation and society. To rewind the above findings we hold that there exists a strong socio-economic impact of television on women and society at large. Indeed television scores the highest rank in preference than newspaper, magazines and radio. The newspaper and magazines have fewer readerships compared to Television as generally women and college students read often headlines and the supplements only and not the entire newspaper. Introduction of new Radio stations and Radio jockeys, radio has also clutch its new listeners; but radio as a medium gets much lesser preference over the electronic media. Since, Television sets came into homes it has overtakes even radio. Television requires little effort when compared to read a book or listen to a radio. To enable audiences to understand quickly what is going on in narratives, television script writers use very conventional, stereotyped characters and storylines. So even if a couple of episodes are missed by the viewers the story would not have progressed that far. Watching television is a pervasive experience, as one simply sits and watches. Also television is very formulaic and avoids challenging material as it requires a minimum amount of effort by viewers to watch and entertain themselves. The roles women are given in television dramas and serials and the way they are portrayed in television commercials exploit their sexuality, use them to create sexual excitement and sell products. Even though feminists have criticized the roles women are given in serials and the way Television exploits female sexuality, there has been little improvement. Women are not portrayed in realistic ways; generally speaking the focus is on their bodies and not on their minds, characters or personalities. The general entertainment channels are the favourite channels, whether news or niche channels and the family serials are the most popular. We noticed that even during the discussions regarding Television programmes and serials respondents discuss the story, actions and the appearance of the characters in the serials. The medium has a diverting and pervasive impact on consumerism on society and it is observed that respondents in our study have accepted as the prime responsibility of buying goods and services for the household. Majority of the advertisements target women as consumers of products as discussed earlier and show them using highest users of the products. All these eventually reveal that even advertisements on Television have a deep and strong impact of consumerism on the viewers through the medium of television.

To recapitulate the foregoing analysis, we have two popular serials as our sample with high TRP rates to examine the gender stereotypes through mass-media. We have tried to cross tabulate the patriarchal value system with different variables such as area, education and gender. We noticed that the higher educational level brings more awareness amongst the respondents, as Post Graduate students in the University system (VNSGU) are more conscious then the under graduate students in the college (SPB and OLPAD Colleges) respectively. Our study also reveals a correlation between viewing of television programmes and the level of awareness of the patriarchal value system. Thus, we submit that the impact of television serials and advertisements on the students in the era of globalization is strong and powerful in general and the mass-media (Television) in particular a tool of legal and justifiable of capitalism and consumerism at large.

As mentioned the media have been a vital conduit contributing to a radical reshaping of the profile of stereotypes. However, the problem persists as the dimensions of racism, casteism, and class and gender bias have become more subtle and pervasive. While appearing to adopt feminist perspectives, the media seem to have failed to take on the more radical critiques of how society supports and perpetuates gender stereotypes. Instead the media reproduces stereotypes from social structure generating new dimensions and problems in the society and it would be simply wrong to blame media. Nonetheless, the media only are reflecting popular assumptions I have highlighted the way in which media reflects and its implications and how the society enhances and perceives in their daily lives. In this chapter we have tried to present overall picture of media on gender stereotypes and patriarchy and its reproduction in the society.

We believe that there is considerable wisdom in the collection of data and findings about where women are today in their relationship with both traditional and new media. Meanwhile, we tried to present a fair analysis, but sometimes failed due to lack of proper understanding of the researcher as well as the respondents. We live in a mediated world, but scrutinized through a gendered lens, the picture is perhaps a little clearer and perhaps a little more hopeful.

5

Conclusion

In the present research, we made an attempt to understand the complexities of women, culture and mass-media from a larger 'perspective in the context of capitalism today'.

Communication amongst the society is a fundamental part of human civilizations. According to Harold Lasswell any act of communication whether face-to-face or mediated can be dissected into five processes that require separate methods of analysis is shown below:

WHO	Control Analysis
↓	
Says What	Content Analysis
↓	
In which channel	Media Analysis
↓	
To Whom	Audience Analysis
↓	
With what effect	Effect Analysis

Lasswell's chain of communication (cited in Key themes in Media theory by Dan Laughey pp. 9, 2007).

Returning of Lasswell's chain of communication it is clear as to how propaganda plays a vital function when its correspondence with different parts of a society is able to affect human behaviour and action. Effective propaganda can therefore provide a powerful stimulus for a targeted response and can enable recruitment of civilians who will fight for the cause. Propaganda in communication is considered a specialist and vital function in modern societies.

Communication is now aided by new and modern technologies. Telecommunication and mass-media technology is controlled by multinational global conglomerates. The inventories of printing press by Johann Gutenburg brought a drastic evolution in media. Printing of the Bible reinforced marketism. We can say that mid 19th century brought a revolution in social theory influencing the theorization of media. Media's new revolution declined the dissolution of traditional forms of social relationship and scattering of humans. This created on adverse effect on the new invented processes such as industrialization, urbanization, democracy and the emergence of contemporary forms of mass communications. The initial world wars enhanced that mass-media had brainwashed the people. Hence, mass-media stands as the powerful propaganda agencies brain washing a vulnerable and defenseless public. Indeed, this proves that media is a powerful tool of propaganda and there is no doubt regarding it.

Mass-media did not have an overwhelming influence between the late 1940s and 1960s. It had to a limited extent. This we became aware through various empirical studies on selection of exposure, uses of studies, opinion of the leaders, thesis etc. The main influence on media research was found during the 1970s Marxist and neo-marxist traditions. These theories proved and enhanced that media was the sole agency in maintaining class dominations through reinforcement of dominant social norms and values to legitimize the social system.

In this context Frankfurt school, started the mass society critique. Marcuss and Adorno's critique of culture industry was the first Marxist attempt, to engage theoretically with media, Athusser was influenced by structuralism and so on.

Accordingly, the sociological and anthropological research explored the use of media in development and theorized that it played an important role in breaking down traditional values considered inimical to development in increasing industrialization and the process of modernization (Learner, 1958 and Schramm, 1964). This empirical administrative research resulted in transplantation of western concept of development and technology (and subsequently the liberal plural media system) to the third world economies under the guise of modernization like green revolution in India (Roger, 1962). Hence, we can conclude that mass communication has been drawn from many social science principles consisting anthropology, sociology, economics, political science, psychology, and even social psychology.

In the 1980s, the emergence of globalization in the market brought a radical change in the organization of production. Before this the needs of the people were given prime importance and market used to produce the related materials, whereas the invention of globalization changed the market strategy leading to far reaching changes in inter-related section of mass-media, telecommunications and information technology too came under its domain. The info-communication sector divided between telecommunication (46%) computers (33%), and the media (only films and broadcasting 21%) by 1994 became an enormous part of global economy with an output valued at $1.5 trillion (Inter-national, Telecommunication Union, 1995: 10). The global media market was valued at 766.57 $ billion in 2001 while the media in India generated approximately Rs. 246 billion in 2003 (Kohli, 2003:4-6). The initiators and amalgamators amongst the global media enterprises that followed in the last decade led to an oligopoly in the global communication sector which proclaims and circulates capitalist ideology to strengthen the globalization.

Relatively to production sector, the socio-political and cultural institutions which are a part of mass-media and has its base in economic structures consisting modes of production at given point of time. As a result, the dominant class created its various institutions to control conflicts that arose with the class division. According to Charles Darwin's theory "Survival of the fittest" and "Struggle for existence" relates here relatively to exist and surviving over the centuries. The dominant class has always oppressed a section of humanity whether of a particular race, class, caste or gender. For existence, the dominant class uses the power of the state by perpetuating the capitalist mode of production through material and ideological means. The dominant class involves a massive political indoctrination, propaganda authorization, legitimization and building up of consciousness. Forces of production and distribution of ideas has been controlled by the dominant class. This class is dispersed worldwide and control's thinking of the general (consumer) class. Because of all these factors easy acceptance of a capitalist social order and its value has increased. This fact certifies one pattern of life i.e. owners of means are the dominant class which dominates the consumer. Even Karl Marx have accepted and highlighted in his theory that society has been divided into two classes i.e. the ruling class and the ruled class. Religion, caste, family and education system are the prominent tools for the principles domination while mass communication media have been added to this stockpile of ideological control and its influences which falls under capitalism.

The mass-media especially television which is the dominant medium globally, in several ways enhances and propagates an ideology which leads to capitalism. In the present study we have attempted to understand the impact of electronic media i.e. television serials and advertisements on college students.

Globally and nationally women have made a landmark in proving their labour power. This has resulted through women's struggle which has ultimately changed the social spectrum. However, no one can deny the persistence of oppression, exploitation and inequalities of women. Females have constituted two-thirds of total world's labour, but they receive only the one-third of the world's income. Gender inequalities have become an integral part of social organization.

Due to unequal socio-economic distribution in India, position of women varies, considerably from rural to urban areas among different classes among different religious, ethnic and caste groups. There is a huge division and infinite variations in the status of women according to the culture, family structure, caste and class. In the past few decades positions of women particularly in urban areas, in upper middle class and in dominant castes has changed positively. These women are excelling in education institutions, and in various professions at par with men.

Occupation like politics, military, law, bureaucracy, law enforcement, and arts are some areas where woman has marked her visible appearance. On the other side there are women who are socially and economically marginalized. Backwardness of women is reflected through poor literacy rate, female feoticide, skewed sex ratio, etc. There are various areas where women work for long hours and are found least paid. In addition to this she bears the full responsibility of her home which is unpaid labour for her. There is a growing incidences of violence against women i.e. neglect of the girl child, eve-teasing, rape, domestic violence, dowry death, prostitution and so on. Oppression of women can be sighted back in our history which has its foundation where male used to own private property that finally resulted in class society. Men have controlled women's sexuality even in savagery and barbarian stages. This oppression finally leads to women's secondary positions, her control of labour which was always in interest of male resulting in patriarchal value system. Patriarchy has been used by class societies and capitalism in their own interest to survive and perpetuate itself across time and space. Family and monogamous marriage are the institutions which reproduces the labour power. The wife performs domestic labour for free which ultimately serves capital. Biological reproduction is also one of the major factor which leads labour power, and this is controlled and initiated in the social formation. Through the patriarchal value system, whether it is private or public sphere the domination of patriarchal system is noticed. The relations of production that are of subordinations and domination are also reproduced at the workplace and the family. The patriarchal system includes control of women and their very selves i.e. their labour power and hence their sexuality and even fertility. Norms indicate a patrilocal, patrilineal and monagomous family where women are submissive to men, and therefore woman's labour is not regarded a social labour but meant only for one man and his family. Society disseminates and reinforces this ideology through religion, educational system and family and now through mass-media. The mass-media especially televisions through television serials and advertisements glorifies, reinforces and portrays the patriarchal family institution. The portrayal of woman as mother, housewife, nurturer and caregiver is not treated equally but as subordinate to the male in his and his family interest.

As mentioned earlier in the current period capitalism has found a powerful tool in mass-media, especially television, its serials and advertisements, for enhancing and reinforcing patriarchal value system and even reinforcement of gender disparities.

Patriarchy reflects the control of women's fertility and thus sexuality manifests as the exploitation of her body by the male for personal or commercial gain. Whether it is advertising, television, film or pornographic industry media commodifies woman's today to provide entertainment and pleasure to the male viewer. Degradation of the female body and degeneration of the idea of aesthetics media encourage of beauty pageants, fashion shows, model hunts, item songs in films, music albums and so on have contributed lot pornography. Besides these also depict woman as a source of pleasure to male and not as an individual or a human being thus reinforcing objectification of women and her non-empowerment.

Meanwhile, in the present research we observed that in television the family portrayed in the top ranked serials like "Balika Vadhu" and "Bandini" reveal that the institution is a male construct while female leading character families are absent; she either has a single widowed parent or is brought up by her relatives like grandmother or aunt. She leaves her maternal family behind when she gets married. Woman does not have a universe of her own and hence is termed and defined her husband's family. These serials are found to be the most popular across socio-economic categories and the popularity of these serials reveals that women residing from different backgrounds at some level enjoy the serials which apparently fulfil their emotional and psychological needs. The women characters are depicted as bold, taking independent decisions in the family and fighting for injustice against them. The problems faced by the women are tackled realistically and familial which each women can identify with it. The storyline deeply reveals that women are projected as doing this as part of their responsibility as they like to be considered 'good and ideal' wife and daughter-in-law to safeguard family honour, values and tradition. Research by the Center for Advocacy and Research (CFAR) indicates that much of the popularity of the serials comes from the manner in which the family is constructed (Center for Advocacy and Research, 2003). The plots of the serials reinforce and reflect the patriarchal (traditional) norms and women in the serials are the receptacle and the guardian of this value system. Their job is shown safeguarding patriarchal value system in the face of change and modernity. Women performing celebrations of rituals and festivals like *Karva Chauth*, and *Vat Savitri*, culture code, submissive role, economic dependence on the male and so on safeguard the patriarchal value system in the television serials. The women characters in the television serials speak English, drive cars, move independently, wear latest fashion and jewellery which proves to be apparently modern. Women characters do job for financial reasons and the few positive characters that are ("Jyoti of Jyoti") are exceptions (Ridhini of Dil Mil Gaye) Birwa of 'Bandhini'. In spite of the modern story lines and contemporary situations, the representation and roles allotted to the women are restricted to the particular area i.e. households and family following the paradigm of patriarchy.

Since 1990's the women have become an inseparable part of television serials both as consumers and as protagonists of television fiction, especially daily soaps which gets the highest ratings. Our data reveal a very high percentage of regular women viewers than men. It is reported that (10%) of television advertising revenue target women directly and prime television is dominated by women-oriented family soaps (Krishnamurthy, 2003).

In marketing of television serials and creative planning women play a very important category. Televisions holds a very strong potentials which cannot be underestimated, as it has become a dominant medium in India and even other parts of the world. There are 80 million sets (half of them cable connected), attracting 48 per cent of advertising and subsequently earning 41 per cent of the entire media revenue in 2002, has more than 200 channels and is in the forefront in both information and entertainment (Kohli, 2003). One television set placed in the living room offers varied combination of entertainment, education on information, which cannot be offered by any other medium such as radio, film, magazine or newspaper. The television includes vivid programmes such as films, music, serials of all kinds, animation, religious programmes, cartoon programmes for children, wildlife, natural history programmes, news and current affairs, programmes for women, sports, reality television, talk shows and so on. Television is a multi-purpose electronic box which has the other something for every one. Just by clicking one button a person has its comforts at home and with wide range of alternatives at one time monthly payment of between Rs. 120 to 300 to the cable operator and very nominal cost of electricity. Compared to movies in theatre, circus shows, dramas and stage shows television is a cheaper alternative to other entertainment packages. Television holds the leading position amongst the electronic medium i.e. colours, lively moving images, drama and fast paced editing intermixed with attractive advertisements. Television as compared to other medium has won successfully in maintaining and sharing audience views and opinion through live shows, game and music talent shows and so on. Private owned channels, and state channels get millions of responses to their contests on the subsidized Indian Postal Department, SMS, emails, etc. Thus, through live shows even the mobile companies reap huge profits and this potentiality of television has been exploited by capitalism to propagate its ideology. Television mesmerizes viewers and unconsciously cultivates a passive acceptance in them, which is meant to be extended at the workplace and in the public sphere. The medium hypnotizes viewers into not discussing anything beyond the most childish and extravagant, fashion or story of serials and soaps.

Television serials project largely one community i.e., Hindu, North Indian, upper caste and dominant group generally depicting business as profession while other professions, classes, religions, communities are absent on the screen. Televisions fails to show working class, vast cultural diversity of India; which consists marginalized sections, various communities, the rural population, farmers and tribals in the serials. Gujarati, Punjabi, Marwari or Bengali are some of the trading communities are depicted in the televisions serials. Many communities from South are absent on the national entertainment channels. Apart from these regional channels like Malayalam, Telegu, Tamil, Kannada, etc. have a vast viewership in the respective states and their serials fall in the same direction of dominant class. Television successfully projects a uni-marginal hegemonic picture of society where only dominant class and dominant culture exist. Thus, it is very essential to study women's issues from the current socio-political and market economy. Thus, globalizations is used as economic integrations of the nations to compete in the world market, sharing of informations, technology transfer and this is done with the help and usage of expanding media and satellite communication. Thus, in 1980's the capitalist countries initiated a project to overcome the depression in the economics and termed its as "globalization". In this regard, they conceived Structural Adjustment Programme (SAP), International Monetary Fund (IMF) and World Bank to encourage open trades with their markets and investments from West. This resulted in encouragement of the entry of foreign capital into each sector, privatization of industry and forced the state to disinvest in the public sector, which ultimately lead to broadening of women's oppression. For example, agriculture traditionally has been the mainstay for women's employment and 80 per cent of women workers are employed in this sector. The programmes have replaced women's control over this employment by shifting the focus from food to cash crops. In each section whether it may lie multinational corporations, privatization of water and forest resources and removal of agricultural products has enhanced the exploitation of women. As this lead to decrease in rural income women's condition became victims of malnutrition and related disorders because of eating last and left over food and reductions of nutritional intake. New Economic policy has increased women's marginalization as they are the first to go when exit policy and voluntary retirement schemes are implemented by the organized sector under liberalization. The media has rarely focused this exploitation of women's contribution to the economy through paid labour or related to domestic labour and lack of her control over per sexuality and fertility.

The most popular on television are soaps, serials and other fiction based entertainment make up the brick of most people's media fare. Television as a medium has a potential to be truly mass-media, has been observed to have a stronger influence than other media, and strongly influences the cultural change. At the outset, we hold that television medium is a ubiquitous phenomenon particularly in urban areas. This is visible from our data that as much as 99 per cent of respondents in both the areas i.e. urban and rural own television sets.

There are more than 250 channels broadcasted on television in India like music, film, religion, sports, health, animation, news and current affairs, wildlife, comedy, cartoon, business and general entertainment channels. The entertainment offers a variety of entertainment of all genres: programmes for children, music, film and film related programmes sports, game and stage shows cookery shows, religious discourses, talk shows, travel shows, programmes for women sitcoms, films, health programmes and serials like detective, horror and supernatural religious, comedy and family serials that may be daily or (4 to 5) days a week. In this genre, the channels are Sony, Star Plus, Sahara Manoranjan, NDTV Imagine, Zee TV. According by Television Rating Indices these channels are among the most popular with the serials on them getting the highest rating. Our data reveals that these channels and the serials on them are the most popular among the respondents. More than 100 channels offered by cable operators in Surat, Colours is the most popular channel watched by 26.33 per cent of the respondents, while NDTV Imagine, and Star Plus are watched by 24 per cent and 13.69 per cent respondents respectively. Rest of the respondents are interested in watching Sab TV, Zee TV and Star One i.e. 20 per cent, 8.35 per cent and 7.67 per cent respectively. Few respondents do watch news channels like NDTV Imagine, Star News and Aaj Tak. The data reveals that the male respondents viewed channels such as Discovery, Bindass, Ten sports, Zee business but in minority. This reveals the strong preference among respondents for these general entertainment channels that have something on offer to everybody. These entertainment channels obviously have an attention grabbing effect on women as they show a marked preference for them rather than other channels.

The respondents perceive the influence of television on society primarily as positive. They view television as a medium that offers information, entertainment and education and as window to the world. This medium opens up new vistas especially to the rural class who have a limited exposure to the world beyond their experience. The rural class has less exposure to the print medium, the world of books and knowledge. Thus, television is their window to the world and also a source of entertainment and information. The urban class is offered television as a source of entertainment as a fantasy and a "good and rich life that they aspire for. Television offers them a variety package of entertainment, education and information that to within the safe boundaries of their home. Even cinema in the theatres does not offer the variety of entertaining fare as cheaply as television does.

Television is a passive medium which demands physical and mental inactivity during the time spent in front of the television set. Increase in aggression levels, use of drugs, increase of obesity, passivity, trauma etc. are some of the effects observed which creates a negative effect on children. This is because of the viewing of distressing scenes both in the news and in the fictional fare. Television brings to children images of war and disaster, divorce and violence, sex and pornography making them a witness to scenes that they would otherwise never see in daily life. The same is true for adults being exposed to images which they would never see in their real life. Thus, constant supply of images and words, oftenly which is disturbing in nature, does not relax or energize but increases stress and tension. In fact, studies reveal that television aggravates anxiety and insomnia.

However, negative effects of the medium are perceived by fewer respondents like having a negative effect on children, affects culture negatively and conditioning reasoning, serials helping to handle interpersonal relations, reducing interaction within the family, etc. (from 49.45 to 36.33% respondents} while many respondents depicted positive effects of the medium (from 85% to 50.66%) which reveals a socio-psycho paralysis in society where the medium has so hypnotized the viewers that it is only viewed in positive terms. None of the female respondents watches education oriented channels like Discovery or National Geographic. A large number of respondents discuss with their husband, friends and neighbours about the acting, storyline or fashion in the serials while only fewer respondents discuss the news or information.

Thus, our study points out the most popular programmes i.e. the daily family serials on Colours, Balika Vadhu (26.66%), and Bandini on NDTV Imagine (22.66%). These are the longest running television serials that will complete the third consecutive year of telecast shortly.

Both the serials depict the lives and times of the Hindu, upper caste and class industrial family that lives in a joint family. The ambience is rich and luxurious lifestyle with palatial bungalows, elite interiors, mobile phones, cars, air travel, men always heavily dressed in suits and '*Kurta-Pyjamas*' and women in silk and heavy jewellery celebrating festivals and rituals with great pomp and show. The atmosphere in the house is cordia as the entire family is a close knit joint family that enjoys living, eating and socializing together, cushioned from the external world whose problems do not exist for the characters. Family unity and integrity is paramount and when whether a family member or an outsider threats or wants to disrupt this that is stopped by the protagonist. The family is apparently patriarchal, monogamous, patrilocal and patrilineal. The protagonist who is depicted as the daughter-in-law of the family defends this family structure, as she does not have any other activity except the safeguarding of the family against any disruptions. Often the negative character is an economically independent woman while few serials show a woman doing paid labour for its own sake. The protagonist in Bandini serial is a housewife whose world revolves around her family, upholding the patriarchal family structure. A conspicuous culture code exists for the married women. Once married the female character adapts sari or Salwar Kameez, the external signs of marriage are mandatory for a 'suhagan' even for the negative character, carrying all its outward signs 'sindoor', a long 'mangalsutra', bangles, earrings, and bright saris. The commonly shown rituals are '*Karva Chauth*' and '*Vat Savitri*' where women fast and pray for the long life of their husbands.

As mentioned earlier women in these serials speak English if needed, are bold, initiate problem-solving take decisions and speak out their minds in the presence of the patriarchy, and appear as strong and confident. They do not wear '*ghoonghat*' (covering the head). In the serial Bandini, the surname Mariyavanshi and the rituals followed suggest that the family belongs to the traditional trading and agricultural landlords from the state of Gujarat. In reality most married women in business families hold a secondary position to men and are subdued in the presence of elders, wear the 'ghoonghat', economically dependent and perform domestic labour while the men handle the family business. In fact, in the two serials mentioned earlier, has a dominant position in the household reinforcing that women's place is in the home. The patriarchal value system in the guise of Indian traditional culture is propagated and reinforced through some women who are projected as bold, modern, initiative taking and decision-making women but remain strictly within the dominant patriarchal system. The popularity of these women and the serials are its to package and appropriate manner of presentation to the female viewers.

Women viewers identify themselves both at the material level and the level of consciousness with the serials and their characters. The women character's clothes, hairstyles, accessories and even makeup on the television set the trend of fashion for the people which the market is ready to thrust on the masses. Thus, the market immediately follows the track which is demanded by the consumers. Thus, Balika Vadhu sarees and Bandini sarees and even hairstyles are spotted by the younger generation irrespective of classes and communities. Initially the fashion trends were followed from the feature films but now television serials and audio/video albums are the ideal trendsetters. Thus, the fashion trend is now extended even in small towns and villages and not to speak in metro cities. Even the college going students both male and female have adopted the latest fashion trends from the media.

As discussed earlier media commodifies women as consumers by creating wants in them and then offer their goods and services to fulfil them. Television serials depict images of the "good and happy life" endorsing a consumer society. Television fiction depicts images of luxurious lifestyles and material wealth, thus endorsing consumerism, and commercialism. Women have adapted the patriarchal norm of being an ideal housewife, mother and daughter-in-law and thus it is used by the advertisers to turn them to consumers of goods and services to fulfil her duty towards her house and society. Women's responsibility is exploited by the media by persuading her that an 'ideal' woman title can be achieved only through the use of products and services advertised on television. Hence, it proves that television is the favourite medium to advertise mass consumed goods and products.

Our data reveal that respondents do not wish to see advertisements on television but are forced to do so due to its flicking in between the serials. Many respondents agreed (12%) that they get information on new products through advertisements. Thus, advertisements remind, generate and reinforce the desire for products to the consumers and manufactures grab this opportunity. Television creates a want of a lavish lifestyle, beauty, status and other wants maintaining the capitalist system. In an half an hour serial advertisements are shown 8-10 minutes distributed over three breaks presenting 22-25 advertisement of consumers' products and services. More than 15 per cent of the advertisements are of consumer household items which feature women as consumers of the products as mothers, housewives and daughter-in-law, etc. Rest of the advertisements i.e. nearly 25 per cent show women as sex symbols where women do not use the product or buy it, but are used to add to the glamour for e.g. the deodorant name 'X-effect for men' where women are presented in Bikinis though the deo is used and marketed for men. Thus, advertisements target women as consumers and also as householders in the family like housewives and mothers, who are prime users of products and therefore depicted in advertisement to present them as contended and satisfied consumers of goods and services. Advertisements are also watched for the entertainment and the humour as revealed by many respondents. Advertisements also depict film stars, cricketers and television stars to attract the audience.

Respondents from the urban area are the most aware group with regard to the impact of television advertisements in promoting consumerism. While the respondents from rural area feel that they have internalized the responsibility for buying goods and services for the family. Consumerism is thus reinforced in women as a contended consumer who fulfils the needs of her family. In our study respondents from all economic categories mentioned that patriarchal value system is packaged in advertisements. Respondents from urban area i.e. S.P.B. College and VNSG University are the most aware group on gender perception and consumerism in advertisements. This could be due to higher education levels combined with economic independence resulting in higher degree of awareness.

Reinforcement of patriarchy is reflected in television serials through depiction of a specific culture code for married woman, depiction of women as secondary individuals as sexual objects, centrality on housewification, etc. The level of the internalization of unequal value system is more in female respondents than male respondents. The men are in the public domain of work (business), while the women are in the private (domestic) world, showing the clear division of labour in our society. The lifestyle, the pattern or job profile, in short life choice of a person is decided by the gender. In the rural area female respondents have internalized the unequal system that they do not perceive gender inequality while urban class are more aware of the gender inequality among the women as reflected in serials. As for majority 90 per cent of the respondents from the S.P.B. College and VNSG University in our sample believe that women should fight against the injustice and the importance of career and education for women to lead an independent life. Awareness regarding planning future was also found amongst the Olpad College (rural) respondents, but they had to face a lot of personal and family problems.

Patriarchy manifests unequal gender relations between men and women both in the family and in every sphere of society where the power and authority lies with the men. Besides, the internalization of secondary position by women reinforcement of gender, division of labour and control of their fertility and sexuality through the institution called marriage lies with the men. As discussed in the empirical chapter, women across economic categories and class legitimize the patriarchal value system and adopted it as a natural phenomenon. They even have internalized patriarchy and its institution endorsement of women's subordination to men. The respondents support certain dimensions of patriarchy and not its entirely. Female respondents from all areas feel that women's labour is not inferior to that of men's and disagree with the stereotyped sexual division of labour in society. They neither accept the submissive secondary position of women nor control of women's sexuality is agreed to them. Many respondents think the decision regarding the number and sex of children should be jointly taken by both the husband and wife. But they definitely agree and feel it is the women's responsibility to buy goods quality goods for the health and hygiene for the family. Women have not only accepted but also internalized their role as consumers. A quick glimpse of the advertisements on television reveals that women are always users, buyers, motivators or influencers in the buying process shown as mother, daughter, sister, etc.

Women have also internalized the patrilineal and patrilocal family structure that prevails in India across castes, communities and religions which is not surprising. In India marriage is an important institution and the ultimate aim of every woman's life. The wedding ceremony includes various rituals no matter the class, caste or community. The marriage institution is glamorised in the media especially in television fiction and feature films with elaborate depiction of the marriage rituals which ultimately leads to reinforcement of the patriarchal marriage institution. Female respondents compared to male show relatively liberal views on women in society.

We conclude from our data that female respondents and some male respondents also believe in the value of their labour and also hold that is in any way less than that of men's labour. Apart from this most of the respondents in our sample favour equal inheritance rights to both the sexes. Some serials depict the ongoing women's struggles and the women's movement which have contributed to the positive perception of women of the value of their labour. Thus, we observe the positive role of media particularly electronic medium and its contribution into the overall social awareness and consciousness.

An analysis of the perception of respondents across educational levels regarding the patriarchal value system prevailing in the present economic system revealed that respondents with high educational qualification point out critical views regarding the oppression of women in society as compared to respondents with lower educational levels. Thus, the respondents from VNSG University were more conscious and aware regarding the suppression of women in society as compared to respondents of S.P.B. College and Olpad College. Accordingly, they do not believe in the lower value accorded to women's labour, oppose sexual division of labour in society and control of women's sexuality by men. Whereas in the case of women's role as consumer and their secondary status is no difference in the perception across educational levels. This clearly points out the degree of internalization of patriarchal system and its pervasiveness among respondents despite different economic and high educational backgrounds. Secondly, this also stresses and signifies the stronghold of patriarchy in capitalism as in other types of modes of production, though capitalism is relatively liberal than other modes. Television is one such tool to reinforce patriarchy in the society.

Cable and satellite television in India has emerged as the dominant medium of this epoch and its impact is ahead of other media. Satellite and cable television systems in the house hold a central place in India without the basic facilities like sanitation, public health system, efficient transportation, etc. As mentioned prior television creates unnecessary wants through advertisements and serials paving the way for the entry of multinational companies. Advertisements promote idealistic images to be aspired by all. Due to its divergent approach, audio-visual effects, graphics, and editing it has acquired (television) a very important place as compared to other media. Our data show that television as a medium is preferred that in all economic categories. Because of this medium patriarchal value system, consumerism and individualism have penetrated in the society. Many respondents believed in the negative impact of medium but they could not point out exactly. This is because a large portion of respondent's perception of this medium is positive.

Finally, we submit that this is only a modest attempt for measuring the impact of media on college students and further investigation is required to understand its complex phenomenon women. Institutionalization of patriarchy through colourful stories has been encouraged by media. In this connection, mass-media is a tool which relates capitalism to enhance consumerism. Because of this, a cultural hegemony of privileged classes over the underprivileged is widespread, thus resulting in submissiveness of the underprivileged classes.

These are only a few findings from the present exercise on many others were discussed in detail both in empirical as well as in conclusion chapters.

Some Significant Findings at a Glance

1. As regard to channel preference of the respondents, we found a huge difference depending upon the area. For instance 30 per cent respondents from Olpad College, 24 per cent from S.P.B. College and 25 per cent from University (VNSGU) preferred Colours Channel. As Olpad College respondents resided in rural area they preferred more to watch daily soap operas as they found connection between their own culture and customs with the television serials. It is revealing to notice from the respondents from the Olpad College that television characters are very familiar and matching to their family members, while S.P.B. College respondents were comparatively less interested in Colours Channel, as they were more interested in reality shows whereas University (VNSGU) includes multi-cultural combination of respondents we had mixed view of perceptions and attitudes.
2. In our empirical analysis we tried to understand the frequency of reinforcement of gender stereotypes which is reflected from the television serials. Majority of the respondents did not believe that the prevalent stereotypes are generated from the television serials. We analyzed this perception area-wise and we found that women were more in number than men who did not believe that the reinforcement of gender stereotypes is created or initiated by media through television serials and advertisements. In our sample 35 (70%) men and 47 (94%) women from S.P.B. College disagreed with the statement of reinforcement of gender stereotypes. Whereas only 15 (30%) men and three (6%) women were in favour. Thus, it is not a surprise that 39 (78%) men and 40 (80%) women

from Olpad College were not in favour of the assumption while only 11 (22%) men and 10 (20%) women agreed with it. Similarly, 40 (80%) men and 31 (62%) women from the University (VNSGU) disagreed with the assumption of gender reinforcement, while 10 (20%) men and 19 (38%) women agreed.

3. The patriarchal mindset subordinates women from birth till their entire life cycle is internalized by women as well as men equally. This process begins from the earliest childhood through socialization process and then reinforced through cultural, social, and economic arrangements in the society. Women in our study sample serials do not enjoy equal status and do not have decision-making powers. The family upholds the gender contract based on limiting women's decision-making as their husband, in-laws and other elders do not allow the women's participation while patriarchy is emphasized and reinforced in the two television serials which brain washes the viewers eventually. The families in the serials follow strict rules and regulations where incision, importance of family's pride and honour, rights and rituals are given prime focus. This gives a clear picture of patrilocal and patrilinial system existing in the daily soap operas. Even though women are projected bold they accept the patriarchal value system and also projected the dominance of male supremacy willingly. Most of the women in all the categories in our study revealed the family and social disapproval of women's decision-making and conservative patriarchal attitudes on the one hand and on the other subtle resistance and struggle towards change within the family structure.
4. We noted that the polarities of male and female behaviour are largely shown as aggressive and confident, while women as shy and responsive in the two serials under study. Women are shown worshipping their husbands, being dependent on them and competent with each other for male favours. Analysis showed that both in fiction and commercials there is a sharp polarization of roles along gender lines. Beauty soaps, toilet soaps, and fairness cream commercials feature glamorous light skinned women

depicting them as desirable princess. Advertisements for energy drinks and health products feature mothers serving the young sons dreaming in their glory of their bright and prosperous future achievements. By and large in commercials, films and advertisements women are depicted as homebound serving men and children seeking male approval, whereas men are depicted outside home. In case of male characters the range of occupations presented is very wide. They are industrialists, bureaucrats, businessmen, journalists, executives, police officers etc. Advertising agencies reap huge profits by making sexist advertisements featuring women. This form of advertising has become an important tool of perpetuation of male supremacy, which exploits women's sexuality and their physical appearance. The effect is also highlighted by showing equally men and women sharing recreational activities but not work. On the contrary, women are relatively shown with less working roles. Our prime effort through this study is to reveal the fact that how women are being portrayed in media specially advertisements and television serials. Media always depict women in two major roles i.e. prime caretakers of the family and sex symbols. During our field work we came to know that not only men but also women have accepted the fact that the prime responsibility of the children, husband, in-laws, house and family totally falls on women. The growing acceptance of the idea that men should also share the task of housework is absent despite globalization and technological changes. This social perception certainly reveals the status of women as well as the perpetuation of gender subornation in family notwithstanding the technological shifts.

5. Our respondents who are college students also agreed to the fact that television has both negative and positive effects on the society. The respondents revealed that they viewed television only as a medium of entertainment 225 (99.6%), window to world 120 (97.5%), relaxation and relieving stress 105 (97.2%), respectively. Negative effects like increasing belief in super natural and fantasy with a negative effect on children (87% to 96.5%) and reducing

interest in reading and making adults and children inactive, 73 (98.6%) are clear cut findings from the study. During the interaction with the respondents in our data collection we came to know the negative affects diverting from the real issues thus resulting in less socialization, reducing interaction amongst the family members and so on. The impact of television is largely adverse especially on children. Children are initiated to violence by the electronic medium. Television is reported to encourage and influence early sexual activity, drug and alcohol abuse. Our data reveal that as much as 94 per cent respondents watch advertisements on television while six percent do not. But we were told by our respondents that those who watch advertisements are not really interested but they do not have any choice as they are forced to do so, as advertisements are flicking in between serials. Needless to mention that the children learn without much effort at early age what took many years for their parents to learn.

6. Television advertisements successfully reinforce the consumerism on the respondents. Market economy has harnessed the medium between the producers and consumers. It is a fact that advertising on television is used to maintain the economic system which creates a demand among consumers for excellent services, status, lifestyle and other fashionable items and commodities. Thus, we found that students across all economic categories hold that patriarchal value system is packaged in advertisements. Not surprisingly, the respondents from urban area are more aware of patriarchal implications and consumerism portrayed through television advertisements than the rural areas. The respondents from the rural area are the least aware and the University (VNSGU) respondents fall between the two. Thus, the urban college i.e. S.P.B. English Medium College stands out as the most aware group on gender perception and consumerism and advertisements. This is so due to not only higher educational level but also better economic condition that results in higher degree of awareness.

7. In our empirical analysis we tried to understand the level of awareness to know the attitude and perception of women

about their status and its larger impact on women. With regard to the perception and awareness women across all economic categories justify patriarchal value system. However, gender inequalities in our study serials namely Balika Vadhu and Bandini are related to themselves more by respondents of the rural area (Olpad College) as compared to urban area respondents (S.P.B. College) and University (VNSGU). This clear difference across classes in the perception of gender inequality as reflected in television serials also reveals the level of involvement and internalization of the unequal value system more by the Olpad college students. More than 90 per cent of the respondents from S.P.B. College and University (VNSGU) believe that women should fight against the injustice and similarly a large group believed that career is important for a woman to lead an independent life. Olpad College students also expressed awareness of economic independence but they had to face a lot of personal and family problems in this connection. This is so due to lack of education and ignorance parents did not allow specially girls to study more and earn to be independent. Our study shows that S.P.B. College and VNSGU students are more career-oriented and are aware of gender equality. The girl respondents from the Olpad College (rural) feel more of the need for women to fight for justice as portrayed in television serials while those from S.P.B. College and VNSGU students the priorities are earning money, achieving success through education and to be independent in their lives.

8. In our empirical analysis we tried to evaluate the level of perception of women on patriarchy and its implications on women through television serials and advertisements. We look patriarchy broadly as the economic and sexual control of women by men. Patriarchy reinforces the gender division of labour and control of their fertility and their sexuality through the institution of society called "marriage". The data show that female respondents across economic categories legitimize patriarchal value system and do not raise their voices. However, the researcher was glad to know that the new generation is becoming aware

more of themselves and social implications and thus agrees with patriarchal values only to some extent but not like their parents. Meanwhile, male respondents have denied about the existence of gender difference as they argue that today women's presence is felt in all professions.

Field Daiiy

As per the planned schedule, I went to S.P.B. College which is situated at Parle Point. I reached there by 8 O' clock in the morning and it was Wednesday. My first day of interviewing the respondents started smoothly because of my friendlier approach. The month was January, and as it was winter season the climate was cool and pleasant. Many of the respondents were familiar with me as I already completed my pilot study in the same college. The S.P.B. College is situated in a posh locality of Surat city and students belonged to elite families and upper middle classes. Most of the respondents belonged to business families. When I entered the college, I found the students rushing to attend the lecture. I waited for the students to come back from their respective classes. In the meantime, I was also looking for other students from different years to start my data collection. Suddenly, I found a group of four students sitting in the lobby area and approached them; after explaining my area of research, I noticed their level of interest in my study and particularly the topic as it is related to media (television serials and advertisements). It was easy to interact with them as the students were aware of the topic. Gradually, I started approaching other students and found girls participated more enthusiastically than boys to fill up the schedule did. Some students found the schedule lengthy. However, as we interviewed them they started analyzing questions of the interview schedule and story plot of the serials. Mention may be made that the male respondents were not much concerned as they do not watch daily soaps, but the overall review about the questionnaire was positive as it has covered all the main perceptions and ideologies prevailing in the society. The next group interviewed was of final year students. Review amongst them was mixed i.e. some accepted the patriarchal value system while the others did not agree. Male respondents which were quite co-operative, but their perceptions and ideologies related to serials were that it spoils and brainwashed women and thus this ultimately leads to disputes in the family. In this connection our study also shows more interest and attraction of female respondents compared to males. In our study we observed that the maximum mothers of the respondents were regular watchers of the television serials. This proves that television serials as a medium has a mesmerizing impact on women's lifestyle. One of the striking facts is that the serials' impact profusely the lifestyle and choices of the college students as they imitate the character's in the serials. In short, there presentation and dressing showed that they belonged to elite class and maintained their status. Even they appreciated the questionnaire and commented that it was framed in an intelligent manner with ideologies and perspectives in mind and agreed that they will start keeping values in their mind related to gender differentiation and henceforth keep their minds open to analyze what they watch. Significantly, we noticed different perceptions of male and female respondents. Male respondents did not prefer television serials and they even do not allow their mothers and sisters to watch it. We noticed a strong view in the study that boys began stressing the need for beauty for success. This clearly depicts the impact of advertisement commercials with reference to whitening creams. One of the male respondents even suggested that there question should be an open ended question on success so as to know the youth's perception.

Our next college was Surat Jilla Sahakari Spinning Vidhya Sankul, Olpad district visited the college with a prior permission and dates given by the principal of the college. The professors in the college also liked the topic and appreciated as well as helped to interview the students. Here, we found a majority of respondents from Patel community. Their dressing and speech was different from that of S.P.B. College students. They spoke their mother tongue, generally most of the females were dressed in *Churidar, Salwar-Kammez,* and only a few wore jeans and t-shirts. Even their hairstyles were different from the respondents of the S.P.B. College. In addition, they found it difficult to understand the questions so it took a lot of time to fill in the questionnaire. We found some were not taking interest in replying the question. This may be due to their ignorance regarding the language and topic. It took more time to fill in the questionnaire in the college. During the fieldwork we noticed their conservativeness and closed perceptions regarding the patriarchal value system. Not only male but even female respondents agreed and accepted the patriarchy without questioning. Majority of female respondents mentioned that they ielp their mother and "*bhabhis*" in the kitchen in their household chores. One of the respondents said that she is allowed to attend ollege because it is morning time so after 11 O' clock she helps her mother in kitchen and also they help in tailoring. One of the rspondents had a different storyline as she identified herself with tle serial named "Jyoti" which is telecasted on NDTV Imagine. Sle recited her story while continuously kept crying and conveyed tht her life is becoming disastrous day-by-day. She recited her wbole story that they are three sisters and one brother. She is the elost one. She works a part time tele-caller in one private company. He mother holds beauty parlour at home itself. After college she go t job which is four hours and then helps her mother in parlour andfter that she makes her younger sisters and brother study as theyre in S.S.C. and H.S.C. Her brother instead of helping the fami roams here and there and spends money lavishly. Her father work in a cottage industry earning Rs. 2500 per month but spends morehan that on alcohol. She is the only member was has to take care ad earn as well for the family.

Oe noticeable point we noticed during our study was the differce of perceptions of the college students and career buildi. S.P.B. College students studied for making their future bright cessarily reflect their career orientation ambitions. While Olpad ollege students were just interested to earn their livelihood and to hd a stable life without ambitions.

Moof the female respondents were aware of the latest fashion trends al were interested watching T.V. serials and advertisement to follop the latest updates. The students from Olpad College (rural) fod difficult to understand the terms and so we translated the schede into their mother tongue. They were not aware of the existing reotypes in the society and believed that it is their culture arevery men has to earn i.e. man is the breadwinner and woman heo stay back looking after the child, family and house. Even theirarents socialized them according to their gender as boys were en more freedom and authority while girls were kept under certa rules and restrictions. Hence, we can say that Olpad College stu was quite revealing in more than one way regarding their views d perceptions.

Our next area of field included the Veer Narmad South Gujarat University students that included faculties of Mass Communication, Interior Designing, Statistics, Sociology and MSW programme respectively. University respondents belong to a mixed category of working, business and service groups. We interviewed the mass communication and journalism students with the prior appointment of the head of the particular department. We took one class explaining them the topic and lots of discussion and query took place. As the topic of research was related to their subject they found it more interesting. The respondents were aware of the perceptions and believed that acquiring education and success takes a top priority as well as a necessity. The group was quite matured and clear in its visions. Overall the observation was above an average as the students were already having first hand information. The session was interesting. The next department interviewed was Comparative Literature in Humanities. The respondents belonged to rural areas i.e. Kamrej, Udhana, Khatodra, Ved, etc. We found that the respondents were less aware than the Mass Communication students and took time to grasp the questions and theme of the questionnaire, as they were from Gujarati medium. Apparently, it took time to make them understand and at times it became a tough task. Thus, we could relate them with the Olpad College students largely due to their similar background. Like Olpad College students we found the respondents from this department especially females were more interested in T.V. serials. They felt proud to reveal the awareness of knowledge regarding T.V. serials. But when the questionnaire turned to stereotypes they were blank and ignorant about it. They were not ready to accept that these are the stereotypes shown on television. They believed that men and women are allotted different kinds of job or duty that they have to perform. Sometimes, they even took the research topic lightly. This showed their level of interest in filling the questionnaire and involvement during the interview schedule. So the researcher felt let down for a while.

The next department we interviewed was Bachelor of Interior Designing, who were in total contrast the above mentioned faculty as the respondents here were well aware of the existing stereotypes on the whole. There were career-oriented and had clear vision of achieving their goals in life. Maximum respondents interviewed in this department belonged to far flung rural area and around Surat city. They have shifted to the hostel to pursue their studies.

They were well dressed and well versed about their hopes. They found the topic of research very interesting and happening too! We found them hard working and talented. Their talent is recognized when one enters the department as the respondents themselves have decorated it beautifully and creatively. It took very less time for us to explain the topic and interview schedule. To know the perception of the family members some of the students took certain copies of questionnaire along with them. There was a group of students who were staying in hostel against the wishes of their parents as they opted for a career which nobody else has opted in their respective families. The consequences which these girl respondents faced by opposing the family was shocking indeed as the two respondents revealed that due to gender difference they were not allowed to complete their studies by staying in a hostel. While their brothers in the family are permitted and allowed to opt their career options and even stay wherever they want to pursue. However, they were happy and satisfied with the decisions they took as they were career-oriented and ready to struggle for achieving their goals. Indeed, it was refreshing field experience.

The next department of sociology and MSW. The respondents belonged to rural and urban areas. So we can say it was a mixed group and apparently the perceptions also were mixed i.e., both progressive as well as conservative. Some respondents said that girls are more interested in television serials, daily soaps and reality shows. Some believed that if the economic condition of the family is good, there is no need for women to work. Some of the respondents were not aware of their father's or family's income. Respondents belonging to business category did not know their family income while the respondents from service class were of their family's income. This showed a clear demarcation in the attitudes of the service class and business category respondents. Respondents from the service class were very open about their income and had more literal views on the status of women in society. Again, the question regarding the respondents from business category mentioned that it is difficult to gauge the monthly income further said that they do not know the income of their father as they could not dare to discuss with him; father gives them (male respondents) enough money for their expenses and they are satisfied with it. However, they want sisters to have an good education and then only get married.

It is a very good refreshing as well as learning experience for the researcher to know that the fieldwork is a significant part of research and goes beyond mere data collection. Precisely as observation, give pulse of the problem, an understanding of the objective reality of the people and an exposure to the research problem in proper perspective. More so as the status of women with reference to media specially televisions serials and advertisements and their awareness of their problems were enlightening for the researcher. Many aspects of mass-media and its impact on the college students became clear by interviewing young boys and girls. Hence, we can say that televisions is not only ubiquitous in most households, it also gets a prime and prior importance in the family. Children are seen glued to the set and generations together view it. Many respondents especially from the service class in rural areas expressed happiness that the researcher was asking them questions regarding **their views and perceptions on media and stereotypes** reveals the satisfaction and feelings of the respondents. As expected, fieldwork was very tiring but at the same time very fruitful and interesting.

Appendix

Gender Stereotypes in Media with Special Reference to Television Serials and Advertisements

INTERVIEW SCHEDULE

I am doing Ph.D. in the Department of Sociology, Veer Narmad South Gujarat University, Surat. The topic of my research is "***Gender Stereotypes in Media with Special Reference to Television Serials and Advertisements***". I will be grateful to you if you kindly co-operate in collecting the information for my study.

The information is purely for academic purpose and would be kept strictly confidential.

General Background

Sr. No.	*Details*	*Code*
1.	Name of the Respondent	
2.	Age	
3.	Sex	
4.	Religion	
5.	Caste/Tribe	

Sr. No.	Details	Code
6.	Native place	
7.	Mother tongue	
8.	Education	
9.	Medium of education	
10.	Monthly household income	
11.	Economic Assets 1. Movable ____________ 2. Immovable ____________	

2. **Do you watch T.V. Serials?**
   1. Yes 2. No.

3. **Exposure to T.V. Serials and Channels? (in order of preference)**

Sr. No.	Channel	T.V. Serials	Code
1.			
2.			
3.			
4.			
5.			

4. **General Perceptions of T.V. Serials (Tick '*')**

1. Entertainment ☐
2. Window to the World ☐
3. Affects culture negatively ☐

4. Sets trends in fashion ☐
5. Pass time ☐
6. Affects children negatively ☐
7. Creates awareness amongst the women ☐
8. Relaxation and relieving stress ☐
9. Viewers identity with some characters in T.V. serials ☐

5. **Values reflected in T.V. Serials. (Tick '*")**

1. Importance of joint family ☐
2. Culture code for married woman ☐
3. Emphasis on rituals ☐
4. Reinforcement of Gender Stereotypes ☐
5. Household unity ☐
6. Consumer culture ☐
7. Depiction of women as secondary individuals ☐
8. Depiction of women as sexual objects ☐
9. Increases career awareness ☐
10. Serials help to handle interpersonal relations ☐

6. **Please give your opinion on the Advertisements.**

Sr. No.	*Advertisements in T.V.*	*Agree*	*Disagree*	*Neutral*
1	Promote consumerism and profit			
2	Reinforces gender roles			
3	Leads to status competition			
4	Glamorizes life			

Sr. No.	Advertisements in T.V.	Agree	Disagree	Neutral
5	Promote unnecessary wants			
6	Forcibly set the taste			
7	Portray women as sexual objects			
8	Humorous and entertaining			
9	Enables to watch celebrities			

7. General Perception of Women about women in T.V. Serials (Gender Stereotype)

Sr. No.		Agree	Disagree	Neutral
1	Women should support men			
2	Men have more power than women in sexual relationship			
3	Women should not have extra marital relationship			
4	Women's labour is controlled and appropriated by men.			
5	Women's work is not important like men's work.			
6	Woman should be feminine in appearance and submissive in behaviour.			
7	Child care is women's work.			
8	Main care taker and bread winner of the family is man.			
9	Men should earn and women should look after the family.			

8. What is necessary to achieve success?

1. Education ☐
2. Intelligence ☐

3. Personality ☐
4. Beauty ☐
5. Smartness ☐

9. **Advertisements promote only women as prime caretakers specially related to health and hygiene like the following:**

   1. Health drinks such as Bournvita, Complan, Horlicks, etc. ☐
   2. Soaps such as Dettol, Savlon, etc. ☐
   3. Food items: Saffola Oil, Tata Salt, Snacks ☐

10. **Advertisements promote patriarchy as reflected in insurance policy ads.**

    1. Yes 2. No. ☐

11. **Whether according to you, who is more depicted in insurance policies?**

    1. Men 2. Women 3. Both ☐

12. **Who are more likely to be shown advertising cars or business products, solid products such as steel and cement, etc.?**

    1. Men 2. Women 3. Both ☐

13. **Who in general largely appear in the advertisements in domestic products, mobile phones, two wheelers, soaps etc?**

    1. Men 2. Women 3. Both ☐

14. **Do you agree T.V. serials such as Balika Vadhu and Bandini reveal men's dominance and supremacy while showing women as dependent and submissive?**

    1. Yes 2. No ☐

15. **Whether or not media responsible for the stereotyping of women?**

    1. Yes 2. No ☐

16. **Whether or not stereotypes restrict progress and control women?**

    1. Yes 2. No ☐

17. **Do serials such as Balika Vadhu and Bandini have impacts women's lifestyle and social context?**

    1. Yes 2. No ☐

18. **Whether or not media reinforce, racism, casteism, class and gender bias?**

    1. Yes 2. No ☐

Place:
Date:

Signature of the Investigator.

Bibliography

Acker, J. (1989). *Fast Capitalism,* University of Oregon.

Acker, J. (1989). *Teachers, Gender and Careers.* Johanesberg: Sage Publications.

Acker, J. (1990). *The Problem with Patriarchy,* Delhi: Sage Publications.

Althusser, L. (1971). *'Ideology and the State' in Lenin and Philosophy and Other Essays,* London: New Left Books.

Althusser, Louis. *Structuralism,* London: Penguin Books.

Anderson, R. (1995). *Consumer Culture and T.V. Programming,* Boulder: Colorado Westview.

Ansari, Mohd. Swalesh (1983). *Media Problems and Prospectus,* New Delhi: National Media Centre.

Anthony, Giddens (2002). *Where Now for New Labour,* Cambridge: Polity Publisher.

Bagdikian, B. (1988). *The Media Monopoly,* Boston: Beacon.

Ball-Rokeach, S.J. (1985). The Origins of Individual Media-System Dependency in Communication Research, 12(4).

Ball-Rokeach, S.J. and Defleur, M.L. (1976). A Dependency Model of Mass Communication Effects in Communication Research, 3.

Bandhu, Pranjali (2001). *Dancing to Global Capital Media in India.* Mumbai: Vikas Adhyayan Kendra.

Barbara, Santa (1999). *The Determinants and Consequences of Workplace Sex and Race,* California.

Belson, W. (1978). *Televisions Violence and the Adolescent Boy,* Hampshire, England, Saxon House.

Bhasin, Kamla and Agrawal, Bina (1977). *Women and Media.* New Delhi.

Centre for Advocacy Research (2006, April 23). Contemporary Women in Television Fiction, Deconstructing Role and 'Commerce' and 'Tradition', *Economic and Political Weekly,* Mumbai.

Chakravarty, A. (1989). *The Indian Testimony.* Bengal: Amitya Publications.

Chakravarty, Jaya (2007). *Women in Media and Journalism: Media and Women's Development,* New Delhi: Sarup and Sons.

Cockburn, R. (1981). *The Sexuality of Organization,* London: Sage Publications.

Comstock, G. (1975). *Television and Human Behaviour: The Key Studies*, Santa Monica, CA: Rand Corporation.

Comstock, G., *et al.*, (1978). *Television and Human Behaviour*, New York: Columbia University Press.

Connell, R.W. (2000). *Male Roles, Masculinities and Violence: A Culture of Peace Perspective*, UNESCO Publishing.

Cornell, West (1987). *The Truly Disadvantaged, the Inner City, the Underclass and Public Policy*, Chicago.

Dakley, Ann (1984). *Taking it Like a Women*, London: Jonathan Cape (Paperback published Fontana 1985; also published by Random House, New York.

Daphne, Spain (1992). *Gendered Spaces*, Chapel Hill: University of North Carolina Press.

Daphne, Spain (2001). *Continuity and Change in American Family*, London: Sage Publications.

Defleur, M.L. (1970). *Theories of Mass Communication*, New York: David Mckay.

Desai, Rajani (2001). *Controversies on the Women's Question and Women Globalization*, Mumbai: Rupe.

Devas, D.A. (2003). *Surveys in Social Research*, Jaipur: Rawat Publication.

Dhar, Sunil and Pattnaik, S.N. (2002). *Portrayal of Distorted Image of Women by Indian Media: Issues in Mass Communication*. New Delhi: Kanishka Publications.

Dobbs, James (1929). *Research Projects and Methods in Educational Sociology*, Chicago: University of Chicago.

Engels, Friedrich (1891). *The Origin of the Family, Private Property, and the State*, Moscow: Foreign Languages Publishing House.

Foreman, Ann (1977). *Femininity as Alienation, Woman and the Family in Marxism and Psychoanalysis*, London: Pluto.

Freedman, Jane (2002). *Feminism*. Buckingham: Open University Press.

Freud, Sigmund (1901). *The Psychopathology of Everyday Life*.

Gallagher (1992). Women and Men in the Media, *Communication Research Trends*, 12, New York.

Gandhi, P. and Shah, M. (1992). *Hinduism, Doctrine and Way of Life*, Delhi: Rupee News Publications.

Garnham, N. (1979). *Contribution to a Political Economy of Mass Communication, Culture and Society*, 1(2). New York: Sage Publications.

Gatan, S. (1992). *Inner Staden* (2nd ed.), Stockholm: Komitten for Stockholmforskning.

Gauntlett, David (2008). *Media, Gender and Identity: An Introduction*. 2nd Edition.

Giddens, A. (2002). *Alibris UK: Sociology*, Cambridge: Polity Publisher.

Gideon, Sigfried (1952) *Space, Time and Archition: The Growth of New Tradition*, London: Cambridge University Press.

Government of Gujarat (February 2003). *Socio-Economic Review, Gujarat State 2002-2003*. Gandinagar: Directorate of Economics and Statistics.

Government of India (2002). Ministry of Labour, *Report of the National Commission of Labour*, Vol. Part-I, 53.

Gramsci, A. (1971). *Structure and Superstructure (1929-1935)*, New York: International Prison Notebooks.

Grobel, J. (1998). The UNESCO Global Study on Media Violence, in U. Carlsson and C. Von Feilitzen (eds.), *Children and Media Violence*, Gotegborg: University of Gotegborg.

Gupta, V. (1991). *Role of Women in Muslim Countries*. New Delhi: M.D. Publications.

Gyanaranjan, S. (2004). *The Hindu*. Mumbai.

Hacker (1993). *The Politics of Respect*. New York.

Hacker, S. (1993). *Why American Sociologists are Racist*, New York: Basic Books.

Hall, Staurt (1979). Culture the Media and the 'Ideological Effect', in Guran, Gurevitch and Wollacott (ed.), *Mass Communication and Society*, London: Sage.

Hasan, S. (2004). *Global Media Publications: From Pluralism to Separatism; Qasbas in Colonial Awadn*, USA: Global Media Publications.

Hasan, Zoya (2004). *Unequal Citizens: A Study of Muslim Women in India*, Delhi: Prajashakti Book House.

Hermen, E.S. and McChesney, R.W. (1997). *The Global Media: The New Missionaries of Corporate Capitalism*. Delhi: Madhyam.

Hevwood, Leslie L. (2007). *Women's Movement Today*. Jaipur: Rawat Publications.

Innis, H., (1950). *Empire and Communication*, Oxford: Clarendon Press.

International Telecommunication Union (1995). *World Telecommunication Development Report*, Geneva: ITU.

Jacob, H. (1979). *Importance of Sociology in Nursing*, Germany.

James Curran and Michael Gurevitch (ed.) (1996). *Mass India and Society: Feminist Perspectives on the Media*. (Second Edition), London: Arnold a member of the Holder Headline Group.

Jani, Lovenduski (2005). *State Feminism and Political Representation*, Cambridge: Cambridge University Press.

Jeffery, R. (2003). *India's Newspaper Revolution Capitalism, Politics and the Indian Language Press*, Oxford: Oxford University Press.

Jha, Umashankar and Pujara, Pranlata (1996). *Indian Women Today*. New Delhi: Kanishka Publishers.

Jhally, S., (1987). *The Codes of Advertising*, New York: St. Martin's Press.

Johnson, Kirik (2000). *Television and Social Change in Rural India*, New Delhi: Sage Publication.

Joseph, Ammu and Sharma, Kalpana (1994). *Whose News*. New Delhi: Sage Publication India Pvt. Ltd.

Joseph, Velacherry. (1993). *Social Impact of Mass Media in Kerala*. Delhi: CISRS, Bangalore.

Kaur, M. (1999). Globalisation and Women, Some Likely Consequences, in Sethi Raj Mohini (ed.) *Globalization, Culture and Women's Development*. Jaipur: Rawat Publication.

Kimmel, M. (2006). *Gender, Class, Race and Sexual Preference*, Oxford: Oxford University Press.

Kimmel, Michael (2006). *The Gendered Society*, New York: Oxford University.

Klasen, A. (2000). *Development Politics*, Germany:

Kohli, Vanita (2003). *The Indian Media Business*, New Delhi: Response Books.

Krishnan, Prabha and Dighe, Anita (1990). *Affirmation and Denial of Construction of Femininity on Indian Television*. New Delhi: Sage Publications.

Kumar, R. (1993). *The History of Doing: An Illustrated Account of Movements for Women's Rights and Feminism in India*: Cambridge: University Press.

Lasswell, H. (1948). The Structure and Function of Communication in Society, in L. Bryson (ed.), *The Communication of Ideas*, New York: Harper.

Learner, D. (1958). *The Passing of Traditional Society*, New York: Free Press.

Lowery, S.A. and Defleur, M.L. (1995). *Milestones in Mass Communication Research*, New York: Longman.

Mark, K. and Engles, F. (1848). *A Manifesto of the Communist Party*, Moscow: Foreign Languages Publishing House.

Marriot, M. (1990). *India through Hindu Categories*, New Delhi: Sage Publications.

Marriott, Mckin (1990). Construction an Indian Ethno-sociology, in *India through Hindu Categories* (ed.), New Delhi: Sage Publications.

Matlelart, A. (1980). *Mass Media Ideologies and the Revolutionary Movement*, Sussex: Harvester Press.

Mead, Margaret (1949). *Male and Female: A Study of Sexes in a Changing*. France.

Mead, Margaret (1963). *Sex and Temperament in Three Primitive Societies*, New York: Morrow Quill.

Menon, R. (1999). *Men on Women*, London: Penguin Books. Millet, Kate (1971). *Sexual Politics*, London: Sphere.

Mitchell, Juliet (1974). *Psychoanalysis and Feminism*, New York: Pantheon.

Mohan, Kamlesh (2006). *Towards Gender History Globalization and Cultural Invasion*, Delhi: Akar Books.

Mukherjee, R. (1970). *Rise and Fall of the East India Company: A Sociological Approach*, Bombay: Popular Prakashan.

Murphy, D. (1976). *The Silent Watchdog*. London: Constable.

Nandy, A. (1983). *The Intimate Enemy: Recovery of Self Under Colonialism,* London: Oxford University Press.

Niranjana, Seema (2001). *Gender and Space: Femininity, Sexualization and the Female Body,* New Delhi: Sage Publications.

Ortner, S. (1997). *What is Practice Theory,* France: France Publishers.

Palanithurai, G.; Parthiban, T. and Vanishree, J. *Empowering Women: Grassroots Experiences from Tamil Nadu.* New Delhi: Concept Publishing Comp.

Patel, Ila (1995). *Representations of Women in Mass Media* (Working Paper), Anand: Institute of Rural Management.

Patel, Jubi (2008). Poor Muslim Women in Bangladesh, in *Issues of Mass Communication.* New Delhi. Kanishka Publication.

Pathy, S. (2010). *Sexual Division of Labour,* Delhi; Serials Publications.

Pfefferbaum, B. *et al.,* (2001). Television Exposure in Children After a Terrorist Incident in Psychiatry, 64, London, United Kingdom: Sage.

Pilcher, Jane and Imelda, Whelchan (2005). *Fifth Key Concepts in Gender Studies.* New Delhi: Sage Publication.

Pinchbeck, D. (2000). *Women Workers and the Industrial Revolution,* New York: Times Publication.

Pokharapukar, Raja (1993). *Rural Development through Community Television,* New Delhi: Concept Publications.

Purvis, Tony (2006). *Get Set for Media and Cultural Studies.* Edinburgh: Edinburgh University Press Ltd.

Raheja and Goldi (1996). *Women's Resistance—A Review of Literature,* Delhi.

Raheja, D. and Goldi (1996). *Women as Subjects: South Asian Histories,* Bhuj Publications.

Rege, Sharmilla (2003). *Sociology of Gender: The Challenge of Feminist Sociological Knowledge,* New Delhi: Sage Publication.

Rode, S. (1990). *The Generations of Adam,* Italy: Free Association Books.

Rogers, E.M. (1962). The Diffusion of Innovations, Glenco, IL: Free Press.

Salzman, Philip (1993). "The Electronic Trojan House: Television in the Globalization of Para-Modern Cultures" presented at the Plenary Session '*Societies, Evolution and Globalization*', Thirteenth International Congress of Anthropological and Ethnological Sciences, Mexico City.

Sangari, K. (1993). *"Independent Women": More than a Century of Feminism in Egypt,* New York: Pantheon Books.

Schramm, W. (1964). Mass Media and National Development, Stanford CA: Stanford University Press. Scott, John (1988). Sociology Paper, Vol. 22, No. 1.

Shankarwa (1993). *Canadian Review of Sociology,* Delhi: Rawat Publication.

Storey, H. (1993). *Organizing the Sexual Division of Labour,* University of California.

Syed, M.H. (2006). *Research in Mass Media.* New Delhi: Anmol Publication.

Thakur, B.S. and Agrawal, Binod (1988). *Media Utilization for the*

Development of Women and Children. New Delhi: Concept Publishing Company.

Tine, Hribar (1995). *Slovenci Kot Nacija*, Ljubljana: Enotnost.

Tinker, L. (1976). The Adverse Impact of Development on Women, in I. Tinker and M.B. Bramsen (eds.), *Women and World Development*, Washington DC: Overseas Development Council.

Unnikrishnan, Namita and Bajpai, Shailaja (1996). *The Impact of Television Advertising on Children*, New Delhi: Sage Publication.

Vachani, Jagdish (2007). *Public Relations Management in Media and Journalism*, Jaipur: Rawat Publications.

Varis, T. (1975). The Impact of Transnational Corporations on Communications, Tamper Peace Research Institute, Reports No. 10/ 1975. Finland.

Vilanilam, John. (1989). *Television Advertising and the Indian Poor, Media, Culture and Society*, 11. New Delhi: New Century Publications.

Viorst, Judith. (1986). *The Art of Loving*. USA: Perennial Publications.

Warren, Farrell (1993). *The Myth of Male Power*, Oxford: Oxford University Press Book.

Williams, G.A. (1960). Gramsci Concept of Egemonis, *Journal of History of Ideas*, Vol. 21, No. 4.

Williams, R. (1974). *Television, Technology and Cultural Form*, London: Fontana Publication.

Williams, R. (1989). *A Common Destiny*, University of Minnesota.

Wimmer, Roger D. and Dominick, Joseph R. (1987). *Mass Media Research: An Introduction*, California: Wadsworth.

World Bank, (1991). *Gender and Poverty in India*, IBRD.

Yadava, J.S. and Mathur, Pradeep (1988). *Issues in Mass Communication: The Basic Concepts*. New Delhi, Kanishka Publishers.

Yamini, K. (October 2008). Women and Mass Media, *Indian Journal of Women and Development*, Vol. 1.

Zemmerman, Don (1987). *Gender and Society*, Sydney: University of Sydney.

Zemmerman, Don (2005). Doing Gender. *New England Journal of History*.

Zoonen, Liesbet Van (1996). Feminist Perspectives on the Media, In Curran, James and Gurevitch, Michael (Ed.) *Mass Media and Society*, London: Arnold.

Websites

- www.allindiaradio.org (Website of All India Radio)
- www.censusgujarat.org (Website of Census of India, Gujarat State)
- www.censusindia.net (Website of Census of India)
- www.ddindia.com and www.dd.india.net (Website of Doordarshan)
- www.rni.nic.in (Website of Registrar of Newspapers of India)
- www.smc.org (Website of Surat Municipal Corporation)
- www.trai.gov.in (Website of Telecom Regulation Association of India)

Index